S0-BEA-118

SELLING DREAMS

HOW TO MAKE ANY PRODUCT IRRESISTIBLE

GIAN LUIGI LONGINOTTI-BUITONI

with Kip Longinotti-Buitoni

SIMON & SCHUSTER

SIMON & SCHUSTER
Rockefeller Center
1230 Avenue of the Americas
New York, NY 10020

Designed by Ruth Lee

Manufactured in the United States of America

1 3 5 7 9 10 8 6 4 2

Library of Congress Cataloging-in-Publication Data

Longinotti-Buitoni, Gian Luigi.
Selling dreams : how to make any product irresistible / Gian Luigi
Longinotti-Buitoni ; with Kip Longinotti-Buitoni.
p. cm.
Includes bibliographical references and index.
1. Selling—psychological aspects.
2. Marketing—psychological aspects.
I. Longinotti-Buitoni, Kip. II. Title.
HF5438.8.P75L66 1999
658.85—dc21 99-21735
CIP

ISBN 0-684-85019-2

I would like to dedicate this book to
every person for whom the most basic necessities
are still distant dreams.

CONTENTS

	Introduction	11
1	The Shaping of Dreams	21
2	The Business of Selling Dreams	52
3	Dreamketing: Reaching the Customers' Dreams	94
4	The Customer: A Dreamer in Search of Surprise	146
5	The Dream-Makers: The Creators	190
6	Redefining Excellence	233
7	Financing Creativity	274
8	Conclusions	299
	Acknowledgments	313
	Selected Bibliography	315
	Index	319

SELLING DREAMS

INTRODUCTION

WHEN I WAS FIRST ASKED to take charge of the North American market of Ferrari, I did not take the offer seriously. Having been a customer for several years and a dreamer of great automobiles all my life, it was difficult for me to recognize Ferrari as a company where one could perform "serious" things such as work. To me, Ferrari was a factory of dreams, just as New York's fantasy toy store, FAO Schwarz, is to any child. Ferrari meant the thrill of very special and rare occasions. I feared Ferrari was not a place where I could shape my competitive business skills, since promoting the ethereal dreams of a fortunate few had little relevance in the global scheme of things. Was this going to help me develop a more versatile business sense that I could apply elsewhere in the working world?

But, because I loved those fast cars so much, I took the job, even if only on a part-time basis. This part-time status, however, did not last long. I started during the recession of 1992, a time when very few people were dreaming of driving very expensive, uncomfortable, 180-plus-mph automobiles in the United States and Canada, the two countries blessed with the most stringent speed limits and toughest cops in the world. The job required my full attention because what was selling at the time was everything but Ferraris: Inexpensive cars were busily getting people where they needed to go, both comfortably and most cost-effectively. While I was "testing" Ferraris on tracks around North America, professionally I felt out on the fringe of the industry. After all, we were selling only a few hundred cars in a market where some 13 million units were sold every year. My sense of exclusion vanished as soon as I realized that Ferrari, the smallest company in the automotive industry, had the most famous brand of all. Actually, Ferrari is one of the five most famous brands in any type of industry, right up there with IBM and Coca-Cola (not bad for a company that practically never even had an advertising budget). I found this to be invaluable in today's suffocating competition, where attracting the customer's attention has become as expensive as it is difficult. Take an auto show, for example. Ferrari is the only company that doesn't have to pay for the exhibition area, since the organizers are painfully aware that these beautiful sports cars help them sell tickets. We do not have to spend fortunes on creating shows that feature beauty queens and dancers, singers, and special effects to vie for our many visitors' attention. Just parking our exciting automobiles is fireworks enough to draw the crowds. We do not have to spend on advertising, since trade magazines are eager to write articles about our automobiles. The fact is that a cover story on Ferrari increases the magazine's sales. Nor do we have to pay for product placement in order to have our cars featured in movies. A scene starring a Ferrari at any speed always seems to add to the film's thrill. As a customer and then as an employee, I realized what is most impressive about Ferrari. It is not the car's speed and road-holding abilities, but its speed in attracting customers and its hold on their imagination. If Ferrari is the most famous automotive company on earth with the least marketing resources, it is for one reason only: Ferrari has transformed an automobile, a product built to satisfy the very precise need of transporting people, into a dream.

Ferrari best embodies what companies must do to succeed in today's overly competitive business world: They must hold their customers' fleeting attention by connecting with their dreams.

THE TERM "DREAM" is not easy to use, particularly when discussing business. Some could say it's clearly a cliché, both difficult to define and too vague to clearly express a business concept. Often people resent being associated with such an ethereal term, feeling that it belittles the seriousness of their business activities. Yet a dream is a catchy image that best describes what ignites our imagination and desires. In this book, the term "dreams" will refer to all of those products and services to which we feel drawn because in the end their emotional link to our imagination transcends their functional purpose. For example, the excitement I feel driving a Ferrari has nothing to do with the fact that this is a means of transportation. It has everything to do with the sensation of speed, fun, and freedom. It is a car fueled by emotions. I still remember when I was six and my father bought his first Ferrari. For an emotionally reserved man, on this day he was gleaming with excitement. Of course, it is easier for Ferrari, a company that builds a very limited number of rather expensive automobiles, to create a dream car. Being harnessed by fewer cost constraints than other companies certainly makes it easier to create a product rich in emotions. Yet even companies selling inexpensive products or services can connect emotionally with their customers. Just look at the Volkswagen Beetle, a car that ignited the dreams of an entire flower-power generation, so much so that its latest relaunch, some twenty years after the original was discontinued, has received a worldwide ovation. A company's creativity can transform common products into dreams. For example, today Levi's jeans are about as far from the coal miners' trousers as you can get; Nike sneakers are a lifestyle statement more than exercise shoes; the movie *Titanic* is far more than a well-documented story on the ship's tragic sinking; and Viagra represents much more than just an anti-impotence pill.

Connecting with the customer's imagination has become an obligatory path to business success. Thanks to the miracles of technology, customers have learned to expect the beauty and performance of a Ferrari even in their everyday commuter cars. They are no longer content just satisfying their needs—they want to fulfill their dreams.

THIS BOOK will closely examine companies, creators, and managers who have successfully engaged their customers' emotions. From these examples, I will mark the critical steps to selling dreams in order to formulate a strategy for tapping the customers' imagination. I found the following points to be helpful:

Interpret the spirit of the time in order to understand which dreams will capture the customer. Dreams are shaped by culture. It was the "flower-power" generation's love for the underdog that created a cultlike emotional following for the Volkswagen Beetle. The baby boomers' desire for independence and freedom cinched success for the Sony Walkman and Nike sneakers.

Artists, people of culture, scientists, and thinkers foresee and often provoke the changes that shape a culture. By integrating their intuition into the organization, a company can better tune in to the times. Just as artists search endlessly and randomly for inspiration, a company should constantly explore unrelated fields and approach business eclectically in order to create dreams. Because truth is best reached by expanding the search for knowledge to include the widest possible spectrum of unrelated fields, it is hardly surprising that the companies with the most eclectic approach to business are ground-breakers when it comes to initiating trends and tastes.

Create products and services designed and engineered to convey intense emotions. Companies cannot survive on merely satisfying consumer needs. Today, most companies can provide zero-defect quality, products that perfectly perform their function. This is no longer a differentiating quality that, on its own, can sway the customer. Companies that rely strictly on marketing and discounts to promote otherwise common products will never win any emotional hold on their customers' minds. To achieve the type of commercial success that establishes a brand for years to come, a company has to infuse emotional qualities that connect with the customers' strongest desires into its products and services.

Practice "dreamketing." No matter how fantastic a product is, it cannot stand alone to represent a dream. A Ferrari in the potholed hell of a city traffic jam is anything but a dream. A dream is not a product, it is an experience. I coined the word "dreamketing" because our job is to create that fantastic experience. Reaching the market is no longer enough: We have to touch (in an emotional sense) our customers' imagination. The first concern of the "dreamketer" should be to create an evocative and seductive brand, one that can spark desire and set the customer's mood. Since customers should never be awakened from their dreams, the dreamketer should ensure that the company's communication, distribution, special events, and any type of customer relations consistently support the brand's mission to build that dream in the customers' minds.

Choose the customer. There is a fundamental difference between a customer and a consumer. The consumer is a statistic, a hypothetical figure symbolizing millions of indistinct people who mechanically buy goods for their functional and utilitarian worth. A customer, on the other hand, is an identifiable individual, with a specific personality and highly selective and distinct tastes, who is emotionally bound to the company's creations. Being a consumer or a customer is a question of purchasing attitude. The same person could be both a customer and a consumer. It is up to the company to make a customer out of every consumer. After all, a company is only as worthy as its customers are.

Choose a creator. Dreams are the realizations of very creative people. Companies cannot rely on market studies or customer clinics to decide what to do. Market analyses tell you what customers want today. Customers are not experts, since they have neither the knowledge nor the intensity of creators, designers, craftsmen, and engineers. To surprise the customers' imagination, you must prophesy what they will want tomorrow. The inspiration must come from within the company. A company must develop, at all levels of the organization, a culture that actively promotes original experimentation and aesthetic research. In order for this to happen, it must hire creators who can lead the organization toward an original and recognizable company taste. Products or services cannot be revolutionary: Customers have to be ready for them. It's up to the creators to heed their aesthetic sensitivity in determining which dreams can become commercial successes. Creators, just like Hegel's heroes, express "that for which the hour has come."

Support creators with a creative organization. Creators alone cannot create dreams. They can provide the vision and the inspiration, but dreams are not made by a single person. Dreams are emotional experiences that require many ancillary activities performed by many gifted people. To create dreams, creators must be supported by a group of individuals with profound product knowledge who can crystallize the vision and the ideas into products and services that exalt the customers' desires. Creativity is the most important quality for achieving business success (or any type of success, for that matter), and companies selling dreams are key examples to which any type of industry should turn to learn how to enhance this most precious and scarce resource.

Seize any possible chance to magnify the customer's perceived added value. Art, which appeals mostly to our emotions, is the foremost example of the maximization of added value: Consider the astronomical prices paid for some colors on a cheap canvas painted by a famous artist. Since a company that sells a dream is actually selling an experience rather than simply a product, it has several chances to influence its customers' perception of added value. Château Rothschild is a perfect example of this concept: It is one of the best wines in the world, and its beautiful labels are nearly as prized as the outstanding contents of its bottles. To achieve long-lasting financial well-being, companies must welcome impulse and steer clear of typical short-term pressures from shareholders and analysts. A company must build a financial structure that allows risk-taking. The role of the financial manager should not be to help a company avoid risks, but rather to enable it to take the risks. With no risks, there are no dreams, since dreams, by definition, are never born of the norm.

SELLING DREAMS is what every company aspires to do—for the media visibility, the customer recognition, and the potential profits. It is hardly surprising that nearly every mass-consumption company carries a "dream" line. No longer a business of marginal interest, selling dreams promises tremendous growth. In this world, there are some 6 billion customers and potential customers craving dreams!

This book offers an approach to business that not only engages our emotions and our senses, but also captivates us with its eclectic approach to knowledge. It suggests that companies not limit their sources of inspiration merely to the rational and the analytical. Reason alone has often failed to select winning strategies or solutions for companies operating in today's chaotic business arena. The business world can no longer navigate solely by reason. Today, changes are fired off so rapidly and unpredictably that experience is often a poor guide, leaving entrepreneurs to surrender all analytical reasoning for that spontaneous "gut feeling." Intuition, perception, improvisation, sensations, and unstructured research can all contribute to more divergent interpretation of today's challenges. I sincerely hope this book can help guide us away from our own over-rationality.

1

The Shaping of Dreams

When we dream at night, the majority of our dreams are nightmares, but how is it that the few sweet dreams we enjoy last us a lifetime? Somehow we cling most to them, because they unleash us from the frustrating limits of reality, unlocking the inaccessible and expanding our own abilities.* A dream acts as an equalizer of social differences: What we can't have we can always dream of having. Dreams enunciate our latent desires, creating a mood in which everything is possible. Dreams let us discover another dimension of ourselves, our fears,

*Many people believe in the direct correlation between a rich dreaming life and enhanced creativity. Dreams stimulate creative activity by unshackling the imagination from the rational decision-making so common in our waking reality. No wonder so many scientists, poets, musicians, and others have enjoyed such enlightening dreams. Einstein (1879–1955) was believed to have dreamed his theory of relativity, Goethe (1749–1832) many of his poems, and Beethoven (1770–1827) his Sixth Symphony.

our inhibitions, and our passions. We cannot help but be moved by our dreams because in them we soar—we meet magic on our wild adventures. While they are very personal, some dreams are expressed in common archetypal patterns by people across cultures, religions, and social classes. For every age, some dreams die while others are just unfolding, yet, as mythology teaches us, there are also dreams that live forever.

In ancient times, a civilization was only as strong as its ability to decipher dreams, a study known as oneiromancy. In 2000 B.C., dream temples were erected in Egypt to enshrine visions, prophecies, and extrasensory perceptions. The Greeks wrestled at length with the question of what was more real, a waking or a dreaming reality. Today's more scientific and less romantic outlook may have finally slammed the book shut on this age-old quandary. In our world, where "seeing is believing," reality seems to be what we wake up to every morning. Not that our innate desire to exceed reality has changed in the slightest. More than ever, we are desperate to escape the shackles of scientific examination with anything that stimulates our imagination. Dreams are not an escape route from our reality—they offer an opportunity to enrich and enhance our reality.

Dreams are slippery, often difficult to recall. Dream interpretation is not an exact science because dreams have multiple meanings, themes, and symbols. Dreams cannot be explained like simple needs.* Dreams, in their most common meaning, re-

*Sigmund Freud (1856–1939) believed that deep in the core of our dreams lie our most profound, often sexual, desires, which our dreams hide away from our waking minds. Carl Gustav Jung (1875–1961) believed that dreams are vital messages that need to be heard, not hidden away. Dreams help reveal many of our wildest wishes to our waking minds and, in doing so, let us fulfill our ambitions.

fer to an ideal, an aspiration, or a state of mind in which the proper perception of reality is rearranged. When translated into business terms, dreams lose their ideals and become the products and services whose aspirational contents can elevate us to a state of mind that transcends reality. In other words, these are the products and services we crave to stimulate our imagination and emotions. This is certainly not a new business. Since the beginning, fulfilling dreams has been one of man's most important urges and, up until the Industrial Revolution, it marked an important force in world economies. From common objects with surprising aesthetic qualities created to please our ancestors, to pyramids built to fulfill pharaohs' dreams of immortality, to the continents discovered during the search for precious metals and exotic spices, to palaces and monuments erected to glorify kings and emperors, history has often been influenced by man's most extreme aspirations. Unfortunately, most of the time, satisfying material dreams has been considered a luxury,* the prerogative of a lucky few, since too many people were too busy worrying about basic survival. Luxury best expressed man's aspiration for what is rare or out of reach, as well as the sublime desire for material pleasure that has often been branded sinful. This urge to aspire to more than nature or social status can offer is not only fundamental to human nature, but also as ancient as its first evidence in the story of Adam and Eve. As far back as Genesis 3:3, this burning desire got its first bad rap: **Man's material aspirations lead to all that is not necessary and is forbidden.**

*Etymologically, the word "luxury" is derived from the Latin *luxus,* signifying sensuality, abundance, splendor, or refinement. Linked to two other Latin words—*lux,* or light, and *luxuria*—it refers to the extreme sensuality and sexuality usually associated with sin.

This obsessive desire for what was out of reach brought the punishment and expulsion of our two destitute ancestors from the Garden of Eden. How could Adam and Eve, who, at the time, were leading a life that even the Sultan of Brunei would call extravagant, lose everything over a simple apple, something that even the most impoverished human being can now afford? Because desire is defined not by that which one has, but by that by which one is tempted. Of course, that simple apple was more than just a cursed fruit. It represented the fruit of knowledge, which was solely God's prerogative and thus forbidden. Unfortunately, in surrendering to temptation, Adam and Eve committed the original sin that still weighs so oppressively on our conscience from the moment we are born.

This was just the beginning of the curse against man's material dreaming. Crucified by a majority of religions and doctrines as the fundamental cause for the demise of all humanity, the desire to fulfill our material dreams has become (and still is at times today) the cause for condemnation. By instilling in man a sense of guilt for his search to relieve existential anguish, church and state have often cast the desire for material pleasure in a sinful light. The greatest fear was that, upon tasting pleasure, people would free themselves from their obedience to God, to moral principles, or to the establishment, and therefore would pervert the social order. Material aspirations threatened institutions with their destabilizing force, so much so that the state felt compelled to subjugate them through sumptuary laws* or

*While such measures applied to the entire population, men in power were usually free to do whatever they wanted. Suffice it to say that two of the most aggressive enforcers of sumptuary laws were Nero (37–68) and Louis XIV (1638–1715).

through forms of specific taxation that would discourage consumption.

Starting with the Middle Ages, these "wicked" aspirations took on an iconographic dimension, usually feminine and seductive in appearance and dangerously laced in sensuality and beauty, and always ready to pounce on human virtue. However, medieval times brought new splendor to man's material dreams. Chivalry's code of honor glorified spending as altruistic. Feudal lords were supposed to spend their fortune, not on their own personal desires, but to declare their superiority and to please their entourage. While living in abject poverty, common people accepted their condition as an immutable birthright, feeling no jealousy toward the rich, since they saw no human chance to improve their own social stature. Material aspirations had suddenly acquired an aesthetic dimension with the embellishing of community living through opulent and romantic theatrical displays. The Renaissance stripped those aspirations of their predominantly military and religious stature, appointing them a newfound political role. Here, the king's mission was to protect his citizenry and to promote splendor in his kingdom. Material aspirations were mainly aimed at promoting a ruler's political greatness, a far less expensive or risky feat than waging war. Artists, artisans, and men of culture suddenly proved more useful than generals in aggrandizing the king's political strength. With this, a hearty slice from the military budget was divvied out to purchase art and construct grandiose buildings and statues. Material dreams had grown more accessible and less futile. Now heralded for improving the quality of life, they had gone from a seduction cursed by religious guilt to an experience in which pleasure was permitted. The seal of social acceptance came with the financial and industrial revolution during the eighteenth century in England, when a new economic and political order emerged. Ceasing to be a nontransferable force solely reserved for one social class, power and wealth were opening out into every reach of society. Material dreams had lost their image of decadence and destruction to become a symbol of freedom, education, refinement, and art, and a critical factor in the redistribution of wealth and the generation of industrial expansion.

THE FULFILLMENT of material dreams represents a relative concept, born of a subjective perception rather than an objective reality (what is common to one may be the ultimate dream to another). It's a concept likely to evolve over time and space. Periods of cultural effervescence, like the T'ang dynasty in China, the Golden Age in Athens, or the Italian Renaissance, have occurred wherein material dreams swung toward aesthetic considerations by becoming **the possibility of acquiring the time, knowledge, and soul of imaginative and talented people.** However, since fulfilling dreams has historically been reserved for the most fortunate and successful members of society, it has usually represented **the possibility of overcoming social indifference** (considered a measure of success, a human condition society admires). This discriminatory status may be headed for change, since technological advances are spreading dreams to a much wider population. Dreaming is no longer a luxury.

We live in an era of accelerated change. The universe was created 12 billion years ago with a big bang while man, or better, *Australopithecus afarensis,* first appeared only 4 million years ago. In prehistoric times, changes did not come easily. It wasn't until the Cro-Magnon moved through the region that is now France thirty-five thousand to ten thousand years ago that art and technology began to develop. With sophisticated mixtures of manganese and iron oxides, their lives and dreams were beautifully painted on their cave walls. Consider the 4 million years it took man—or, better, woman, since Lucy was, after all, a female—to toddle away from her mother's tree just to reach that decorated cave dwelling. Now, compare the mere thirty years it has taken us from sending a monkey up into space to disengaging from planet Earth altogether when we rocketed to the moon and beyond! A trip up to Mir, our condominium in space, makes Lucy's little stroll look like kid's play.

The world is now reinventing itself almost every ten years through new technologies. Some believe that the period from 1850 to 1903 may have been the most prolific period of new technologies: the lightbulb, the phonograph, the telephone, the radio, the automobile, the refrigerator, and the airplane. These breakthroughs, however, were distant dreams that only the fortunate few could enjoy. For a technology to be relevant to mankind, it must improve the life of more than just millionaires. A real indicator of technological progress should be the time it takes for a new invention to go from dream to necessity. Today, this time frame has been reduced to the blink of an eye—"never in your wildest dreams" is already passé.

We live in the Age of Speed. The computer has delivered communication at the speed of light. We've grown so impatient that instant gratification has become the rule: instant coffee, instant pancakes, instant microwave-hot, instant replay, instant sex on easy-access cable. Attention spans have shrunk. Speed makes us feel we are getting more of life, but in our race to download so much data into so little space, we are left desperately trying to create more of something we cannot: time.

Speed is efficiency, since less time is needed to get the job done. With technology offering us faster and better methods of achieving vital tasks, we are freer to enjoy more leisure* time. On average, leisure time has almost doubled over the course of the twentieth century and will continue to do so in the future. Leisure time and television have boosted the number of middle-class dreamers striving for the things previously reserved only for the rich, whether they be material dreams, exciting entertainment, or cultural and intellectual activities. Today, people may be weary of the possibilities that constantly confront them, either through the many channels of their cable television or the endless options they can click on their computer. The truth is that people are only beginning to appreciate this new wealth (or apparent wealth) of choices. A click of the remote control and instant dreams fill our homes twenty-four hours a day. Television programs, hosted by supermodels, take us backstage where leggy bombshells dress up or down to prepare for runway catwalks. Tabloids, magazines, catalogues, and newspapers deliver our dreamscapes in Technicolor, a vivid way to fill the gaps in our own lives.

* * *

*Leisure only exists when material goals are satisfied and a surplus of means can meet needs which are not essential for survival. Today, leisure is restored to its original meaning, as a time for thinking and exercising the mind without constraints. The word "school" comes from the Greek *skholé,* meaning leisure, or the employment of leisure in disputation, as in highly civilized ancient Greece, where learning and becoming educated was held to be the best way to spend leisure time.

NEVER BEFORE has life so mimicked a Hollywood movie, turning mass murder into mass media and total destruction into happy endings. The world seems set to head in a new direction, managing to create more than it has destroyed. And, despite the amount of wealth destroyed by wars alone in this century, the world's total estimated GNP still seems able to explode, from a few hundred billion dollars at the start of the century to an estimated $40 trillion in the year 2000. **Over this past century alone, we have managed to create more wealth than in all of the preceding 4 million years of our civilization.** This growth is bound to accelerate. Over the next twenty years, the world economy—its output in goods and services—should double, while the average living standard, after adjustment for population growth, should rise by almost two-thirds. The world political order, though full of small crises, seems momentarily calmed by the allure of a *Pax Economica.* Wealthy and poor nations work alongside one another on a new global activity: generating wealth. Adam Smith's prediction that commercialism would prove to be civilizing seems to have become a reality, since even just sitting back and watching war on CNN depresses sales. Commercialism is luring man away from the battlefield and onto the businessfield. It is also changing customers' choices. We used to sit down to only two choices at breakfast; now we're using logarithms just to count our way down the cereal aisle.

We live in an era in which dreams are much more accessible to many more people than ever before. Fulfilling customers' dreams is no longer a marginal activity dedicated to pleasing a few spoiled individuals. It has rapidly grown into a substantially influential business that affects the rest of the economy.

* * *

ONEIROMANCY, the interpretation of dreams, is becoming a critical skill for the successful businessperson. Since interpreting dreams is more an art than a science, there are no precise rules to follow. Looking at various phenomena that share some elements with dreams should help one better understand how they are formed and shaped.

For its theatrical excessiveness and desire to constantly surprise, fashion shares many characteristics with dreams. The business logic behind fashion is designed to arouse the customers' emotions by influencing their perception of reality.

FOR MANY CENTURIES, dress codes have determined different class hierarchies. Each class would, by tradition, wear its own clothing style ordained by a strict dress code (the French *droit vestimentaires*), which would enforce the rules of this tradition. Sumptuary edicts would forbid people of the lower class to dress like nobles. The thirteenth and fourteenth centuries saw the advent of the *parvenu,* a successful bourgeois class that craved social recognition in its desire to imitate the aristocracy. According to a model ascribed to Herbert Spencer (1820–1903), the lower classes, in their search for social acknowledgment, imitated the behavior and appearance of the higher classes. The higher classes, in order to preserve their social distinction, were obliged to change and modify their appearance once it was imitated. It has been this dual action of imitation and differentiation that has fueled the constant innovation we call "fashion."

Favoring the decay of an inflexible order that defined the traditional *parure* and class differences, fashion fostered risk-taking and the acceptance of change among the classes, legitimizing the desire for social promotion of the working population. The right to distinction was no longer limited by birth, but could be gained through competition and upward mobility. Fashion depreciates the collectively accepted past by insisting on novelty. It creates change by kindling aesthetic initiative and originality.

Almost theatrical in its ostentation and caprice, fashion has succeeded in fostering the refinement of taste and the sharpening of aesthetic sensitivity. It has educated the eye to discriminate and find pleasure in the subtlest of details, to accept new forms, to search for grace, elegance, and originality. The pleasure lies not only in seeing but, even more important, in being seen. Fashion becomes a message, the expression of moods, feelings, and tastes that are not limited to a specific action or moment, but to a personality and a lifestyle. It is the source of many pleasures: seduction, surprise, impression, excitement, and shock. In its quest for happiness in life, an escape from the ordinary and the vulgar, fashion longs to promote one's individuality.

Anna Wintour, *Vogue*'s present editor-in-chief, prizes the influence of her magazine in shaping fashion and recalls the time *Vogue* ran a little blurb on a man selling orchids down in Miami. She remembers when he came all the way up to New York City to hand deliver an orchid in thanks for the piece and for how much his business had taken off. She smiles remembering how he told her that he "could pay off the rent for the next ten years just from that one little mention in our magazine." Praised for her intuitive ability to recognize and even guide the mercurial changes of fashion, Anna Wintour says, "Fashion is always reflecting what is happening on the outside.

Sometimes it's hard to see it when you're closely involved in it, but when you look back and see what we all wore in the nineties when everything went black and plain, we were in the middle of a recession. Fashion photographs can tell you just as much about what is going on in the world as the newspaper headlines. It is a real signal." Ms. Wintour thinks that great designers are those who can influence the fashion of a certain period. "They direct the ideas and taste of their time and they have brilliant designs. Whereas certain designers might represent the last decade, for example, I think Gucci and Prada are the designers of the moment. Everybody wants them, that's what fashion is about. And they're not cheap, we put a six-thousand-dollar red crocodile handbag in our February '98 issue and now there is a waiting list of hundreds of people just from that one picture."

As Ms. Wintour sees it, "Fashion has everything, it has sex and glamour and gorgeous girls. What else do you need? It has escapism, it's fun, it's basic, it's nothing more intellectual than that." Its innovation applies to temporarily shaping appearances, manifesting its energy in changes that are short-lived. Fashion addresses social recognition, risk-taking, glorification of glamour, and the right to distinction, characteristics it shares with many dream products. Dreams, however, are usually not as transient as fashion. While fashion accelerates the passing of time, many dreams are capable of withstanding the judgment of time: They never "go out of fashion." If fashion buys youth, dreams buy time: Dreams often stop time, because controlling time is the ultimate dream. In order to endure fleeting trends, dream products or services should adopt a lasting aesthetic dimension.

* * *

AESTHETICS* pertain to the science of art and beauty. People grasp the concept of Beauty because they can appreciate it through their senses and their minds, and can reproduce it through the power of their imagination. Beauty is a value experienced when perception is not guided by a practical need but purely by an aesthetic impulse: A beautiful object does not interest us for its functional utility, but for its emotional content. One reads an income statement for the information it contains and a poem for the emotions it sparks. Beauty attracts us with its profound pleasure and serenity. We cherish beauty so much because it makes us feel good about ourselves.

Kant† maintained that aesthetic judgment aspires to be universal: An individual who believes that a person, a work, or an object is beautiful is convinced that it is an objective judgment that everyone else shares. When saying that Catherine Deneuve, Michelangelo's *David,* or a Ferrari is beautiful, the individual believes that this is not just his personal taste, but

*The word was first introduced by Alexander Baumgarten, a German philosopher (1714–1762), who made a major distinction between *noeta,* facts of intellect, and *aistheta,* facts of sensitivity. His most significant contribution, *Aesthetica* (first edition 1750, second edition 1758), associated *aistheta* with true knowledge. Baumgarten acknowledged the difference between a knowledge guided by the senses and one guided by the intellect, calling it a "sensitive" knowledge. The three fundamental issues of aesthetics are: 1) the relationship between art and nature; 2) the relationship between art and man; 3) the role of art in society. Today, the word "aesthetics" has grown to include all analysis, study, or speculation whose objective is connected with art and beauty.

†Kant also claimed that our sensitivity to beauty is a testimony to our inclination toward morality (defined as a set of values and prescriptions, pertaining to an epoch, a civilization, or a person). He believed that aesthetic perception projects and prepares moral awareness (in both, there is a strong sense of direction and an equilibrium between freedom and the rigor of values).

rather something everybody will agree upon. Beauty is what pleases universally. It is not founded on any *a priori* concept, because there is no imposed idea of beauty, no simple model on which we can base our judgment or define our standard. Is Catherine Deneuve the universal model for the beautiful woman, or is it Marlene Dietrich, Ava Gardner, Brigitte Bardot, Sophia Loren, Cindy Crawford, or even Hillary Clinton?

The idea of beauty does not float in some transcendental state but is actualized through the work of the genius, the artist, the creator, or the craftsman: Beauty is born of labor. The creation of beauty is rarely an improvisation. It requires a learning process through which the artist and creator achieve technique and a means of expression that free their creative potential. Because no universally accepted definition of beauty exists, just as no set rules can produce a beautiful object, artists and creators must develop their own vision. A Ferrari automobile, a Girard-Perregaux watch, a Feadship yacht, and the movie *Casablanca* are not, no matter how beautiful they may be, models that once copied will guarantee the absolute beautiful automobile, watch, yacht, or film. The different expressions of beauty can act as examples, yet, since beauty does not follow objective criteria, those expressions cannot be simply imitated to reproduce beauty. As Hegel said, *"Art does not imitate, art idealizes because it is able to express the universal in the particular."*

Hegel believed that any form of aesthetic expression depends on the culture and the vision of the world for which it is the expression. What may have been regarded as a "fact of Nature" (a perception of beauty that is *a priori* or genetically inherited, therefore given to us by Nature) is, in reality, a "fact of culture" (an *a posteriori* perception learned from the cultural environment). Certain harmonies appeal to our ear, or certain plastic forms to our eye, because those organs have been conditioned by a certain environment earlier on. While stemming from the realm of senses and emotions, beauty still represents a call to knowledge. The more we know about art, a craft, or a technique, the better we can appreciate it. A *grande complication* watch is even more beautiful once we're more attuned to its technological sophistication and complexity. The perception of beauty can thus be instructed and even influenced.

Those products and services that ignite our dreams come from a particular cultural environment in which time and exposure have contributed to a deeply rooted appreciation for art and objects that possess strong aesthetic value. Artists, creators, and craftsmen make common objects so beautiful that the aesthetic appeal overwhelms the functional. Some of those objects become the heirlooms, handed down over generations* through inheritance, collections, and museums, that enrich the perception of beauty for future generations and contribute to the historical evolution of beauty.

MATERIAL DREAMS are often the expression of exuberance, since they usually surpass the functions for which they were first conceived. They are the "symptoms" of culture, since they reflect the worst or best a given culture has to offer. It is society's taste that determines to what extent material dreams express aesthetic values.

*Until the practice was finally prohibited by Catholicism, people were buried with their most precious belongings. These significant objects have been unearthed by archeologists and used to assess the cultural development of ancient civilizations.

The word "taste" defines the criteria by which to judge an object or the expressions of man's feelings. Beauty, for example, is a feeling, and taste is the canon by which to judge the various expressions of beauty. Kant distinguished between "taste," a faculty with which to judge, and "genius," a faculty with which to produce. It is the artists', designers', and creators' task to help refine their constituencies' collective taste by imposing their own norms, both in how they create their products and in how these products are "consumed." Success for artists, designers, and creators often means exceeding the norms accepted by society to present original works representative of their genius, style, craft, or technique. For original works to be properly appreciated, some guidelines are required for their interpretation. For an artist, this process of "education" may not be immediate. Many times works of art are not perceived as such until long after the artist's death. In business, on the other hand, educating the customers' taste is crucial, since their immediate acceptance is what keeps a company alive. In other words, Caravaggio (1573–1610), van Gogh (1853–1890), Utrillo (1883–1955), Soutine (1893–1943), and Modigliani (1884–1920) are still deemed "great" even if during their lives they starved trying. However, you can bet there will never be a company in the business of selling dreams that will achieve greatness without feeding its bottom line.

THERE IS ANOTHER COMPONENT in every dream that pertains to our desire to entertain ourselves. Perhaps it is why many materialistic dreams are referred to as "grown-up toys." Sports cars, yachts, airplanes, watches, and so forth are, to some, just toys for adult boys, and jewels, dresses, perfumes, and so forth toys for grown-up girls (thus preserving the sexist segregation toys have usually carried). The word "play" conjures up ideas of relaxation, pleasure, moderate risk, and general abilities. In an environment of fantasy, where freedom is the indispensable engine, a player participates in a game free to quit at any time. Only with continual and unpredictable renewal of the action does interest last. Many historians and psychologists consider the spirit of play to be one of the principal resources of society as well as one of the highest expressions of culture.

Play fosters creativity by provoking the players to constantly improvise and invent new responses that are free within the limits of the competition's rules. What sparks interest is the game's continual and random surprise. In every form of play, rules tend to bind and confine the creator. They do not, however, eliminate freedom, they only provide a framework. Rules* also beget recognizable styles wherein a sense of taste, a mixture of technical difficulties, and the whim of genius all come together.

Play is a means of managing energy and working through primitive impulses to compensate for life's many frustrations and the boredom of the daily nine-to-five grind. Play is a consolidation of intellectual operations, a way of learning the difference between fact and fiction. More important, play represents a major force in sustaining the creative spirit, which is

*Several parallels can be drawn between play and aesthetics. In the domain of aesthetics, as in play, freedom is usually shaped by rules and rigor. In painting, the law of perspective must be respected; in music, rules of harmony; in poetry, prosody and metrical rhythm act as the confining structure; in sculpture, there are proportions; in choreography, rhythm and motion pose limits; in theater, stage directions.

often left behind in the attic toy box. If, for the child, play fills the important role of "growth regulator," teaching positive adjustments in life, for the adult, it represents a re-creation or renewal of life.

FASHION, aesthetics, social taste, and play all have relevance to the shaping and understanding of customers' dreams. Companies eager to sell dreams should study the world of fashion. With fashion's constant quest for newness, its fostering of risk-taking to surprise customers, its legitimization of social promotion and individuality, its theatrical settings, its educational role in finding aesthetic pleasure even in details, and its glorification of glamour, fashion companies create a business environment filled with dreams. There is also a great deal to learn from art. Neither frivolous nor fleeting like fashion, art generates pleasure by exposing people to the beauty of all its expressions. Through the power of the artist's imagination, art brings us beyond functional utility into a world of emotions. From the world of art, companies can see that aesthetic research is not based on improvisation but comes from the arduous development of innovative techniques. Original work requires guidelines for interpretation established through a process of education. Just as various leading artists can influence social taste, companies can also impose their norms, both in how their products are created and in how they are "consumed." However, unlike artists, companies can make use of their substantial communication resources to accelerate the learning process so that their products can be readily accepted. Companies can influence their customers' taste. For example, the more customers know about a style, a craft, or a technique, the more they will appreciate its complexity. Since the goal is to sell dream products and services to generate profits rather than create art to gain immortality, companies cannot push aesthetic research too far. Their creations cannot be artistic ego trips, they must fulfill their customers' dreams. When dreaming, customers are not art critics, they are players who want to be surprised. And with so much more leisure time, they will want to indulge in diversion even more. Just like players, today's customers have very short attention spans: Their interest must be renewed constantly and unpredictably or else it's lost. Play has often been considered one of the highest expressions of culture, often an activity in which freedom exists within a framework of rules. Many companies could kick up their creativity (the "substance" dreams are made of) with a more playful approach to work.

THE DEMOCRATIZATION of dream fulfillment has become one of the enjoyable consequences of the unprecedented wealth our society has generated over the last few decades. Today, purchasing products and services of extreme quality is no longer the sole prerogative of a lucky few. Even those people who cannot afford them have been swayed more by the riches offered up through television and gossip magazines than by the size of their bank accounts. The world at large wants to indulge in the pleasure of material well-being. The technological revolution has saturated our needs and enabled us to stimulate our imagination. "Give me the luxuries in life and I can dispense with the necessities," once a famous wish from Oscar Wilde, has now become the demand of the masses. So widespread is the phenomenon that the word "luxury" seems to have grown obsolete, no longer able to express this pervasive desire for pleasure, comfort, wonderment, and surprise. The word "dreams" better characterizes those products and services that, exclusive or not, can elate and surprise the customer.

This amplification of customer expectation is shaping the way companies do business, since customer spending is shifting away from the satisfaction of necessities into the fulfillment of desires. Customers have become so spoiled by the miracles of technology that they want luxury even in the most common object or service, be it bread, water, or toilet paper. Satisfying physiological necessities is now considered the bare minimum. Customers prefer to spend their hard-earned money on products and services that improve their emotional well-being. In other words, companies are more likely to attract more customer spending power by selling dreams.

To fulfill their customers' dreams, companies need to expand their sources of knowledge by adopting a much more eclectic approach to business. How does a company fulfill these dreams? Obviously, this is not an easy task, since dreams, by definition, must surprise and excite, must produce wonder and intrigue. So-called luxury companies best exemplify an industry of dreams in which products and services, unique, exclusive, beautiful, rich, and glamorous, are created to exceed the customer's imagination. A Ferrari is a perfect dream product: It is not purchased because of its function as a car, but rather because it transports us to the exciting and romantic world of racing (with all its symbolic, aesthetic, and hedonistic appeal). In the same way, all of the most successful movies ignite spectators' dreams. As Michael Mann, one of the most insightful Hollywood directors, says, "To fulfill one of the preconditions of cinema, spectacularly successful pictures must transport people into a world for two to three hours that is not their normal world and a world that they have not been in before or have not been in for a long time. It's a completely different world that when re-created with consummate artistry can do that fundamental thing that only cinema can do: placing you in a large darkened room, you get to collectively, with the rest of the audience, dream away. You are truly in that world, you lose yourself in the world of the film."

To inspire its customers' dreams, a company has to transport them to a world that is more exciting, more seductive, more romantic than the one they live in.

The luxury and movie industries' business missions both play upon the customers' dreams. It is certainly more difficult, but nevertheless possible, to captivate customers with more common products and services. For example, the huge success of the Volkswagen Beetle, Nike sneakers, or the Sony Walkman could be attributed to the way each product ignited the dreams of an entire generation. Through these products, companies managed to interpret the latent thoughts and moods that motivated the desires of customers in different times, whether the love of the underdog that the "flower-power" generation saw in the unpretentious little German car or the love of freedom and leisure that have forged the success of both Sony and Nike.

TO SUCCEED in the age of constant change, in which everything seems possible, a company must be able to launch a product or a service that answers a corresponding dream. In a sense, it must interpret the spirit of the times, or the *zeitgeist,* and discover the leading ideas that influence how people behave, respond to their environment, form their aspirations, and make their purchasing choices. How can one interpret the spirit of the times? As this is usually the prerogative of artists and thinkers, we asked Luc Gauthier, one of Europe's rising painters and a professor at the École Nationale Supérieure des Arts Décoratifs in Paris, for his thoughts.

Q: "Are real artists those who interpret the 'spirit of the time'? If so, how can they shape it?"

L.G.: "Flour is the raw material of the baker, money is the raw material of the businessman, and time is the raw material of the artist. The artist must understand what in his time differs, even if imperceptibly, from the preceding time or times, and then shape it. This means creating a reality which is tangible and alive, thus fragile and imperfect, like any human reality."

Q: "Does this require a supernatural sensitivity or an ability to constantly listen?"

L.G.: "Certainly one needs natural gifts and a particular aptitude, for this 'job/profession' of artist, as with any other vocation. Maybe people should feel like they were being called, or maybe they feel they simply cannot do anything else. After that, it requires a veritable exigency, a total giving of oneself, so one can perceive the silence so difficult to hear against the noise of any complex society. It is as difficult as when the Resistance desperately tried to listen to Radio London [during World War II] so indecipherably scrambled by the Germans."

Q: "Since this is a business book, how should an artist feel about being poor when some paintings sell for millions?"

L.G.: "Gold exists because it is rare, thus it is precious, and the one who finds it, the gold digger, relies on the wholesalers, the retailers, the banks, etc. Each one is part of the chain, and even if it sounds unjust to say that the gold digger is far less rich than the banker, one cannot forget that he has chosen his life.

Some get confused, and, at times, the gold digger aspires to become the banker and the banker, the gold digger. Of course, there are moments when a penniless artist may be struck by the blues and feel like a great French chef who goes bankrupt and has to surrender his lease to McDonald's."

Q: "Can art be viewed as a business?"

L.G.: "In today's confusion, is business not perceived as art? Everyone claims the artist's status/condition without assuming the obligations. If van Gogh is very expensively valued today, perhaps it is because our civilization no longer has confidence in its living art."

Q: "How does art influence the business world?"

L.G.: "Since 1945, the world of art has become a world of business. In the stock exchange, values may be fictitious; the guaranteed value of art is also fictitious."

Q: "How can creativity be enhanced?"

L.G.: "By giving a real value to the work of art, which is the price of the work, of the talent, but nothing more than a human wage. Too much money for an artist may be as detrimental as not enough."

Q: "Do you think it possible for businesses to operate like artists and find inspiration in their own souls rather than from numbers crunched out on market studies?"

L.G.: "All creators, and evidently, the innovation in the business world are born of intuition. Their intuition bears a new vision that can be embraced even though there is still no real demand."

WHILE MR. GAUTHIER may espouse a very romantic view, Christopher Buckley, an American writer and political commentator, expresses his pragmatic opinions on how to interpret the spirit of our times.

"We live in very materialistic times. It seems that we have gone from the age of the *Logos* [reason as the controlling principle of the universe, in other words the power that begins the entire world] to the age of the Logo, the trademark, the brand name. More and more people seem to be defining their lives according to the brand names. We are no longer 'what we eat' or 'what we read,' we are 'what we wear and drive.' As a reflection of the materialism of the age, even James Bond has lost his aristocratic taste and is now more impressed by brands than by blondes. Particularly in the American culture, it is hardly a new phenomenon that people identify themselves with the products they wear and use. Yet, as we are approaching the year of the triple zeros, we seem to have reached some kind of explosion of the form, to a degree that makes you wonder whether or not some core values are missing. When I was growing up, the label used to be on the inside, you had to look under the other person's collar or inside the jacket. Now, it is stamped on the outside big and bold. Why is it so important to people to announce to the world that you are wearing Tommy Hilfiger or Donna Karan? Labeling has become a way of defining cultural and tribal identities: It is better to say Italian-American or Irish-American than say Hutu or Tutsi, at least one gets in less trouble. The current obsession to identify oneself according to the things one buys, drinks, drives, wears, and smokes is an extension of the kind of need to identity which we have always innately felt. Maybe in America it is more ingrained because this is the most consumerist nation of all, where people are bombarded from infancy with commercial messages (a typical seven-year-old absorbs 180,000 commercial messages a year!).

Yet, we are not the leaders in materialistic identification: Japan and Russia top that list. The Japanese identify themselves even more with material objects, possibly as a reaction to the fact that theirs is a society which emphasizes homogeneity and conformity.

"People want to be associated with icon products because they spark people's dreams. For instance, Henry Ford's huge success stemmed from his ability to reify a dream. In a revolutionary way, he interpreted the desires of the American people, who dreamed of owning 'something' that would set them free. That car, the Model T, represented one of the most ingrained American dreams, the dream of mobility (America being a big country, it needed to be explored). Levi's, an icon product of very humble beginnings (originally the uniform of poor miners), is connected with another primal dream: striking it rich (the search for gold). Every great American personality, at the acme of their career, looked best in jeans: James Dean, Gary Cooper, John Wayne, Clint Eastwood, Ronald Reagan, even Dolly Parton. Jeans are so extravagantly popular because they also tie in to the utmost American symbol, the one you would send out in space to define the essence of America to the Martians: the cowboy. Any American male, no matter what his origins, at a certain point in his life has dreamed of becoming a cowboy. It is primal because it involves mobility and freedom, and you get to shoot the Indians. Perhaps Marlboro is the most recognized logo in the world because it celebrates the image of the cowboy."

So I asked Mr. Buckley what he feels culturally motivates the latest craze in terms of television sitcoms. "Why is the most watched television show in the world *Baywatch,* frantically seen by 2.3 billion people every week?"

"I think you can deconstruct that one pretty easily: tits and ass [isn't this guy crude?]. It is a television program that is no more than a 'moving' *Sports Illustrated* swimsuit issue."*

While Mr. Buckley believes that those commercial successes are "due to everybody's dream of getting laid," on a less trite note, it could be the expression of an Adonis/Venus dream, attracting social admiration through physical beauty.

He adds, "Some dreams are changing. Last year, for the first time since the poll was taken, the majority of parents no longer share the dream of wanting to raise the next American president. It was much more fun in the past to be president; one could have an affair with the secretary, call an air strike without asking Congress for permission. Now the paperwork alone will kill you. To paraphrase Mel Brooks, 'it is no longer good to be the king.'"

Mr. Buckley does not believe that the spirit of the times can be interpreted, not even by great artists.

"One cannot consciously interpret the *zeitgeist,* because it is sort of like the Heisenberg principle in physics, the closer one gets to an object, the more unreliable the information one can draw from it. Great artistic interpretations of an age are wonderful accidents. For instance, Hemingway did not consciously set out to interpret the age of 1920s when he wrote *A Moveable Feast,* a [memoir] that was not even published until after his death because he did not think much of it. He was simply writing about his world. The interpretation that most endures is

***Sports Illustrated*'s swimsuit issue was created to fill the void during the single week of the year when no sporting events occur and has become the magazine's biggest moneymaker with spinoff videos, calendars, TV special programs, and accessories.

the one that explains the age most economically and universally. For instance, Tom Wolfe, possibly the greatest American writer of this half of the century, has often been able to portray the spirit of the American times. It is of no wonder that his theme is 'status' and that his literary signature is 'branding' since he constantly refers to it."

WHILE IT MAY BE DIFFICULT to decide whether artists' or writers' interpretations of the spirit of their times is due to a special sensitivity and commitment as Gauthier preaches or to the wonderfully accidental luck that Buckley describes, it is certain that a company, with its need for profits, cannot rely on luck. A company should have an easier time interpreting the desires that motivate its customers than an artist or writer, who must interpret the cultural spirit of the times. Companies, unlike most artists and writers, who usually work on their own, can count on a wide range of collaborators to generate creative ideas. Most important, companies can also promote their products through incisive advertising and public-relations campaigns that help educate and possibly influence their customers' and even society's perceptions. A company's precise purpose is to generate wealth, while artists and writers are torn by complex spiritual and cultural motivations. It is easier to influence the customer's material dreams than a civilization's artistic and poetic vision.

AUCTION HOUSES prove to be the definitive place where art meets business. Didi Brooks, Sotheby's president and CEO, has a clear idea of who is responsible for interpreting the spirit of the times: "The artists. The critics have a point of view and sometimes they can influence the views of the time. Look at the Impressionists, who were absolutely destroyed by the critics of their time, and yet sixty years later they have withstood the test of time. Critics probably have too much control during the time that art is being made. Some time must pass for one to really declare who created great art and who created art which was interesting at the time but that did not stand the test of time."

It seems to me that Sotheby's does influence the tastes and desires of its customers. At times, it's as if Sotheby's even promotes a form of art that customers may not have been aware they liked, but that becomes a huge success.

"For example," Ms. Brooks recalls, "when we sold an Andy Warhol in Maryland two months ago for $17 million, we played a role in creating a value that was placed on that work of art. Our contribution is marketing works of art in such a way that value is created. Another example was the *Tyrannosaurus rex,* which some figured might have been difficult to sell. But the way we marketed it and the context in which we wrote about this extraordinary fossil, I think, caused the price to become $8 million. So, our role is not as a cultural institution to opine on the aesthetics of the time or on what is good and what is not good. It is not Sotheby's responsibility to determine if something is art. We are a secondary marketplace. We do not represent artists, we do not sell primary works of art. There has to be an established market for us to sell it. And that is an aesthetic judgment made by someone before we get there. Our role is to place art in a context, to create an environment in which you market works of art. We do everything in our power to increase the value of works of art. Our contribution is creating an active marketplace. A lot of people do not like Warhol. And a lot of people like Warhol. The fact that we were able to achieve the price we did took Warhol to a price level he has never been before. We play a bit of a role in terms of the evaluation of art."

I asked Ms. Brooks whether she felt technology has changed taste. She agreed to some degree: "Yes, but I don't think we will feel the impact for some time. We will see more of it in people in their twenties or thirties than in people in their forties, fifties, and sixties. Our customers are mainly in this second group. So, even if we are trying to attract new customers and introduce them to art, we have to be careful not to put our buyers off by being too contemporary or too technology-oriented. We have done a few CD-ROMs, yet the collectors are not interested. It may be changing but it is much more dramatic in the younger ages. We are starting our first Internet auction this week on books. How can we make the Internet as exciting as the auction? How do you re-create the electricity that you have on the auction floor, the palpable energy and excitement that seems to give everything that is sold a bit of a lift? On the other hand, if people do not want something, they won't buy it just because of the excitement. You cannot create something out of nothing.

"Look at the JFK auction, for example. It gathered so much interest because of its meaning: the Great American Family, the tragedy of the Kennedy assassinations, the glamour and the mystique of Jacqueline Kennedy, her marriage to Aristotle Onassis, her children. We did not hype the auction. The press did. Our catalogue and the collection's setting made it really fun for people to come and see, offering them a real sense of the Kennedy family. By looking at the objects which filled their lives, the customers could understand the family history. The customer lived the Kennedy dream. Our job was to create an aura such that people wanted to own a piece of it. We want them to go away knowing that they can be part of this history and this dream."

While Sotheby's job is not to influence the aesthetic values of its time, its financial success depends on its ability to influence its customers' desires and taste. By selling works that best interpret the spirit of the times, Sotheby's attracts customers eager to buy time and a piece of eternity. Through careful selection and the exciting auction settings that Sotheby's constructs for its art and relevant objects, this company is able to increase the value of these works. Simply stated, Sotheby's builds a dream that customers want to live.

THERE IS a new breed of customers in the business arena. Their attention span must be reloaded as quickly as the rapid-fire rounds of change brought on by technology. Overindulged by the numerous options, they are, quite simply, spoiled! They are real "kings" who have much more money to spend and much more time to enjoy it. This new breed of customers is much more difficult to please. Their minds are triggered by emotional impulses that override all rational thinking. They live in a constantly frenetic state. To attract them, companies must sell products and services that can excite their dreams.

Dreams form within a certain cultural environment and are inspired by many different phenomena, such as fashion, aesthetics, society, taste, and man's desire to play. Interpreting them requires dedication. Artists often foresee and influence the dreams that shape the cultural environment. By integrating artistic intuition into its organization, a company is better suited to reach these dreams. Just as artists wander endlessly for inspiration, companies should constantly explore unrelated fields to increase their chances of understanding how their customers' desires are formed. Just like artists, they must learn to extrapolate from their cultural environment the spirit that drives their customers' dreams. This will let companies introduce new trends rather than just follow them.

Market analysis, consumer studies, and product clinics are no longer enough to succeed in this highly competitive and rapidly changing world. To sell dreams, the type of products and services that ignite customer spending and a company's future forever, means companies must interpret the spirit of the time.

DREAMS ARE ETHEREAL, existing only in our imagination. To transform them into business successes, companies must learn how to create products and services designed and engineered to excite intense emotions.

2

The Business of Selling Dreams

JUST AS WE NEED to carve out our own identities for a space in society, so do companies need to establish their brands to secure their business success. Fame is crucial in the business world, because it translates into name recognition, company image and reputation, customer awareness, and, most important, sales and profits. A company spends, over an entire lifetime, as much as 10 percent of total annual sales promoting and advertising its name and brands. No matter how crude it sounds, in today's competitive ring, it is often hard cash that buys fame. Maybe that's why one major Japanese corporation was so stunned to discover that Ferrari was among the three most recognized brands in the world, the other two being IBM and Coca-Cola. What makes this such an impressive statistic is that Ferrari never even had an advertising budget until 1993 when the racing and sports **automobile** manufacturer, founded in 1947, finally created a marketing department! It is fascinating (or frustrating, depending on which company you're working for) to think that the few million dollars Ferrari has spent over the last twenty years to improve its name recognition has achieved an effect comparable to what the billions spent over the same period by such powerhouses as IBM and Coca-Cola have achieved.

Ferragamo is a company that has turned the most pedestrian exercise into an art. Rubbing his hands together like a priest on the receiving end of a most delicate confession, Massimo Ferragamo secretively ushered me toward his company's most prized treasure: the "museum" of lasts, wooden blocks built to perfectly replicate the world's most famous feet. Actresses and actors, artists, members of royalty, industrialists, and politicians have all been faithful yet demanding Ferragamo customers over the last seventy years. In the precision of these lasts lies the secret to what makes these handmade **shoes** so comfortable. Curiously morbid, they look like prostheses on parade, yet the "museum" sparks our curiosity as we discover the intimate anatomical secrets of so many beautiful stars and powerful people. From Sophia Loren to Anna Magnani, Audrey Hepburn, Ava Gardner, Marilyn Monroe, Rita Hayworth, and Marlene Dietrich, Salvatore Ferragamo could distinguish each foot just by handling it. It turns out that, when barefoot, Ava Gardner's flat feet saved her from having to vacuum, while Greta Garbo needed no flippers when scuba diving. Of all the different fittings, I asked Massimo Ferragamo what type of special shoe he wore. Ironically, the king of custom shoes doesn't even wear custom shoes himself, since he was endowed with man's most standard foot size: a 10E.

In a large room with massive wooden beams in La Chaux-de-Fonds, Switzerland, Girard-Perregaux displays its history through a collection of **watches** dating as far back as 1791, when the company was founded. Off the museum, six watch masters hunch over their work in the modest laboratory. With utter skill and dedication, as if they were performing open-heart surgery, these doctors of time assemble and construct the internal parts of their famously complex watches, such as the *grandes complications.** One master meticulously whittles away a wooden stick with his minute knife. What's most fascinating is that, though this wooden stick has been so carefully prepared, it is obviously never going to be part of the watch. It is simply a tool that the watch master will dab into a diamond paste in order to sand down the edges of the internal mechanism. Such intense dedication and so much precious time is invested simply to embellish parts of a watch that its future owner will never even see. This is the creation of an invisible beauty. Some might call it a wasted effort, yet it is the dictum of a craftsman's pride, reflecting his deep respect for those watch technicians who will, in the years to come, open the back and peer into his creation. In any efficiency-driven business, this translates into a squandering of costly energy. At La Chaux-de-Fonds, where the business strategy is also driven by the profound aspiration to create beauty, this story clearly demonstrates the supreme dedication involved in the concept of quality.

*In watchmaking, *complications* and *grandes complications* are terms for the functions of a watch that are not limited to showing the time. Examples of *complications* are date indicators, calendars, phases of the moon, or alarms, while *grandes complications* are combinations of the above, together with complex precision systems such as the perpetual calendar or the automatic *tourbillon.*

Château Margaux appears noble, austere, even a touch solemn, like some ancient temple devoted to the cult of **wine.** Vineyard or dwelling, Margaux disdains all embellishments. But, just as the wine must be served before it unfolds all its charms, so does the château await its visitors' entry before revealing its inner treasures. The wine and the château share the same elegance, distinction, and mystery that come from many generations of dedicated attention. A wine well-aged, a house well-inhabited, Margaux the vintage and Margaux the château are by-products of the rare combination of rigor and time.

Crissier is a small Swiss village where fifteen hundred inhabitants live perched in the hills near Lausanne. This seemingly common village has become world famous not because it houses the Swiss headquarters for McDonald's, the fast-food giant, but because of Le Girardet, a small restaurant responsible for some of the most sophisticated cuisine in the world. While it is strange to find such a temple of **haute cuisine** located outside France, the countryside surrounding Crissier naturally authenticates this dining experience. With the theatrical sense that often unites actors with great chefs, Fredy Girardet diffuses the complexities of haute cuisine with a simple look at his craft. "Enhancing the richest flavors which Nature can offer, I carefully select and combine the freshest ingredients. Time is the key ingredient to creating a great meal. The time of year when specific produce is harvested, the time needed for that produce to mature, the time required for their preparation and cooking to perfection, and of course, the precious time it takes to savor the delicious meal."

The post–World War II era brought an impressive prosperity that was ideologically shattered by the student revolts that swept the Western world in the late 1960s. Protesting the social differences that this economic recovery had generated, enraged students and workers exploded in revolt, hailing the communist manifesto of their hero, Ernesto "Che" Guevara. Very closely linked to Fidel Castro, Che Guevara, a doctor then, landed a very important role during the Cuban revolution. He was placed in charge of the most prestigious **cigar** factory in the world, Cohiba. Made from the finest tobacco crops on the island and prepared over a patient three-year period, today Cohiba is the best expression of Cuba's domination in the world of fine cigars. Ironic as it may sound, while Cuban communism goes up in smoke, cigars, one of the greatest expressions of capitalism, represent the most enduring legacy of the last bastion of the Marxist revolution.

In revolt against the czar's unrestrained luxury, the Marxist revolution rolled across oppressed Russia. The czar fled, seeking asylum at—where else?—the Ritz. While today the name Ritz appears on many **hotels** around the world, there is still only one that serves up the magnificence and *grande vie* that spurred the opening of so many grand hotels around the turn of the century. The Hôtel Ritz in Place Vendôme, Paris, was opened in 1898 by a hospitality professional and a visionary, César Ritz, who came from a mountain valley in Switzerland. In the former townhouse of the duke of Lauzun, the Ritz was one of the first hotels to offer the supreme luxury of electricity and fully equipped bathrooms in each room. Unlike most grand hotels at the time, it also offered superb food by the celebrated chef Escoffier. The grandeur of the Ritz can still be found in the refinement and polish of its employees (as many as two per guest), some of whom have worked at the Ritz for more than twenty years. After so many years of close contact with the most distinguished and sophisticated customers in the world, they have developed an ingrained *savoir faire* that epitomizes luxury service. Who could have ever demanded better attention than the Ritz's eminent sojourners: King Edward VII, the czar of Russia, F. Scott Fitzgerald, Truman Capote, Winston Churchill, Coco Chanel, Lady Di, and many others who have represented important pages in world history, politics, and culture.

For centuries, bankers in Geneva have managed the world's most wealthy accounts. On the surface, Lake Geneva is calm and placid, yet the rivers that flow into this lake are as wild and powerful as the money that has come to rest in this quiet little town. Perhaps that is why the entrance to the Pictet Bank reminded me of an impenetrable set of **bank** vault doors. I was ushered into Nicholas Pictet's office without ever even being asked my name. When I suggested to Mr. Pictet that not knowing a visitor's name could result in the wrong person's being introduced to the meeting, a smile stretched across his face. Geneva, one learns, is the only place where not acknowledging a customer's name is the ultimate measure of social recognition. At Pictet, the lure is anonymity.

"Blue screen" is a technique often employed to reproduce a dream or a vision in a **movie** by superimposing several elements. The more elements are superimposed, the more depth is given to the scene, and the more complex and credible the dream becomes. In Louisville, Kentucky, where I am sitting in on the shooting of a scene in Michael Mann's latest movie, which is based on the cigarette industry, blue screen is helping depict the protagonist's psychological struggle. Overwhelmed by his world crumbling all around him, alone in his hotel room, Dr. Jeffrey Wigand (played by Russell Crowe) longs for his daughters, who were wrenched from him along with all the furniture and much of his life when his wife decided to leave him. The mural decorating the wall of his room suddenly dissolves into his girls playing in the garden of his former Louisville home. Several scenes were shot separately. The first included the actor sitting alone, back to the world, the next the empty room and the mural, and the next the daughters playing in the garden. This last scene, which lasts only a few seconds, is being shot more than thirty times to appease Mann's fanatical search for perfection. Mann is certainly one of the few directors able to remind us that filmmaking is not only a business but can also be an activity akin to art. His commercial successes and the respect he enjoys in Hollywood have earned him a certain leverage with producers and distribution companies, letting him dynamically execute his films without stooping to external pressures. This is what lets him create movies with such complex psychological dimensions, stories often shunned by producers who deem them a commercial risk. This film is about an investigation into the cigarette industry's denial of nicotine's addictive effects. The topic could be perfect material for a lengthy, if not boring, legal case study—more so than the subject of a Hollywood blockbuster. Yet watching some of the scenes already shot, I have become completely enthralled by the plot, and have a craving to see the final product. The story unfolds slowly, not so much in terms of the movie's pace, but rather in terms of the intensity and depth of its plot development. Michael Mann has accomplished the extraordinary feat of transforming cold hard facts into engaging emotions. His painstaking research and attention to detail, coupled with his extraordinary vision, have produced dynamic works, both involving and credible. Mann's unflinching belief in what he does confirms that dreams are born of excruciating dedication.

* * *

AFTER SUCH A MISCELLANY OF STORIES, the question is: What do all these activities have in common? Each sells a different product: automobiles, shoes, watches, wine, haute cuisine, cigars, hotels, banking services, and movies. However, they share one common purpose: to fulfill their customers' dreams. These companies can exceed the mere function of their products or services by offering their customers an exceptional experience. These products and services primarily represent occasions to dream. Ferrari does not sell automobiles, but rather the dream of speed. Ferragamo does not sell shoes, but rather the dream of elegance. Girard-Perregaux is not merely a watch—it reflects the dream of controlling time. The Ritz is not just a hotel room, but a palace of splendor and refinement. Pictet not only manages bank accounts, but satisfies the dream of fertilizing money.

Selling dreams is an important business, which includes all of those products and services that can stimulate our imagination and excite our desires, from the most exclusive luxury to mass-produced products sharpened with an emotional edge. It includes automobiles like the Alfa Romeo Spider (which ignites the dreams of all college graduates) and the Ford Mustang, cultural statements like the Sony Walkman, Levi's jeans, or Nike sneakers, movies, "well-being" products (be it well-being of the mind, the body, or the wallet). We consider all of these "dream products" because their success is not gleaned purely from the function they satisfy, but from how they emotionally engage us. In a *sensu lato,* they fulfill a customer's dream.

Considering such a grouping of apparently diverse companies in a horizontal manner offers a different perspective on how a company can grow its business, because we shift away from the logic of their production and follow the logic of their customers' desires. Traditionally, such companies as Ferrari, Feadship, Ritz, and Chanel would think of themselves as being at the top, respectively, in the automotive, nautical, hospitality, and apparel industries.* However, selling such well-defined products and services as automobiles, boats, a hotel stay, or couture should not be the goal of any of the above companies. Customers do not usually buy a Ferrari or a Feadship yacht simply to get around in, a Chanel dress because they are cold, or a room at the Ritz because they are just looking for a good night's sleep. These companies sell dreams. Customers don't flock to them to buy functionality, but for an emotional boost. This distinction is key, because it helps a company broaden its business horizon and better relate to its customers. It forces a company to define its products and services in terms of its customers' desires rather than its own engineering capacities. Here, we unite companies from a horizontal perspective rather than vertically (see the graph on page 61), shifting the focus from the company and its products to the customer. This different perspective clearly illustrates that a company like Rolls-Royce has less in common with the car manufacturer Toyota than it does with a company like Ferragamo. From a product standpoint, Rolls-Royce obviously shares more with Toyota, since both produce cars. However, in terms of the customer, Rolls-Royce owners are more likely to purchase quality items from, say, Ferragamo than from the mass-production company JC Penney.

*As far back as the Middle Ages when business activities were first organized in guilds, classification has "vertically" referred to a company's specific products and services, since those are what have always defined the company's foremost business objective.

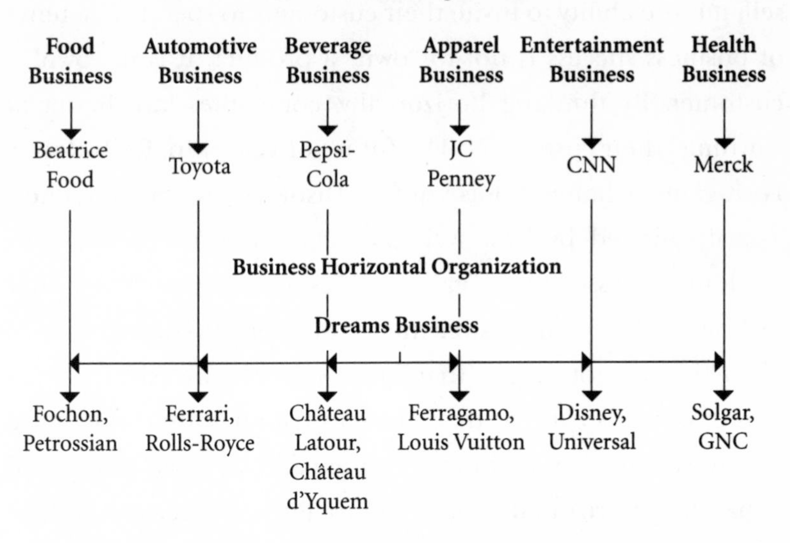

In a supply-driven economy, securing production has always been critical. Historically, companies have vertically configured their activities by selling a certain product, expanding either through an increase in sales or by diversified activities related to the given product. Today, competition is exponentially more difficult and markets far more saturated, turning our economy into one that is demand-driven. Thus, winning over the customer becomes much more crucial than securing production, which explains the dramatic increase in most businesses' marketing expenditures compared to their production costs. To succeed, companies can no longer focus on how to produce more, but must focus on how to gain more of their customers' spending power. When companies think of their businesses from a horizontal perspective, they are more attuned to their customers' purchasing patterns, since customers spend their money in a "horizontal" rather than "vertical" fashion: They buy a car, a house, a vacation, food, and so forth.

What makes companies thrive is not what they produce and sell, it is the ability to invite their customers to spend. The tenet of business success is not to "own" a product. It is to "own" a customer. By thinking horizontally, companies fare better at "owning" their customers. The future of Feadship, Rolls-Royce, Ferragamo, Chanel, Louis Vuitton, Disney, or Solgar is not necessarily gauged by how well they can produce yachts, cars, clothing, accessories, luggage, movies, or vitamins, but rather by how well they can answer their customers' dreams.

This does not suggest that Fochon should diversify from *foie gras* into sports cars, or that Château Latour should start making moccasins. Not all brands can expand in equal terms, and expanding horizontally may be unrealistic for certain companies. Yet having a horizontal business vision lets a company appreciate new opportunities and establish different ways to improve the emotional appeal of its products and services. It helps the company "see" through the customers' eyes and understand where indirect competition comes from, since a customer is more likely to choose between purchasing a bottle of Latour and a tin of Fochon *foie gras* than between a bottle of Latour and some cheaper wine. In the future much more of this type of horizontal expansion is likely to occur. For example, Ferrari's fastest-growing business is licensing. Most likely Ferrari's business will shift horizontally: Selling its sports cars means financing its highly visible F-1 racing activity in order to continue enhancing its technology and expanding the myth of its brand, with which it will win lucrative cobranding contracts in horizontally related fields. This horizontal action will continue to stoke the profit engines.

* * *

BUSINESS MAY BE HEADING TOWARD "polarization": On the one side are the positioned, undifferentiated, and often unbranded products and services that spark no emotional interest in the consumer. Sold like commodities through competitive price-slashing strategies, these products are distributed in a convenient, no-frills manner. The more sophisticated people become, the more products and services satisfying consumers' needs will become commodities, because they are not worth the emotional investment. On the opposite side are the positioned companies vying to overcome market saturation and its compression of profits through product and service differentiation. By offering products and services rich in emotions through powerful brands, they trigger the customer's purchasing desires.

Since gasoline is perceived by many to be the most obvious commodity, we decided to discuss the topic of business polarization with Lucio Noto, chairman of the board, president, and CEO of the Mobil Corporation and one of the masterminds behind the largest merger in history.

I was eager to hear his thoughts on whether there exists a polarization in selling products, with commodities on the one hand and products and services with high emotional content on the other.

"My business is a good example of that. A fair amount of my business is commodity-type business, crude oil that is transformed into a product that has to meet a certain specification. For many years, the oil companies have tried to differentiate their little molecules from other companies' little molecules, and the customer has never believed it. The customer said, 'If I see a brand that I recognize, I am OK.' So the customer has been hard to convince. More and more, the business was becoming selling a commodity. In the meantime, the other side of the business had become the dream-selling business, as you say. We are the world's foremost lubricant manufacturer. There is an absolute demand for synthetics in some usages, for example, aircraft jet engines or very highly sophisticated industrial machinery where there is a very clear payout between the amount of money you spend over regular oil for the premium oil. You can see the results: the fact that the machine will run more hours and will need less maintenance. And that is sort of a technical sale. But we also sell synthetics for automotive use. Mobil 1, for example. We sell in Europe oil that is more sophisticated than the one we used to put in jet engines five years ago. Customers who spend $250,000 on a Ferrari want the assurance that they have the best possible product in that crankcase. In Mobil 1 we have created a product that responds to that desire—and we market peace of mind. We are selling a concept, and that is how we like to position that product. I tell my people: You make the best damn oil you possibly can—that is what the customer wants and I want to be the one to give it to them. And that is how we position it. I see the market going in that direction. I see successful people on both ends of the price/value scale. I do not see many successful people in the middle yet. I do believe that there is polarization.

"Now we go back to the gasoline business and apply similar thinking. Mobil gasoline cannot be positioned as a dream product. Yet Mobil can be positioned as a dream seller of gasoline. Your product, a Ferrari, you can see, touch, smell, and hear. My product—gasoline—nobody sees it. You have to trust. You have a hose that comes out of the ground. You stick it in a hole, you push a button and you never see the product and there is just a little meter that says now you owe me twenty-two dollars. You do not taste it, you do not sense it. And when you actually use it, it does not give the impression that it actually does something. It is the car that is transporting you, not the gasoline. Then, to add insult to injury, you leave my station, not bringing with you our charm or smiles, and you get to the next corner and there are two other gasoline stations with price signs that are six feet tall and remind you how much you just paid for something you really do not take any enjoyment in. The idea to try to convince people that our molecules are better than other molecules is very difficult. But what we have found is that people are more and more concerned with the experience of buying, the convenience and the speed of buying. We put our money into the electronics: Pay at the pump first, and now the Speed Pass, of which there are already 2 million. And the many applications, be they the well-lighted service area or cleanliness of bathrooms, which is a major issue for women, who buy a lot of product during the daytime. Customers have sort of a split personality: They want to be fast at the pump, but they also want to be able to get a lottery ticket, buy the Starbucks coffee, Domino's pizza, beer, tobacco, drop off dry cleaning, they want a convenience package. People go to the pump, use all the electronics to fill up the car quick, they do not have to deal with the dealer, then they go and park in front of the market and do their business. We see customers come more than once a day, even if not to buy gasoline. In the past we were not paying attention to their desires. We were putting in the marketplace what we thought the customers wanted. The customer did not want it. Then we decided to ask the customer. First, the customer did not want to see the Mobil name on the store, because Mobil was associated with gasoline. They wanted to see another franchise on the store, so we had to create a new franchise for them. For retailers, this is ABC. For oil companies we used to have the *Field of Dreams* theory: You build the field and people will come and play on it, you build the station and people will come and buy gasoline. Now, we start to worry how we get the customer, how we keep the customer. It is the buying experience more than the product that counts.

"At a certain level when you're selling a dream, you start to see your business horizontally because you are selling an experience and not a product. Therefore, your interest is in the customers' pockets rather than what you are producing. Ferrari can sell a car, but it can also sell accessories, driving schools, and luggage, for example.

"At Mobil, we are also looking at the business horizontally. It is slightly different than your approach, because you are selling the brand across the board while I am selling convenience and speed across the board. People do not buy the lottery ticket because it is a Mobil ticket but simply because it happens to be available in a convenient spot when they come to buy my gasoline. In your case, you have a different view, but we are dealing horizontally just like you are.

"Our advertisers are starting to try to appeal to the emotional side of the equation. What does the brand mean? Your brand, for example, Ferrari. Wow! In five years, we try to build the brand Mobil so that people can say Wow! Not just because the molecules are better, but because we take care of the customers, we care for the customers, we try to sell them a concept different than just selling them gasoline.

"Differentiating a commodity from a dream is all in how you sell it. It is also true when you have a product as sophisticated and as expensive as a Ferrari. It is the experience of buying it, it is the experience of the relationship with the service, the delivery, the way the car is presented, the little things. The fact that someone goes out of the way to make sure that this is a special event for you as opposed to, 'Oh no! I am down here dealing with a car dealer.' I think you can do as much around the process as you can around the product. In my case, that is essential, because the product does not have the qualities that differentiate it. It is absurd to advertise a quality that no one can perceive. You'd better sell some emotions rather than objective qualities no one can see. You've got to create real value in the future. You just cannot live on cutting costs, because you will drive yourself to distraction. You have to cut costs to be competitive. But to be really successful, you have to create value. Any of these major mergers you are seeing that are done on the theory that they will cut costs may work over the short term. But unless you have value creation, a strategic drive in the future toward doing things better and differently than what you are doing today, then these mergers don't make any sense to me."

Mr. Noto believes that there is polarization in his business, since creating value is, in the long term, a much sounder strategy than slashing costs. Even in the business of selling gasoline, a company can sell emotions by creating the ultimate purchasing experience rather than focusing only on the product. After all, as he says, it is better to sell emotions than objective qualities no one can perceive.

DREAM STATUS is as coveted as it is privileged in the business world. Many mass-consumption companies claim to sell emotionally laden products or services. As the markets grow more crowded and competitive, so must the products grow more differentiated in order to win the commercial visibility that attracts the consumer's spending power. Dreams have become an important market-positioning strategy. Today, even a bottle of mineral water is much more elaborate than its contents justify. Water is no longer the most common element on the planet, here to quench our thirst. Instead, it is unveiled as a potion as magical as it is expensive, claiming such exceptional powers as those that trickle from the fountain of youth. Despite the fact that many bottled water manufacturers market their product claiming that it provides energy, health, status, sexual vitality, and whatever else you could possibly want, it is difficult to classify these companies as producers of dreams. Their product is born on the production line as H_2O, only to become embellished by some marketing miracle and a good swig of consumer naïveté. Dream products or services, on the contrary, usually start out as products or services possessing aesthetic value, be it for their design, for their technology, or because of their cultural impact. Marketing only completes the dream experience. In other words, a Ferrari is a dream car because it was conceived, designed, and produced to stir the emotions, while a Hyundai, no matter what its advertising campaign declares, is a commuter car with functional qualities and four wheels.

A dream is not an object as much as it is a perception. The product *per se* doesn't claim dream status; it is up to the customer's perception to decide that. If a diamond is industrially used to cut glass or as a needle for a record player, it's hardly a product with high emotional content. But when it is shaped and crafted into a jewel endowing its possessor with beauty or power, that's entirely different. The quality of the work performed by the creator, the designer, or the craftsman is what influences and educates that perception.

Since dreaming does not refer to specific objects, but rather to the way those objects are perceived, a company sells a dream also by creating the perfect stage for its product or service. For example, at Versace, a dream isn't merely a dress, it is the embodiment of the entire collection in Piazza Navona on a stage of outstanding aesthetic significance, with its statuesque models, its cosmopolitan crowd, and its mythical dresses. The theatrical setting that unveils the dreaming mood is fantastic, yet still the dresses are what make the entire event so spectacular. To sell dreams, companies must create products and services with specific characteristics: They have to be designed and engineered to be strikingly attractive (a Ferrari, a Gulfstream jet, a Swan sailboat, a Buccellati jewel), original (a Volkswagen Beetle, a Sony Walkman, a Swatch), socially desirable (a Rolls-Royce, a Louis Vuitton bag, a Rolex watch), exceptionally well crafted (the movie *The English Patient,* or a Patek Philippe watch). In other words, they must connect emotionally with the customers. Once the spirit of the time, often the latent desires that define the customers' dreams, has been established, the company must create the product and service that best expresses such dreams. Ordinary products or services will not do. The company must take a risk and distinguish* its creations by reproducing the aesthetic qualities and the originality that unleash the dreaming state. Without that, it is difficult to convince today's customers, who

*While "differentiate" is the word most commonly used to describe a company's attempt at setting its products or services apart from its competition, we prefer the word "distinguish." The word "distinguish" best characterizes the fact that in order to create dreams, a company must "make them prominent, noteworthy" rather than simply "making them different."
Differentiate = make different; modify.
Distinguish = draw distinction; characterize; make prominent, noteworthy, eminent.

are sophisticated and informed. All the products and services in this business share undeniable emotional characteristics: the look of a Ferrari, the elegance of a Dior dress, the distinction of an Hermès bag, the intensity of a Michael Mann movie, the majesty of a Feadship yacht, the charm of the Volkswagen Beetle, the hip appeal of Adidas or Nike sportswear, the electricity of a Sotheby's auction, the mystery of the Pictet bank.

WHILE "DREAM" is an attractive word for its many positive connotations, not everybody agrees upon its use in describing highly emotional products and services. Mr. Leonard Lauder, the eclectic president of Estée Lauder, believes that it is not an appropriate term to describe his products.

"No, I do not agree with that. We do not sell dreams, we sell practicality. Our products work. The concept that says 'using a cream on your face is a dream' is wrong. If you use a cream on your face it helps prevent the aging process. If you use a sun cream on your face it not only helps prevent aging but also prevents cancer. If you use lipstick it helps your feeling of self-worth and your feeling of beauty. Dreams are not in our vernacular."

I use the word "dreams" to describe products and services that satisfy more than a simple function, like fulfilling the aspiration of being beautiful. I asked Mr. Lauder, "Do you think this is also incorrect?"

L.L.: "Everyone aspires to something. Everyone aspires to health, or wealth, and everyone aspires to being attractive in one way or another, and what we do is help those aspirations."

Q: "So more specifically what can your company do for somebody to become more physically attractive, for example?"

L.L.: "We can sell them creams and lotions. We can sell them makeup, we can sell them anything they want that will help their level of attractiveness."

Q: "So, in a sense, you are not selling just pure function, you are also selling an aspiration?"

L.L.: "Well, let me tell you. If you have a good meal, your aspiration is that your hunger will be satiated and that you will get pleasure at the same time."

Q: "That is important. The fact that there is not only a function. The fact that there also is an aesthetic and hedonistic pleasure to it. In a sense you are also selling an emotional product. You have fun and you look better with it."

L.L.: "Yes. Look, I can see where you are going and I am sure that that is going to be the framework of your book."

Q: "Right."

L.L.: "Okay, so I just do not want to get hooked into the concept: 'We do not sell practicality we sell dreams.' We sell practicality. Many of our products come as close to the concept of practicality as possible and many of our products are also in the area of aspiring to be able to look better."

Q: "Since you are a man of culture, how can a company like yours influence customers' taste?"

L.L.: "We respond to the desires of the customers. One can never influence taste where the customer does not want to go. Our job is to determine where the customers want to go before they know where they want to go."

Q: "Do you think that this is a cyclical business?"

L.L.: "No. It is been around since the time of Cleopatra. It perhaps has its ebbs and flows, but it is not cyclical. The cosmetic industry has been hurt far less than the total industry has been hurt in Asia because if you do not want to buy a two-thousand-dollar dress you can always buy a twenty-dollar lipstick. It is a question of gratification. How can you have gratification for less money? I am very optimistic about the future. We represent an aspirational quality that very few other companies can offer: aspiration to be part of the world of Estée Lauder and part of the beauty and look better."

Mr. Lauder's concern is shared by other businesspeople who perceive the association with dreams as undermining the credibility* of their products or services. We believe that "practicality," to use Mr. Lauder's word, is not the antithesis of dreams. Dream products perform their function exceedingly well: Ferrari cars drive very fast, Girard-Perregaux watches measure time precisely, and Michael Mann's movies tell stories both scientifically and enthrallingly. If they did not, they would not carry the credibility they have. It is the way they perform these functions that substantiates customers' aspirations. "Practicality," or the capacity to perform a function very well, is a prerequisite in this business. Yet, apart from performing a function outstandingly well, these products also ignite our emotions and our imagination. They are dream products and services.

SOME SAY THE SKY'S THE LIMIT, and to many the ultimate dream means owning a personal jet. Bryan Moss, the unpretentious vice-chairman of Gulfstream, personally sells most of his company's magnificent airplanes. Mr. Moss absolutely feels he

*To avoid any confusion, it is important we make a distinction between dreams, fantasies, mental masturbation, and alienation. Dreams are likely to occur, while fantasies, mental masturbation, and alienation are flights of fancy.

is selling a dream: "The famous Formula One racer, Ayrton Senna, once told me 'Bryan, keep the dream.' In our marketplace we are very often dealing with dreams in a positive sense. We are selling function, but we are also selling performance, we are selling beauty, and we are selling aesthetics. Customers buying a Gulfstream are associated with high performance, reliability, successful companies. They are interesting and exciting individuals, be they international businessmen or heads of state. While more than 90 percent of our planes are sold to companies, the presidents and CEOs who make the final decision are also moved by emotional factors. Many people say that they have removed all emotions from the equation. I do not accept that someone who has reached such a point as to make a decision to buy this type of equipment is absolutely without emotions. Of course, a great deal that is tangible is weighed in this kind of a decision process, like the metrics, the performance, the operating costs, the fuel consumption, flying capabilities, the cabin, altitude, landing performances, avionics . . . but there is also their feeling of pride, of recognition, concern for safety. Successful airplanes must above all be beautiful. Of all the airplanes that are up there today, the Gulfstream has the sleekness and the appearance of disguised performance. It sits on the runway and you have this great feeling that this is a marvelous machine, that can go fast, high, far, and keep you safe and comfortable."

As I listened, I couldn't help wondering, "If you sell a dream, when dreaming about an airplane, I cannot accept the fact that in the last thirty years the speed of flying has remained practically the same. And since other technologies have improved so dramatically, we would expect by now to go from New York to London in one hour. Don't you think that if feasible that would be the ultimate plane?"

"There is no question that from an intellectual standpoint the idea of a supersonic business jet cruising people in just a few hours between major continents is exciting. It is the kind of subject that would excite any of our powerful customers. There is much appeal. It is doable but is not economically viable at this time. The future of the industry, considering that the last few years have been outstanding, will continue to grow very significantly. First, because of the continuing internationalization of the business, which will not slow down. Second, because commercial airlines do not receive high marks for providing all the services and flexibility that our customers require today. That is not going to improve: There will be larger and larger airplanes between fewer and fewer key cities. It is still a hub-and-spoke system. The third reason I am bullish in the industry is the introduction of the fractional* ownership program, which makes access to our kind of airplanes much more affordable to a much broader customer base. I think by that approach we expose many more people to the benefits of business aviation, and when people get accustomed to how they can use these machines they just do not go back. It has been a cyclical business driven by corporate profits. Thanks to these factors, we have the opportunity to significantly dampen the swing.

"People think that technology might change the need for travel. But take video conferencing. It's been around for a while and, like faxes and all types of communications processes, it

*Fractional ownership is a program that allows a prospective buyer to buy a share or a fraction of an airplane and pay monthly fees that cover the pilots, the insurance, the hangaring, the maintenance, and so forth, together with an hourly fee when he/she is on the airplane to cover the direct operating cost, fuel, oil, catering, landing fees, and so forth.

increases the information flow hugely and enables a larger number of decisions to be made. That generates new opportunities, additional need for travel. Actually, it is working counter to what the current perception might be. We do not see video conferencing as a threat, we see it as a complement."

Bryan Moss reminds us that even in the performance-driven business world, the purchase of a $30 million asset such as a Gulfstream aircraft is not based on sheer facts alone, but also involves emotions. While personal jets are more of a fantasy than a dream for most of us, through more flexible service agreements such as fractional ownership, Gulfstream is flying high in a business where success hinges upon making dreams more accessible.

THE MOST COMPLEX PART of this industry is that it is not driven by well-defined needs but rather by complex desires. To better link so many different companies, it is important to determine what motivates the purchasing decision. In this chapter we have given examples of products that illustrate some specific dreams: Ferrari, the dream of speed, or Gulfstream, the dream of ubiquity. Since emotions are so ethereal, companies position their products and services based on clear images that customers can relate to. Those images, however, do not necessarily represent the "real" dream that motivates the customer. For example, while the dream of speed may conjure up a very strong image in the customer's mind, the underlying motivation for purchasing a Ferrari may not be to set a new land speed record, but might be sheer social recognition. Our self-image might be better if we claim to be buying a car for its speed rather than to fulfill our own craving for social attention.

For purposes of simplification, we will link the various motivations behind the purchasing decision to three fundamental dreams that fuel this business:

1. *The dream of social recognition* (mythologically, you might say, the Adonis/Venus dream). Being such social animals, we crave recognition and admiration. The most immediate way to attract such attention is through physical beauty. Power, or the ability to influence others, is another prized quality in our society. Since power usually relates to money, it is often expressed through material possessions. The following products and services meet the customer's dream of social recognition: cosmetics, perfumes, fitness (relating to beauty), luxury (with its accent on status), icon products (spinoffs of the "classic cool" in personal imaging), motivators (social positioning from the inside out), and Wall Street (where more than just financial assets are sold).

2. *The dream of freedom.* Our ultimate dream is immortality, which explains man's fascination with gods (immortal humans) or semigods, be they living on Mount Olympus or up in the Hollywood hills. History is our saga of overcoming hurdles, the final one being death. While immortality still seems to elude us, technology has stepped up the search to reduce many limitations to our enjoyment of life. For example, the Walkman allowed customers much more freedom in enjoying their own music. Computers have become so ubiquitous because they dramatically facilitate people's acquisition of knowledge. While the dream of social recognition relates more to the symbolic imagery of attracting other people's attention, the dream of freedom is based on more aesthetic or hedonistic considerations. For example, one admires art as an immortal work of hu-

manity or uses a Ferrari or a Gulfstream to go much faster than our physical limits allow. All products and services with high aesthetic and hedonistic content help customers enjoy the dream of freedom. The same products and services can fulfill different dreams. Luxury restaurants, for example, can fulfill the dream of social recognition for some, and the dream of freedom for others: Customers can visit a great restaurant to "be seen" or to educate and expand their senses. By educating its customers a company can influence the way they perceive its products or services.

3. *The dream of heroism* (the Herculean dream) combines the above two dreams. A hero is admired by society, but a hero, in this case a semigod, also enjoys a life much freer of limits. Movies, sporting events, and glamorous magazines offer the role models we look to imitate, letting us live vicariously through their heroic deeds.

WHY IS BEING BEAUTIFUL SO IMPORTANT? No matter how pragmatic a world we live in today, the importance of beauty still explodes in our unabashedly narcissistic society. Being beautiful almost seems to be a prerequisite for success.* We peer up at long-legged creatures as they strut down haute cou-

*Even though many may hypocritically profess that beauty is only skin deep, our attraction to pulchritude is deeply ingrained on our psyche. This fascination with perfect features dates back to our oldest ancestors, so far back in history that it precedes even the mirror. In 4000 B.C., Egyptians had already established perfumeries and beauty parlors. Fashionable women would paint the veins on their breasts blue and their nipples gold. Vanity raged as Roman men and commanders would have their hair done and their nails polished before going to battle. In early Western civilization, beautiful women were rosy and voluptuous, radiating sensuous fertility, while men hoisted strong

ture runways, we are in ecstasy when Hollywood gives us ravishing actresses willing to bare all. Since childhood, we are taught that beautiful people are good, and only the villains are ugly. Attractive children often shine brighter in school, receiving more support, higher grades, and less punishment. Even in the business world, the "beautiful people" seem destined to be hired for more interesting positions and enjoy quicker promotions.* Beautiful women have historically managed to marry their way up from the lower class and poverty, a knack men are trying to finesse today. Aristotle said it long ago: *"Beauty is a far greater recommendation than any letter of introduction."*

Beauty† is one of the biggest businesses with its various industries: cosmetics, perfume, clothing (who dresses only to be covered up against the elements?), diet and exercise regimens

---

muscles and heaved hairy chests as a sign of their virility. In some parts of Africa and India, being overweight was a sign of prestige and beauty, hardly the case in today's Western culture, in which dieting and minimal body fat are preferred. In Japan, beautiful women pride themselves on milk-white skin, something most Westerners consider a flulike symptom as they head for their twenty-five-dollar-an-hour tanning salons (whitening dark people's skin and darkening white people's skin keeps cosmetic companies like Estée Lauder and Revlon very busy). However, there are some qualities that transcend cultural judgment. Youthful, healthy looks (strength for men and fecundity for women) have always inspired artists and poets.

*Height is an important beauty marker for men. Judges of employee achievement prove to be anything but equitable when it comes to height: A 1990 University of Pittsburgh study showed that managers' average yearly salaries rose with their height at a rate of thirteen hundred dollars per inch.

†Plastic surgery, beauty clinics, and, further down the road, biotechnology (through re-engineering the genes) are competing to create a more beautiful human race. The effort may be ethereal. Since beauty is a relative term, without ugliness beauty cannot exist (making the entire human race "beautiful" would only change man's perception of beauty). Still, this fixation on looking better may improve the way many people feel about themselves. Beauty be-

(since, in both cases, "good looks" are the key motivator over well-being), plastic surgery, hairdressing salons, spas, and numerous beauty publications and videos. Men and the elderly have just begun boosting the market even higher, as witnessed by the flood of specialized magazines now available to them. In the United States alone, the recent boom in catering to men's vanity already exceeds $10 billion a year. Since plastic surgery first found its niche in the United States, men have accounted for one in every four cosmetic surgery procedures. American men are no vainer than the rest (until the Industrial Revolution men were very concerned with their looks), they are simply quicker to accept new trends. Modern society is increasingly fixated on stopping the aging process. People live longer and usually healthier lives and seek to continue to stay active and enjoy life (and can afford it). Looks being the most visible sign of aging, elderly people invest more and more in their physical appearance, their bodies, and their attire.

From time to time, sporadic attempts at praising intelligence have tried to humble beauty. Shakespeare (1564–1616), in *A Midsummer Night's Dream,* proclaims: *"Love looks not with the eyes, but with the mind."* Even the legendary Aristotle Onassis, the Greek tycoon, dismissed his own bad looks by boasting of his

---

longs to all of Nature, not just man. A flower uses beautiful colors to lure birds and insects so they will carry out the flower's pollination. In many animal species, the beauty of the male sex attracts the enemy away from the female and her offspring. Darwin's theory of evolution states that the weak and ugly are naturally overpowered by the strongest and most beautiful. Luckily, beauty has many faces and is somehow more justly distributed. For example, Nature's sense of justice and humor award the mandrill, one of the ugliest creatures on earth, with legendary sexual potency, an uplifting consolation for its grotesque looks.

intelligence and wit: "My own disadvantage against any handsome man in seducing a woman lasts no more than ten minutes, the time it takes me to impress her with my charm." Unfortunately, only a few individuals have proven as idealistic as Shakespeare or as rich as Onassis. Beauty continues to be the center of attention, be it in its physical presence (designed by nature) or in the objects and experiences (designed by man) perceived as beautiful or beauty-enhancing.

BODY BY JAKE'S NAMESAKE, Jake Steinfeld, is one of the pioneers in personal fitness. Famous for sculpting celebrity bodies, he chooses to think he's selling hope, but somehow it seems to me hope isn't a strong enough term, not if you're hoping to have a body like his.

Q: "When you want to have a body like yours, Jake, it's more like a dream than hope. You're selling much more than muscles by the pound. Dreams have more excitement and more glamour than hope. How many exercise for physical well-being and how many do it to look good?"

J.S.: "I was the trainer of the celebrities. People were coming to me because they wanted to look as good as those celebrities. I haven't trained a star since 1988, but the perception that I am the guy who trains the celebrities still follows me. I have become part of pop culture as the sculptor of incredible bodies. All the things that I do basically all come back to and stem from my customers' dream of being a celebrity. If I buy Jake's book, or use his equipment or watch his exercise video, I might look like Harrison Ford, or I may be as pretty as Priscilla Presley. It's glamour, it's fame, it's fortune. To be able to sell a dream, you have to believe what you are selling. I believe what I am selling because it works on me. After spending time with unbelievably successful people like Steven Spielberg, Harrison Ford, and Priscilla Presley, I realized that these guys are regular guys, they are just like us. The only difference is that they had a dream, and that they never quit on that dream. I thought, I may never direct an *E.T.* film like Spielberg, but I am going to have my own *E.T.* successes. Steven Spielberg was turned down twice by the USC film school. Harrison Ford was hammering nails at a floorboard at MGM studios when George Lucas came over to him and asked him to run lines with some actors for the film *Star Wars* he was screening, with no intention of ever hiring him. Bette Midler grew up in a trailer park. The secret is to stay in the game no matter what your dream is. In those times when everything seemingly goes wrong and people tell you to quit, you need to go to a person who knows how to support you because he or she is credible and means it from his or her heart. I am selling the dream of self-esteem, of building confidence in who you are. From physical fitness you not only get physically strong, you also get mentally strong. When both physical and mental work in concert you can achieve anything. And also look good in the bathing suit!"

Q: "The symbolics of looking great means much more to people than the results of physical well-being. Am I right?"

J.S.: "Many more people are attracted to a Ferrari because of the possibility of picking up girls or winning social recognition than the number of people who want to become great drivers. The secret lies in positioning the dream by trying to paint the picture of somebody the rest of the world wants to imitate. The immediacy of the message helps get the customer's attention, then later works to uncover other characteristics, like the dream of feeling good about yourself. Fitness has evolved and now more people are into the health aspect rather than solely wanting killer biceps."

Jake is living proof of the hypnotic appeal celebrities have in our society. For example, Hollywood's success may hinge, in part, on its masterful exploitation of our obsession with stardom. People do not go to the movies to simply relax. They go to immerse themselves in their heroes' lives. Michael Mann believes that "Hollywood is so successful because it is in the fortunate position of being in an industry that is in its frontier phase. The frontier is defined by the zone between what is occupied and settled, wherein institutions, be they political or economic, are established versus where the institution doesn't yet exist. The zone in between this gap is the frontier, which is constantly moving outward. We are in a frontier condition in the entertainment industry because of the telecommunications revolution, so we are constantly expanding. However, Hollywood's success is not only based on the making of great movies. Don't forget how Hollywood introduced the star system, promoting the famous 'Hollywood Dream' with all of its glamour and bright lights. Hollywood still towers and this relates more to a worldwide fascination for American culture, more aptly called 'the American Dream.' "

SCOTT GREENSTEIN, coproducer of *The English Patient,* which won nine Oscars, finds the movie business to be so successful because "movies are a way you can see your dreams, parts of life you are fantasizing about feeling, that it is you on the screen while you are watching that movie. Movies allow your mind to roam and think you are one of the characters and ride with it. Actors are beautiful because people dream about being beautiful. For example, many men have dreamed about being like Clint Eastwood and many women, Sharon Stone. Technology is advancing and maybe it will soon be technically possible to make movies without actors. Yet, since at the heart of dreams is always a human being, technology will not be enough to replace human beings. I do not believe too many people fantasize about their lives being run completely by technology."

I looked down and happened to notice Mr. Greenstein's wrist. "You are wearing a Patek Philippe. Can you draw a parallel between your watch and a movie?"

"Both represent a dream. In both cases, you buy emotions. I liked that my watch was handmade by human beings. I liked its appeal, its look, its heritage. *The English Patient* was, in a sense, so much like that, because it was an extremely well-made film rather than simply a fantasy. I liked the depth of the movie, the quality and the human craftsmanship, Anthony Minghella, the director, and that tremendous cast. It was really like a Patek Philippe: a very well-thought-out and crafted product made by human beings. *The English Patient* came out of the independent studio Miramax because no major studio wanted it. Producing it required some special belief."

I was curious. "What makes a great movie?"

"A great script, then a great director, then a great cast. If the script is not perfect, the movie will never be perfect. The director keeps the vision, while the script makes the dream possible. Hollywood is not alone: There are great filmmakers around the world, and there are more and more international movies that have been successful in this country, like the Italian *Il Postino, Se-*

crets and Lies, a British movie, and *Breaking the Waves,* a Danish movie. There are very vibrant movie communities worldwide."

The knowledge behind the movie industry also reaches out horizontally. Proof lies in the not so farfetched parallel between such heterogeneous products as a watch and a movie. Both fall into the realm of dreams because both are exceedingly well-crafted products.

THE ENTERTAINMENT BUSINESS has been revolutionized by the cable industry, which has invited an unlimited choice of programs into the viewer's home. Kay Koplovitz, a pioneer in this industry, has made her mark by successfully building the USA network.

She feels that "people want to satisfy their expectations, their dreams, because they want to obtain something they did not have access to before, things that they think other people have, the fancy cars, the getaways, the movies—all things that satisfy their need to escape. It is another way of saying dreams, instant gratification and escapism in a lot of ways. So whether you say they are dreams, or visions, that is what we are feeding. We are storytellers. We are feeding people's minds, their desire to be entertained, to escape. That is a lot of what entertainment is. It's escapism, escape to something else we would like to be a part of, whether it is something glamorous or something action-oriented. All are part of the dreams of what people would like to have. It is feeding emotional needs. How much would people pay for that? When I started in the cable business, my first job was to get licenses to provide cable to residents of the community. The reaction of the local officials was one of total surprise: 'What, pay for TV? You must be crazy, people do not pay for TV.' "

I asked Ms. Koplovitz what quality she thought was most important to success in the entertainment business.

"Good storytelling. Whether it is live action or animation or a romance. It is all about good storytelling, the way in which you tell it and the tools you have to tell it. Spectators want to escape to a world they do not have. They want to have a romantic story they can believe in, that could happen to them, they want to be scared to death in thriller movies, they want the excitement of action movies. They want to be emotionally moved. It's got to make you laugh, to make you cry, to make you frightened. Nightmares are dreams. They are the dark side of dreams. It's about the edge of the mind, voyages of the mind. It is a positive emotional experience to feel fear or horror, because then you know that it is in you, you have the depth in you to be revolted by something that is scary. It is fun to be frightened. Like going on a roller-coaster ride. Entertainment allows you to have those emotions without getting hurt. I want to have negative and positive experiences. Movies need to evoke strong reactions. A movie has to make an impact on you so that the story lingers in your mind for a long time. It has to engage the viewer. There are different emotions, and in entertainment you need to touch the largest possible spectrum of emotions. This is the best storytelling. We could draw a parallel with Ralph Lauren, who is selling the great American country feel, the Western wealth, and the depth of his quality through years of very consistent positioning. It would not last if he only had image and did not have the quality."

I wondered, "Is technology changing the way people think?"

"Technology is enhancing the experience. For example, the technological advance of the visual image is so enriched, so deep that it brings vividness to the imagination. In animation, computer graphic imaging has more visual depth to it; it does not have the elegance of hand-drawn animation, but it has more color, more definition, and it has the capability of making more real-life movement of the images because there are more frames and there is more depth in the process. All the tools we now have available help us create more emotions. Technology is changing our expectations. Yet I do not know if it makes us more creative dreamers. Our business is still fundamentally about storytelling. That element is never going to change."

From here I went to Leo Hindery, the builder of TCI and the president of the newly launched AT&T entertainment venture, whose pragmatism offered yet another interesting perspective on this emotional business.

I dove right in, asking, "What exactly is the entertainment industry selling?"

L.H.: "Broadcast television was selling sort of just base entertainment. When cable came you got niche channels where you started to sell emotion and intellect, excitement, and sex, sort of niche emotions. When it was just ABC, CBS, NBC, it was the least common denominator and everybody who had an aspiration above that suffered. Now you've got the exotics, you've got adult entertainment, C-Span, Discovery, A&E, History."

Q: "Where is the real business, where are the profits? In the niche or in mass market?"

L.H.: "Profits are in the niche because the advantage of the niche is that it has a much higher CPM, cost per thousand. I would rather sell a high-end magazine to people who are really committed to the subject than a lower-end magazine to a lot of people. There is more relative money. Media is just profits through advertising, through circulation, and a man and a woman who are a niche audience are much more willing to put their money where their aspirations are. Look at the Ferrari. I did not know what the cost of the 355 F-1 was. I assumed it would be fair. But if it would have been ten thousand dollars more it would not have made any difference to me. It is because it is an experience. If I wanted to buy a regular car, you and I would still be arguing about the price. But when I bought a Ferrari, I did not ask what the price was. I asked if you could get me one. Big difference. It is that same phenomenon. All audiences that are niche-categorized are much more profitable because they are much more focused, they are much more decisive, they know their thoughts. Successful companies know their audiences. Do not try to change the audience, react to the audience. Media is about denominators, and by that I mean that everybody in mass media wants his or her denominator to be bigger so that their numerator, the portion of that audience they have, is more profitable.

"Why is Bill Gates getting into the television industry? Because the television industry is the most ubiquitous audience there is in the world. There are more TVs than telephones at this point in time. That is the mass media. The narrow-cast media have to be very careful because their denominator is small. So they have to have high numerators and small denominators. On the other hand, my business, the Rupert Murdoch business, is a small numerator of a huge denominator. Fox television is not going to win a lot of Emmys, it just appeals to a very broad-scale base of American society. Murdoch, with a big denominator, if he gets a small share of that denominator, he makes a lot of money. If you are selling *Town and Country*, an extraordinary magazine with limited circulation sold to a small group of people living in the Hamptons, they have to get most of them. You saw it when Clinton was up in the Hamptons yesterday. I was struck again by how society is big denominator–low numerator, small denominator–high numerator: He got $2 million for the Democratic National Committee yesterday from a handful of people. Small denominator, huge numerator."

Q: "What do you have to do to catch those people?"

L.H.: "Sell them their emotions, do not sell them your emotions. Why is Ferrari so successful? Because of people like you. You know your audience really, really well."

Q: "But we also know the product. When people suggest we do 'clinics' to understand what the customer wants, I decline, because we have to act like artists. We are the ones who are supposed to decide because we are supposed to know much more about cars than our customers."

L.H.: "Right, and that is why mass merchants do not necessarily do well with niche companies. Take Snapple. Snapple was a great success, then Quaker Oats buys it and destroys it, losing a billion dollars. A billion dollars! Just because a mass marketer bought a niche product. In the cable business, you want destination. When you go to the Discovery channel tonight you may get there and find it is nothing you want to watch but you are not disappointed when you get there. When I go to some networks I am disappointed because it is not what I was expecting. A network is a collection of shows and a channel is a destination. Ferrari is a destination. When you get to Ferrari, you may not buy one, but you are not disappointed. A&E, Discovery, History, E!, C-Span, you are not disappointed. The USA network, for example, had a lot of people watching it, but the advertisers were not as supportive. There was no focus. Advertisers would rather run an ad on the Discovery channel with a tenth of the audience than run an ad on USA, because it is a better, more focused audience. It is destination. It is very important."

Q: "Once you get to the destination, what do you think is critical to make the customer happy?"

L.H.: "Do not disappoint them. Ever. Look at the classic '56, '57 Thunderbird. Greatest car ever made in the U.S. Then it went to a four-door and it became just an expensive family car and Ford never recaptured the high-end audience. They had to go and buy Jaguar to get back to the high-end audience they already had. They gave it away. So, do not disappoint people. Do not come down to the least common denominator, stay at the highest common denominator. Give up audience for profit. Give up predictability for heavy emotional involvement. I have people who write me letters and say: 'I will kill you if you drop Discovery, I love Discovery. Discovery defines my life.' They get 2 percent of the audience, which is not a high rating. But that 2 percent is so committed. You can charge anything you want, just do not disappoint people. People are so committed to you that you can even expand horizontally. We have the Discovery and A&E monthly magazine. We've got T-shirts that say Discovery."

GILLES BENSIMON, top photographer for *Elle* magazine, believes "we are all kids who live through the dreams we have. A woman could buy an Hermès lookalike bag or an imitation Chanel lipstick at a fraction of the price, yet women prefer to buy the original because Hermès and Chanel carry a dream. To be successful, companies must be able to carry a dream. They have to be sexy, they have to have sensuality, be trendy, and bring pleasure. They have to inspire customers to save up their money to buy something they really want. There is an evolution of dreams. Dreams have to be affordable now. I see it in the magazine. Every time there is elitism, if the dream is not affordable, it kills the product. At some point you have to have access."

Bensimon believes that the products *Elle* is promoting "are more a dream than luxury, since luxury has become more available. Companies are introducing affordable products that still represent their spirit. For example, if you cannot afford a Ferrari, you can still afford a Girard-Perregaux 'Tribute to Ferrari' watch, so that you can still experience the dream."

DREAMS ARE BECOMING MORE ACCESSIBLE, and Leo Hindery's denominator is becoming larger. This business is all about credibility. The dream state enables the customer to "let go" and bear all emotions. To "let go," the customer must trust the product or service. This very receptive state is a highly privileged position that companies should never take advantage of; if customers are disappointed, they will not come back. No such thing as short-term solutions here, because without outstanding quality, there is no dream. Quality here means products and services that are designed and engineered to ignite customers' emotions—first, by offering practicality, to borrow Mr. Lauder's term, performing a function outstandingly well in order to establish the product's credibility, then by powerfully designing the most immediate emotional link, the looks. As Gulfstream's Bryan Moss says, "Even in a business that depends on objective performances, emotions are critical." Just looking at a Gulfstream aircraft convinces the customer that it can perform all it promises. In a sense it has what the French call *le physique du rôle* (the looks to do the job). Looks represent one of the most powerful means of attracting customer attention. Jake Steinfeld has certainly found success in marketing his celebrity clients' glamorous bodies to sell his concept of physical fitness. Scott Greenstein, in his role in the making of *The English Patient,* illustrates that even a product with moot commercial appeal may become a huge success provided that it is outstandingly well crafted.

Products and services have to be able to "connect." USA network's Kay Koplovitz reminds us how important the business of storytelling is. As Hollywood has shown us so many times before, there is no film if there is no story. No matter how expressive the actors, how insightful the director, how spendthrift the producer, you've got to have a story to tell. A strong story is directed by a burning sense of purpose. Ferrari has always been about racing, with all its successes and dramas. Safety features on its racing cars, for example, were not simple design adjustments made based solely on computer simulators. They came with the many tears shed for the lives of young race drivers killed while pursuing their dream of speed. The conviction behind the purpose is what makes the story so strong.

Leo Hindery pragmatically illustrates the logic behind this business: It is all about denominators. The denominator, the number of customers, may be low, yet the numerator, the money spent per customer, is very high. To succeed in the business of selling dreams is not to reduce yourself to the least common denominator, but rather to stay at the highest denominator. This will not prevent, as Gilles Bensimon artistically puts it, the denominator from progressively increasing, since more and more people want to dream. As Michael Mann so poignantly said,

"This is a business perched on a frontier which is constantly moving outward."

COMPANIES ABLE TO REACH OUR DREAMS attract us because they spark life with fun and entertainment. Stories about these companies read more like novels than business agendas. Filled with their anecdotes of famous people, successful artists, celebrities, and entrepreneurs with extraordinary vision and refined tastes, this is a world of glamour, humor, fun, money, and gossip, to which readers are naturally attracted, much like spectators to a movie about love, romance, and wealth. Most of the time, these stories even end "happily ever after." Their glamour, however, provides an interesting twist. Not superficial and fleeting, it is rich and multidimensional in both culture and creativity. Beneath the gilt, their cultural tradition has been painstakingly molded by labor and skill to purposely create products and services designed and crafted to "touch" their customers' emotions.

Glamour attracts attention and generates brand recognition. Each one of these companies is far more famous than its total sales volume. While fame is usually proportionate to sales volume, since a company is mostly recognized by its consumers, these companies are also recognized by people who will never have the good fortune of purchasing their products. This is what I call excellent brand recognition. For example, there are hundreds of companies in the world that have a larger volume of sales and a larger client base than all these dream companies put together. Yet none will achieve such fame, no matter how much they spend on advertising. And fame, in a world overloaded with information, is becoming the only shortcut to business success. What is so interesting about the majority of these companies is that they are like great raconteurs. Everyone wants to listen in because their stories are credible, with plots based on products and services that capture their customers' imaginations.

Since this business has grown much more competitive over the last ten years, it now takes more than just coming up with extraordinary products to succeed (not to mention the fact that mass-consumption products are rapidly achieving very high quality standards). Thus, companies must not only create fantastic products and services, but also induce desire and fascination in their customers' minds. They must create a dream. Companies must promote in their customers' wonderment, feelings of extreme well-being, and the conviction that they too can be freed from the daily grind and head for the impossible.

This is the task of the "dreamketers," marketers who can transform these powerful stories into dreams.

3

Dreamketing: Reaching the Customers' Dreams

A COMPANY SELLING DREAMS can never restrict itself to simply selling products or services but must sell an experience. To better understand the distinction between product or service and experience, let's look at, say, a lobster. It could be considered a "dream food," sold at both supermarkets and first-class restaurants. While a supermarket might wrap the lobster in cheap paper and sell it at some "bargain of the week" price just as it sells detergent or rolls of toilet paper, a first-class restaurant will dress up that same lobster with a seductive selling strategy, including the restaurant's exclusive ambiance (the decor and the spectacle of seeing other customers and even celebrities), its outstanding service and food preparation, the wine selection, and accompanying specialties. Born a "dream food" due to its scarcity, its delicate taste and image, the lobster becomes a competitively priced "commodity" in the supermarket, while at the four-star restaurant, it is elevated to a scrumptious experience. The supermarket limits itself to simply delivering the product at the lowest cost, while the restaurant gets the customers' imagination hopping for that lobster extravaganza. There is little that the supermarket can do to improve the lobster's quality, whereas there are many ways for a restaurant to make that lobster an unforgettable experience, or, in business words, to add value to it. Competition or advances in technology can transform any dream product or service into a common item (a lobster can be sold as a commodity or can be cloned to become as common as sardines). Thus, the strategy for long-term success in the business of selling dreams (as well as in many other types of businesses) is not to simply sell a product, but rather to envelop the customer in the full experience surrounding the product. Companies should take a tip from those first-class restaurants that focus not only on making great food, but also on captivating the customer's senses and imagination. It's not the number of "lobsters" these restaurants sell that determines their fortune, it's how successful they are at attracting the customers' purchasing power. The lobster, no matter how fantastic a product it is, only represents the occasion for the dream.

ONCE A COMPANY HAS CORRECTLY interpreted the spirit and the desires of its time and created a product or a service that best fulfills those desires through aesthetic values, originality, and innovation, it must entice its customers into a dreaming mood so that they can better appreciate its creations. "Dreamketing" better illustrates this task than "marketing," since reaching the market is no longer enough. Companies have to touch (in an emotional sense) their customers' imagination by creating a fantastic experience. Since the market is more crowded than ever with indistinct consumers and equally indistinct products and services, today's companies must address the individual customers, and, most specifically, their dreams. "Dreamketing" acknowledges that blockbuster successes are achieved by interpreting *and* shaping the customers' strongest desires. Marketing defined the company's critical task in order to succeed in business. Now, this task of reaching the market is not as critical, since technology is changing the way companies reach their clients. Traditionally, the market was a gathering place where peasants would bring their harvested goods to exchange for other products such as food, clothing, or tools. It was here that the term "barter" took root. Eventually, peasants would exchange their goods for money and the concept of commerce was born. The market was a specific place, often crowded and dirty, where products were physically exchanged to satisfy the most basic needs: food, clothing, and tools to work the land. Modern markets have since evolved from the physical to the highest degree of abstraction, thanks to electronic devices and telecommunication wizardry that enable the purchasing and bartering of products and services to occur with no need for physical contact whatsoever. Items can now be viewed, even three-dimensionally, on computer screens or through mail-order catalogues and can be shipped directly to clients' homes. The explosive success of such systems as the Internet has made reaching the market less complex or critical than it once was. However, we are still at a point where not even these electronic systems can alter one fundamental fact: Companies still view the market as their main source of inspiration. To this day, a market is still the place to sell or exchange products, to see what other products look like, to find out which sell the best and are most preferred by the consumer or most profitable. Yet simply reciting current product information is no longer enough to please the customers' emotional cravings. A company must address and influence the customers' desires, ambitions, and tendencies, which may not yet be clearly expressed, but which will shape their tomorrow.

Wealth has transformed us from mere economic entities with physical needs into psychological beings with mental and emotional expectations: dreams. Dreams, so difficult to define, are even more difficult to fulfill. They are mercurial, constantly changing, and often affected by puzzling emotions. Dreams are born of our irrational side, where passion tends to prevail over reason. So intricate are dreams that at times even the customers themselves are incapable of clearly expressing them. To capture customers' dreams, companies must go far beyond traditional methods of inquiry, such as marketing research, to adopt a more "artistic platform" on which "feelings" and "intuitions" rule over "figures." Most important, dreams are not specific objects but particular moods: A product can only be the inspiration of a dream. The crown is the object that inspires an individual to wish to be a king: The dream is not to own a crown, it is to be king. The role of the "dream-marketer," or, better, the "dreamketer," is to woo the customer into a mood for dreaming. Of course, it is easier to dream about, say, a Ferrari, than a Ford or a Volkswagen. Yet a Ferrari, no matter how fantastic it is, is anything but a dream in bumper-to-bumper city traffic or when you're standing on the brake to comply with some stringent speed limits. And certainly we all know how the Ford Model T and the Volkswagen Beetle had entire generations dreaming. Even if those dreams were most likely facilitated by historical or cultural circumstances (the Industrial Revolution, the "flower-power" generation's love for the underdog) rather than by a specific marketing strategy by Ford or Volkswagen, the fact is that common products can also spark our dreams. And, when they do, a company's future may be changed forever!

Successful companies all generate wealth by stoking the perceived added value of their products and services. Profits come from the added value, which, in turn, comes from the customers' perception. So the most direct way to generate profits is to focus not solely on the product but also on customers' perception: their dreams. Of course, not all companies create dream products in the traditional sense of the word, but to some extent they all make money on the hypnotic appeal of strong imagery. The role of visionary "dreamketers" is precisely this: to purposely create a dream appeal around the product or service their companies are commercializing, be it a Ferrari or a Ford. Blockbuster successes aren't the pragmatic responses to market needs, but rather a gutsy take on the customers' imagination.

HOW DO YOU actually reach the customers' dreams? The luxury industry is possibly the most immediate example of an industry that makes a flourishing business out of satisfying the customers' emotions and desires. Never geared toward any rational needs, luxury companies have flourished by exploiting man's emotional frailties. This is a business born of passionate creators in a constant search to fashion the ultimate products or services that will capture their customers' dreams. Customers are never given the opportunity to rationally evaluate what they are buying: Is it social recognition, unbridled pleasure, or some sort of beautiful trance? Brains are too busy being numbed by theatrical settings where creators proudly display their genius and ego, while artistic collaborators unfurl their culture, and glamorous customers strut around like supermodels. The art of success in the luxury industry lies not in creating fantastic objects, but rather in making them the accessories to the dazzling experience we call the dream.

Take, for example, cigar smoking, which has been so harshly condemned in most public places, with the result that cigar smokers feel like criminals. Determined to relaunch cigars, Edgar Cullman, Jr., owner and president of General Cigar Holdings, realized that he not only needed to create a fantastic product, he also needed to invent a fantastic place where people could enjoy their cigars.

"When I came up with the idea for Club Macanudo, a club open to the public," Cullman says, "the concept was, if you smoke cigars, you belong to the club. You walk into Club Macanudo and you have a license to smoke cigars and enjoy everything about it and not be disturbed and told you that you can't enjoy this kind of pleasure. All of the decor is dedicated to this. For example, the wall treatment is a plaster wall embedded with tobacco leaves. There are motifs from Macanudo labels all over the place. The lampshades are made from the packaging material from the Macanudo cigar brand. The wallpaper decoration in the men's and ladies' restrooms consists of labels from all of our other brands. The concept was that Club Macanudo embodies the lifestyle of cigar smoking. In the past, everyone would perhaps retreat to a place in their home that was a haven for them to smoke a cigar, but there were very few places in public where they could go to smoke their cigars. Today, Club Macanudo hopefully epitomizes the place where everyone wants to go to smoke a cigar.

"Cigars are in fact very, very social. It's amazing: If you smoke a cigar, you meet people very easily. People share stories about their experiences with cigar smoking. The fact that someone else is smoking a cigar—you feel more comfortable walking up to them and talking about the experiences of that sort. Cigars can be used as a social tool, an add-on as a way to meet people.

"Look at what Marvin [Shanken] did with his fantastically successfully magazine, *Cigar Aficionado.* He really conceived this magazine with great trepidation from members of the cigar industry because they never thought that there would be enough for him to talk about. *Cigar Aficionado* put a wonderful spotlight on cigar smoking. Marvin has really used cigars as a lifestyle key, so that while he has called it *Cigar Aficionado,* the magazine is really devoted to enjoying the good life. I think it emboldens those people who were not necessarily committed to being cigar smokers because it gives an imprimatur of 'This is a socially acceptable activity now.' "

The movie industry is another great example of a trade dedicated to igniting our imaginations in a world with no boundaries, where fiction becomes fact. Hollywood has become the world's undisputed leader in moviemaking, if not in the depth or artistry of its films. By creating a world of glamour, romance, and surprise that extends far beyond the films it produces, Hollywood has established a stardom system that transforms even extras into demigods. Though there are many other great movie-producing centers around the world, none have achieved Hollywood success, since none have managed to build the dream around their core activity. Turning engaging stories into engaging movies is not enough; Hollywood also brings the glamour and glitz to life.

Lifestyle, fashion, and luxury magazines also sell dreams. In a sense they do to words and photos what Hollywood does to action. Today, newsstands are such a blur of magazines that these publications can no longer attract their readers and advertisers through well-written and accurate articles. The magazine's role is not solely to inform but to transport the reader into a beautiful world of fame and success. As Steve Florio, president and CEO of Condé Nast, points out, "This is what sets our magazines apart from others. Our readers enjoy looking at the best of something even when they cannot afford the beautiful mansion in the pages of *Architectural Digest* or the beautiful dress shown in the pages of *Vogue*." Magazines must be convincing. "Readers have to dream that possibly someday they could be able to afford it. Even when they can afford it, they have to have an identity with the product—we have to move them to action, to desire it and purchase it. I do believe that we most definitely sell dreams." The challenge is to consistently "look new and fresh. Luckily, with magazines you have the opportunity to change the product every month. We can constantly rekindle the desire for a particular product by presenting in *Gourmet* a beautiful dinner and photographing it properly; by showing in *Glamour* a beautiful woman with perfect makeup to inspire the reader to look like her in the coming spring; by inspiring readers to dream they are skiing in Switzerland through our *Condé Nast Traveler* January issue, or about going to St. Bart's by reading the March issue. You can change the direction every month, yet the challenge is to always re-create something that has style and quality and rekindles the need for that dream product every month."

Mr. Florio does not believe that the Internet will displace magazines. "The Internet will probably help magazines. If you go back, whenever a new medium was introduced everybody said the old medium was dead—like, for example, when the television was introduced everybody predicted the end of the radio. The new medium always affects the old medium and, in many ways, makes it better. You have seen magazines like *Slate* and a few others that are purely based on the Internet and are not doing well. It goes back to the idea of a dream product. When you are sitting comfortably by a pool enjoying a few hours of sun, you want to read a magazine. You do not want to have a laptop computer. There are places where readers will respond to the portability and the luxury of a beautiful magazine. Once the dream is sparked, they may visit the site afterwards to get more information. You will see a lot of that. The new medium will not compete against the old medium. It will help it.

"Dreams are changing. Every generation creates its own lifestyle, its dreams. For example when I graduated my father gave me a beautiful Swiss watch. I offered a similar watch to my son for his graduation and he told me he preferred an Ironman, a $150 watch, since watches for his generation are not as important as they were for mine. Si Newhouse [the chairman of Advance Publications, the owner of Condé Nast] asked me if I could help him purchase his 'dream car.' I thought he wanted a Rolls-Royce or a Mercedes; instead he asked me about the new Volkswagen Beetle in red. That was the car he dreamed about. Or, for example, the owner of one of the largest yacht builders told me that ten years ago he was mainly building sailing yachts and large motor yachts. Now customers dream about smaller motor yachts with no crew so that they can be conveniently and privately alone with their families and their loved ones. Our goal is to foresee and even direct the changes of our customers' dreams and allow our advertisers to get new, fresh messages out into the marketplace."

Dreams don't only come from the emotional world of luxury, movies, and lifestyles. Even an industry as rational and scientific as pharmaceuticals has understood that growth and bottom line can be better achieved by satisfying customers' dreams than solely by filling patients' prescriptions. Borrowing from its neighbor, the vitamin business, the pharmaceutical industry has introduced a number of drugs that offer customers rejuvenation and well-being. Viagra, the now-famous wonder drug, is just one of the latest to be launched. Vitamins have already proved how much money can be made off people's craze for feel-good living, even with scant scientific proof. The more the FDA warns customers that many vitamin claims are based on very few objective facts, the more muscle the industry seems to build. It may be easy to refute the facts, but it is very difficult to destroy the age-old dream that flows from the fountain of youth. It seems a sign of the times that now, even the world of science is stamping its approval on these dream drugs.

Even Wall Street, today's temple of numbers, is built, share by share, on people's dreams. Wall Street winners are thought to have any dream they want come true. Wall Street is not driven purely by strict disciplines such as accounting or finance, since it makes its fortunes on society's own psychological fibrillation. Companies, after all, are not evaluated solely on such facts as their actual assets, but also on wishes, their future earnings. It is the whimsical p/e (price/earnings ratio) that, by discounting the dream of growth, determines the value of a company. Who is really paving Wall Street with money rolls? Is it the whip-cracking managers and CEOs driving their companies into hyper-performance, or is it the brokers with the get-rich-quick dream that investors want to buy into? The fact is that customers who simply invested on their own on the Dow

Jones index would have outperformed the vast majority of El Dorado–promising brokers during the last twenty years. Yet brokers continue to make fortunes out of their customers' credulous dreams.

Even such common clothing as miner's trousers can become dreams. Paul Marciano, co-owner with his brothers of the jeans manufacturer GUESS? Inc., explains how: "By translating a message of dreams and sensuality and acquiring an image that customers will always identify themselves with. By making them aspire to become the next GUESS? girl: a sensual, voluptuous, very feminine woman, just like Claudia Schiffer, Anna Nicole Smith, or Laetitia Casta, the now-famous models who began their careers by impersonating our dream of women."

Mr. Marciano's job is what most would call a dream job. "I have to work hard every day of my life at finding unknown beautiful women who will become the next GUESS? girl because we have never hired an established model. For example, I once hired an unknown German girl, Claudia Schiffer. Her very first campaign was with us. The very first time I saw her, I saw my dream of Brigitte Bardot. Or, for example, when I saw Anna Nicole Smith, I immediately saw my dream of Anita Ekberg acting in Fellini's *La Dolce Vita*." Transforming jeans, or any otherwise common products, into dreams requires constant reinvigoration of the customers' emotions and imagination.

When I mention the market leader's current sales decline, Mr. Marciano explains, "Levi's has not evolved over the last few years and has stuck to the basics. People get tired of basics. We try to make a difference by introducing a constant evolution of fashion, style, and communication. Our strategy is selling dreams and staying true to who we are: sensual, fresh, and always new and changing. This everlasting evolution of surprise comes by way of new faces, new identifications, and ever-changing models, be they redheads, blondes, brunettes, yet all with that piercing presence in the camera."

No matter what the business is, the secret is to develop a vision that helps the dream become credible. Jonathan Linen, vice-chairman of American Express, says, "What makes us different from any other brand is our ability to deliver dreams and aspirations." American Express achieves this primarily through execution: "We are able to deliver what we promise. While the other card companies are just utilitarian brands that do not connote a lifestyle, American Express conveys prestige, status, and uniqueness. We provide the ultimate service because we control the merchants as well as the services that we offer to our customers. For example, take a platinum card holder who stays at the Ritz in Paris: To ensure that the service that is being provided is perfect, we acquire the transaction on both the back end and the front end. We can deliver a level of service quality on both ends of the transaction that nobody else can." Once the service is provided, American Express also builds a dream around its services, according to Mr. Linen, through "a number of magazines, like *Travel & Leisure* and *Food & Wine,* that tie nicely into the lifestyle of our customers. We also have *Departures,* a magazine that is given to all platinum card members. Through the magazine we create the dreams that inspire our card members. For example, in the last issue there was a story about France and all the great places customers can go to visit, written by an author who has done it and who wants to inspire them to want to go do that. Through exciting articles and advertisements, we also give the merchants, our partners who accept our card, the opportunity to communicate with the members."

Whatever the business, a company's success depends on the leap from merely satisfying the consumers' needs to fulfilling the customers' dreams. Marketers will be more likely to land generous bonuses if they can scrap their scientific market analyses for a more intimate look at oneiromancy (the ancient art of interpreting dreams). As we embark on an era of dreams, marketers must become dreamketers, because dreams are no longer merely elusive respites from life's daily tedium. Dreams are becoming the means to a more exciting life.

But, why do we yearn to dream? Dreams are only as intense as the extent of their meaning, defined by the innovation and originality of their creators and skilled collaborators and through the imaginative communication of resourceful dreamketers. Jewelry, possibly the oldest of dream creations, is one of the most interesting examples of an object charged with meaning. The word "jewel" originates from the Latin word *jocus,* game. Like a game, jewels were meant to amuse, bring pleasure, and embellish. But eventually, the game grew more serious. No longer just an ornament, jewels were transformed into symbols of power, be it military, religious, or civil, often even more credible than the person who donned them. Is it the king wearing the bejeweled crown who possesses the power, or is it the crown that bestows the power on the king? A jewel ceases to be a piece of gold that has been worked and reworked by a skilled craftsman when it becomes an amulet made of "solidified light" (to quote Marx or Lévi-Strauss), which bequeaths strength, protection, and life to whomever wears it. Maybe great jewelers are not the "dispensers of life" as some would lead us to believe, yet, through their creativity, they perform the "magic" of transforming inanimate materials into emotional objects agleam with meaning. This alchemy is what attracts customers to dream products. The dreamketer must transform this attraction into an emotional experience. Traditionally, the marketer has promoted product appeal in the mass markets, since standardization constraints and cost control generally do not permit the production department much creative latitude. In the dream business, on the other hand, products are already emotional expressions. The dreamketer must build the dream around many emotional attributes and transform beautiful jewels into symbols of power.

WHEN PURCHASING DREAM PRODUCTS, the motivations may be different in nature. Since dreams are composed of symbols, we call symbolic consumption those multisensory impulses that emotionally link the customer's fantasy with the physical product. From the perspective of symbolic consumption, products are viewed not so much as objective entities but much more as subjective symbols. For example, a gold chain dripping around a man's neck could be a glittering symbol of very recent financial success. The products and services that dreams are made of naturally carry much more symbolic weight than those satisfying needs. Yet symbolism and emotional imagery seep out into many more messages presenting need-satisfying goods, as companies struggle to distinguish their products and services from the suffocating competition.

Symbolic consumption is tied to reality's more imaginative side, based not on what customers believe to be true but on what they wish reality to be. The most diverse desires are important determinants and consequences of symbolic consumption.

These "absorbing experiences" all but swallow the customer up in the imaginary world of representations projected by the products. The power of symbolic consumption is unprecedented. How often we see the avaricious mutate into compulsive spendthrifts hell-bent on being the most ostentatious.

Purchasing symbolic goods is predominately right-brain-oriented, triggered by our emotional side, in response to visual-spatial stimuli and emotionally charged events. Symbolic consumption is a dynamic experience, one based not on the limited objectivity of a function (to quench one's thirst), but rather on consumer whimsy. When Perrier water was first introduced in the United States, its marketers launched an advertising campaign to masterfully position it more as an expression of social status than as a thirst-quencher. The campaign was so successful that soon it was not unusual to see a consumer order a Perrier and a glass of water (as if it were some single-malt scotch!).*

SEXUAL AROUSAL is typically the most frequent concomitant of symbolic consumption. For example, the shape of the Perrier bottle was designed as a sexual stimulus, with its curvaceous shape and sleek feel. The game of sexual connotation is particularly visible in many dream products and services, ranging from one lover's innocent gift of jewelry, to smoking a large cigar or driving a fast car, to the more provocative act of wearing sensual

*Sales skyrocketed until a chemical called benzene was detected in a sample of Perrier water (a small amount resulting from failure to change a filter at the bottling plant), and for the first time marketers could legitimately say that Perrier was more than just water. Unfortunately consumers did not appreciate the new ingredient, and Perrier sales temporarily collapsed in the United States.

perfume or a transparent dress, to the sex that sells movies, to the recent Viagra craze. It's no surprise that there is so much sex and sexual imagery in this business's communication.

HEDONISTIC CONSUMPTION is motivated by the pleasure of the senses, like a gourmand savoring *foie gras,* or a child eating ice cream. It is a freer and more immediate type of consumption, since it is not as influenced by society as by personal pleasure. I purchase a Ferrari not to gain society's recognition and admiration but because I love the feel of driving it.

Aesthetic consumption is motivated by the mind's pleasure or its search for beauty, like purchasing a beautiful painting by an unknown artist. Aesthetic consumption also provides a degree of freedom, since it too is driven by an internal pleasure, though more refined than the hedonistic one. Customers who make hedonistic or aesthetically motivated purchases are usually less volatile than symbolic buyers, since they are more in control of their decisions.

Symbolic, hedonistic, and aesthetic consumption rarely exist independently, since the emotions are usually complex outcomes of different impulses. In other words, you can buy a Ferrari for society's attention, but also because you enjoy driving it and admiring its beautiful lines and craftsmanship.

In some rare cases purchasing emotionally laden products can be the result of rational motivation—that is, a purchase deprived of any emotional or symbolic impulse. For example, jewelry is the only financial compensation for Saudi Arabian women after divorce (all too common considering the inflationary number of wives each man can marry). Thus, it is not uncommon that, when purchasing a jewel, Saudi women produce loupes to carefully assess the jewel's value before buying it. No emotions, no romance cloud their businesslike rationale. Quite simply, the jewels are what will hedge their futures.

THE ROLE OF THE DREAMKETER is to work creatively on the different purchasing motivations in order to build the most convincing dream. In the business of fine wines, for example, the dreamketer starts with something as extraordinary as, say, a 1982 Pétrus and *expands its reach* beyond the customer's sensory taste buds into the world of imagination. Thus, he/she must transform an *already* extraordinary product into a dream by revealing its emotional qualities and "blending" the mind and soul of the creator with the customer's dream. Satisfying a need is a far easier sell than detecting the many desires for highly emotional products and services. Drinking a glass of water may directly satisfy your thirst, a most basic urge, while the full appreciation of a *grand cru classé* entails a much wider range of motivations, be they symbolic (establishing one's social status), hedonistic (enjoying sheer pleasure), aesthetic (admiring the beauty of the creation), or even rational (making a good investment, since the price of a bottle went from $63 in 1982 to $1,363 in 1998). The dreamketer must decant all of these messages in order to reach the broadest number of customers. The prevailing motivation depends on such factors as the type of product or service, the customer's cultural background, the level of competition, and the targeted volume of sales. Since a strategy based on symbolic and hedonistic motivation can strike a more immediate and wider reaction than one stressing aesthetic motivation, different dreamketing styles are required. For example, appreciating the aesthetic qualities of a *grand cru classé* means savoring the depth of the wine's taste, experiencing the fullness of the bouquet, determining the best temperature, and responding to the color of the wine. It also demands respect for the skills and labor that go into making a great wine, as well as the whims of Nature, the *savoir faire* employed, the complexity of storage, and so forth. Educating customers on aesthetic values is a tough campaign. Not many people care to cultivate an aesthetic proficiency, yet these communication campaigns are important. First, customers interested in aesthetic excellence are usually most faithful, since they fully appreciate what the company has created, thus retention costs (the cost of retaining them as customers) are lowest. Second, these are often taste leaders, able to convince other people of the product's excellence. Third, their sophisticated taste demands that the company creators and collaborators preserve tradition and integrity. And finally, nobody likes to be told that they buy expensive wine only to impress their dates or the sommelier!

SINCE PRODUCTS AND SERVICES that excite dreams are all so distinct, one way to choose a dreamketing strategy could be by following the product's or service's intended life cycle, be it short, medium, or long term.

Products and services with a short-term life cycle, such as fashion and perfumes, require marketing strategies with aggressive and constantly renewed campaigns through either TV, newspapers, or magazines. Because this dreamketing message usually hinges on symbolic and hedonistic motivations, it must be easy and immediate to impress, since the dreamketers must win instant approval from a wider range of customers. For example, the success or failure of a movie is often measured by the first weekend's box-office traffic. Success takes the shape of a pyramid: The stronger the impact of the promotional launch, the wider the base of the pyramid (the larger the number of initial spectators) on which to build by attracting new spectators through positive word of mouth. Medium-term products and services, such as jewels, luggage, and accessories, require a more subtle dreamketing approach that, in addition to symbolic and hedonistic motivations, must also promote aesthetic values, and thus require a more educational message. In this case, direct distribution is often critical in communicating how the creators infused quality into their products. The dreamketing strategy for long-term products and services, such as yachts, specialty food, wine, and furniture, addresses the aesthetic values characterized by the uniqueness of the product or service. The message usually comes across best by word of mouth or through specialized media and special events.

THE COSMETICS INDUSTRY could be called the best example of a business strategy based on fulfilling customers' most fundamental wishes: being desired, or, better, becoming a dream. George Fellows, the president and CEO of Revlon, describes how one of the most famous American dispensers of dreams perceives its customers.

"In the past, the dream of the cosmetic industry was to sell 'hope in a bottle.' You use it and suddenly you become the most attractive, wonderfully alluring person. Women see through this now and recognize that it is not true. Now they watch the product with a more critical eye and want to be sure that it delivers the promise. If I tell you I will be able to make you look healthier and younger, then I have to come up with the product that does it, because if I do not, she will walk away, use another competitor's product, or give up completely on the idea, because we do not have the technology to deliver. The marketing environment that you create lays the ground for why your product is desirable. Revlon sells an aspirational look. For some, that means making them feel better about themselves, for others it means appearing more attractive to other people. It depends on what the hot button is for that particular classification of customer. We find out, now, that women are responding more to things that make them feel better about themselves. They look to satisfy themselves for themselves as opposed to seeking a means of attracting the attention of men. This still plays a part, yet it is no longer the sole attribute."

Revlon uses three words to describe its products: glamour, excitement, and innovation.

"Innovation represents being at the cutting edge of what cosmetics can really do for you. Being able to deliver promises that were not possible to deliver in the past. To growing baby boomers in the United States, we are not selling youth anymore. We are selling the ability to be the best they can be instead of selling a fantasy that they can look twenty. It does not carry credibility. Now it's about being the best-looking forty-year-old woman that you could ever hope to be. Women are no longer willing or likely to delude themselves by believing in things that are just not there. Yet women have a very creative approach to purchasing. The fact is men tend to be very uninspired consumers. They do not listen to new stories, nor do they react to them. Women are much more adventurous. This is why in our business innovation is very important: Women like to experiment with new products."

Mr. Fellows believes that leaps in technology have made his customers more scientific about their dreams, since "the definition of dream today is a more practical, realistic, and achievable objective. It may be an aspiration that is a stretch, but it is still an aspiration that is within a reasonable realm of possibility. Offering incentives to somebody with something that is not reachable demotivates customers. The dreams that we sell are motivational rather than demotivational. We are not in the business of selling fantasies, we are in the business of selling dreams, aspirations that are achievable rather than fantasies that are not likely to happen. I think technology has made this very true. The tremendous number of choices that people have today makes them much more critical about whether the item they have purchased is delivering what it promises. People are taking a more practical view of dreams because they have much more selection, a choice among many options that can get them as close as they can possibly get to what their dream is. This inspires them to be something better than they are."

Customers' emotional involvement varies depending on the type of product.

"The fragrance business is a very emotional category. There is little rationale involved here. We launched a perfume that lasted longer, to address the fact that many perfumes would fade away rapidly. It did not do well, because while it was a nice quality, it did not go to the core need of what a fragrance is supposed to do, deliver an image, an environment, a sensuousness. So the functional benefit, the fact that it stayed on longer, and came in a bottle that makes it easier to apply, had no relevance to the core need. It is a category that is emotionally driven. Whereas a mascara is a commodity, largely, so women buy the cheapest they can buy: They may use a Maybelline mascara and a Chanel lipstick. In terms of lipstick, women objected to the fact that it wears off and that they had to constantly reapply it, and that it transfers onto things, their teeth, the cup they are drinking from. It looked good but the current products performed in a rather inconvenient way. We launched a new product called the Colorstick that had a functional quality: It would not transfer. It made you look good in any color you wanted, but it also addressed the functional deficiency of current products. It instantaneously became the number-one-selling product in the country. In that particular case, a functional benefit to a cosmetic need was very important. They want emotions, but also they want functional perfection, which in this case became the distinguishing quality from the competition.

"In our business there is a wide distribution of products. At one extreme, there are products that offer solely functional benefits. They become commodities. In the middle are products with both emotional and functional qualities, and on the opposite fringe are products that are purely emotional. We are not in the traditional consumer business, like, say, toothpaste. Consumers buy a new tube of toothpaste because their old one is empty. Women do not buy cosmetics because their lipstick ran out. They buy because you have attracted them with a new fashion statement, a new shade, a new technology. A typical beauty care business that is very mature grows at the rate of the population, two-thirds of a percentage point a year. The cosmetic business has been growing at double digits because we have been able to drive that growth with the impulse purchase that a consumer would not have otherwise made."

The sustained growth has been helped by Revlon's success in expanding in foreign markets. A company that promotes the American look, Revlon has overcome regional tastes by adapting to different perceptions of beauty.

"Revlon is selling an aspirational vision of beauty. Beauty may change regionally due to cultural things that have nothing to do with cosmetics, but there are some fundamentals that appear to be transferable. Much of what we do as far as product performance has found acceptance worldwide. In the Far East there are skin-whitening products. Skin-tone eveners are very important in the Asian markets, not in the West. There are tone differences in the makeup markets. Deeper, for example, in Latin America. At Revlon, we sell the American beauty: simple, sporty, and athletic, with a clean and fresh look. This is why we have chosen Cindy Crawford, the icon of the American beauty, as our role model."

UNLIKE many saturated mass-consumption businesses that grow at the same rate as the population, the cosmetics business has been growing at double digits. Selling a dream rather than solely a function, the cosmetics industry generates additional sales through impulse purchases. Revlon succeeds because its brand credibly portrays the quintessential American beauty all around the world. Continued technological research is what substantiates the functional qualities behind Revlon's beauty.

DREAMKETERS can use *rituals* to spur impulse purchasing. Rituals are opportunities to affirm, evoke, assign, or revise the conventional symbols and meanings of the cultural order. They are versatile tools that shape cultural messages. From the very beginning, they have played a powerful role in all cultures, stressing important moments in our lives, such as the ritual of circumcision, an important tradition in the Jewish culture, or the various rituals in which the dead are buried with their most prized belongings. In the classic rites of passage, rituals move people from one cultural category to another as they relinquish one set of symbolic properties in order to acquire new ones: A boy becomes a young man when he exchanges short pants for trousers, a girl becomes a woman when she replaces her bobby socks with stockings, the wild bachelor becomes a faithful husband when the wedding band slips down over the knuckle.

The ritual of exchanging gifts is an important exercise in interpersonal influence. The gifts that parents shower on their children contain symbolic properties in themselves, be it only to express or gain affection or control. For example, the parents who give their child a Steinway concert piano clearly express their ambition to rear the next Mozart. Rituals are a powerful dreamketing method of swaying the customer. In the luxury industry, this gift-giving ritual is an important chunk of business. When you enter a luxury store, ritual is everywhere: from the way the personnel greet you, to the product displays, to the gift wrapping.

Other ritualistic forms are also at work in the business of selling dreams to enhance the products' and services' symbolic, hedonistic, aesthetic, and even rational properties. For example, by understanding the importance of the ownership ritual, some luxury companies have fostered such organizations as owners' clubs, wherein their customers can share their creative experiences with other owners. Clubs like the Ferrari, Rolls-Royce, Feadship, Harley-Davidson, or Baron de Rothschild host meetings and events at which members fraternize, enjoying the privilege of belonging to the same exclusive group. Customers like to spend an amazing amount of time cleaning, admiring, discussing, comparing, reflecting, showing off, and even photographing many of their possessions. This ritual of possession is not a simple assertion of territoriality through ownership, but a complex attempt to highlight the qualities that the creator or the marketer has incorporated into the object. Consumers and customers draw on the characteristics of goods in order to discriminate between such cultural and social categories as class, status, sex, age, occupation, and lifestyle. Through the exercise of possession rituals, individuals award themselves the cultural meanings of the goods, thus aggrandizing their own lives and empowering them with self-confidence or even outward aggression.

The Harley-Davidson club represents one of most striking examples of how the ritual of possession can work to market an emotional product. Founded in 1983, the Harley Owners Group (HOG) offers free membership for the first year to new Harley owners. After that, the annual dues are thirty-five dollars. The annual renewal rate is 68 percent of total members. Membership has grown steadily from thirty-five thousand (representing the number of bikes sold in 1983), to two hundred thousand members worldwide ten years later. Keeping Harley owners actively involved and out on the open road is the company's biggest challenge, the fear being that the customer might stop using his or her Harley after the first burst of enthusiasm wears off. Enthusiasm builds sales by driving owners to purchase Harley clothing and accessories, and, most important, by convincing friends and the world at large to try the Harley adventure. The final goal of HOG is to offer riding events all over the world, providing its members with so many benefits and activities that it turns these mere owners into joyous fanatics.

* * *

SINCE DREAMS are so fleeting, the dreamketer must constantly nurture the customers' imagination through a very creative and consistent campaign. Keeping the customer dreaming is like hovering in a helicopter: You cannot imagine how tough it is until you try. It feels impossible—the helicopter is counter-intuitive, very unstable and incredibly easy to crash (if you slip up). It requires total focus, great sensitivity, gentle coercion, and serious understanding of how the entire system works. Successful dreamketing calls for the same intense understanding. Take the following case.

The various Ferragamo family members have all inherited their father Salvatore's passion for shoes, striving to keep up the tradition of making products of outstanding quality, both in design and in comfort. To keep up with its impressive growth, Ferragamo overhauled its organization, shifting from a totally product-oriented company to one more customer-sensitive. While the company had diversified into many other areas, such as ready-to-wear, accessories, luggage, leather products, and ties, and had also expanded into all major international markets, all with substantial growth in its sales volume, it was still organized around the core activity of making shoes.

Organizational changes were first implemented in the North American branch, headed by the youngest family member, Massimo Ferragamo. Believing that "an excellent product is only a basic requirement in our business," and that "strong brand management can make a company successful," Massimo decided to boost the role of marketing within the organization. In the United States (the most sophisticated market in terms of distribution), Ferragamo struggled with an inconsistent image, ranging from elegant, to understated, to the doomed "out of fashion." Massimo hired marketing director Scott Fellow to re-strategize after his predecessor, a commercial director whose main interest was sales, had drastically narrowed the focus and caused erratic product distribution. Having gone unchecked, Ferragamo had amassed some one thousand points of sale in the United States alone, with 80 percent of sales in less than 20 percent of the outlets. This high number of sales points, which was at least four times the ideal amount, was not the only issue. The mix of products in each store was also inconsistent: Some points of sale were only carrying one product—shoes, for example—when they could have sold the entire Ferragamo line. Even in each category, they only stocked a few models in limited sizes. Thus, these stores were giving customers the wrong message by misrepresenting Ferragamo's wide line of products and models. This, in turn, distorted the company's image. The restructured marketing department had become the sales controller, indicating, through precise rules and regulations, which distribution system to choose, the mix of product and assortment in each point of sale for each season and collection, which area to cover, and which message to communicate. Mr. Fellow hired a visual display director to specify guidelines for each store's look, giving a certain uniformity to the window and shelf displays. He regimented thorough sales training programs and ensured that all personnel wore a Ferragamo uniform and learned how to sell the Ferragamo way. At the beginning, Mr. Fellow admits it was tough to change the old way of doing business. For example, imposing a uniform code for the fiercely independent sales directors was no small feat. Each was basically the business manager of each product line and had extensive authority, yet under the new organizational design, the marketing director could enforce stringent regulations and ensure that they be respected by all sales directors.

After his successful reshaping of the U.S. operations, Mr. Fellow was promoted to head marketing director and moved to the headquarters in Florence, where he undertook the same task at the corporate level. The organizational changes implemented there were more complex in response to how the creative department was organized and how it interfaced with sales and other commercial aspects of the business and with production. Given that the company's organization revolved around production, all decisions about creation, marketing, and commercial policies were generated by Ferragamo's production abilities and inabilities. For example, the timing for the collections (when the designing process begins, when the collection editing starts, the merchandising, the detailing, and the commitment for fabrics) was decided by the production organization, which had originally been established for the shoe division. In the fashion business, this is no minor glitch, since the timing for the shoe season is completely different from that of handbags or ready-to-wear. All worldwide buyers will purchase shoes for fall 1999 in December 1998 through February 1999, therefore the shoe collection must be ready in November 1998. Whereas ready-to-wear, for example, is first seen on Milan's runways in March, and most of the designers work on the collection from the end of December up to the very last minute. The collection is sold immediately after the show. Handbags and accessories also have different schedules. In order for a company to develop a uniform message for all the different lines, the designers must start their creative process together. The process cannot start with shoes in September, since, at that time, ready-to-wear designers do not yet know what the latest trends and fashion are. Since shoes are not as fashion-oriented as ready-to-wear, the creative schedule should obviously start with ready-to-wear. But since Ferragamo had begun as a shoe company, shoes had acted as the driving "culture." Yet the fact is that customers usually first buy a dress, then follow up with all the necessary accessories, including shoes. To ensure that there was common ground in the creative process for the company's wide product line, two fashion directors (one for women and one for men) were hired. They acted as design directors, not directly designing like Tom Ford at Gucci, John Galliano at Dior, or Giorgio Armani (who designs everything and farms out the sketches to all the other designers), but providing uniform and clear direction for all the different designers.

Dealing with different channels of distribution (wholesale, directly owned, accounts), each with different needs, it was crucial that a new position be created, linking the creative process with the commercial needs: the merchandise manager. Designers, then, had two key people to follow: the fashion director, for aesthetic direction, and the merchandise manager, for commercial instructions regarding such issues as the product mix, the sizes, and the cost range. Left to themselves, designers would create only what they liked, often thinking more in terms of what is beautiful than what sells. The new organizational goal was to ensure that the designers follow a specific direction.

The marketing director was to become the interpreter of the family's style in terms of aesthetic value. Taste had always been decided in the boardroom, where the different members of the family (the mother, three brothers and two sisters) sit. After having clearly crystallized the distinctive Ferragamo message, the Ferragamo style, it was the marketing manager who had to clearly communicate it to everybody in the organization, the stakeholders, and the customers. To make the process even easier, an "inspiration room" was started, where key creations of the past were displayed. Here, the Ferragamo taste was accessible to everybody. The new organization enforced clear communication and a stronger advertising campaign, which, in large part, was centered on ready-to-wear, the most powerful point in its brand's image strategy.

Having decided to make the transition from a shoe company into a house of luxury products and services, Ferragamo had to reorganize the way it worked. This new marketing approach organizationally redesigned the creative workforce. No longer focusing solely on the company's cultural inspiration, Ferragamo was now guided by its customers' desires. As Mr. Fellow says: "In the past, if your closet was filled only with Ferragamo dresses and accessories, you'd have been hard-pressed to get dressed, since there was no aesthetic cohesion between the different products."

THE FERRAGAMO EXAMPLE teaches us that there's a difference between creating exceptional products and creating dreams. The first are born of the creators' and designers' inspirations, while dreams are drawn from the customers' perceptions. In an ideal world, these perceptions would coincide with the creators' and designers' inspirations. In business, this is rarely the case. The dreamketer must ensure that the company's creative energy pulses within the customers' dreams rather than solely pumping the creators' and designers' egos. Unlike artists who work at interpreting their own dreams, creators and designers must work to interpret their customers' dreams. The dreamketer must get the company to listen carefully to the customers. This discipline cannot be implemented only at the communication level, but, as demonstrated by Ferragamo, must touch every department of the organization, starting with the product design. After all, in the business of selling dreams, the product is the most powerful communicator. Yet, since the product is only the "occasion to dream," the dreamketer must enlist the entire organization to build the fantastic experience while also educating customers to better appreciate the aesthetic value infused into each product. In other words, dreamketers must align the customers' desires with the company's original aesthetic message. Unlike fellow marketers in mass consumption, dreamketers must preserve the company's aesthetic identity against over-commercialization.

DREAMS DON'T USUALLY COME CHEAP. Their price tag marks both rational and irrational components: the rational being the intrinsically high cost of producing and distributing products of outstanding quality while the irrational draws its high price from the pure emotions of desirability, uniqueness, social recognition, and personal reward. Often prices are not based only on cost factors, but also on the strength of the customer's desire. For example, certain (new) products such as wines and cigars and the vast majority of preowned luxury items are sold at auctions where the customers themselves set the price. It is up to the company to boost its brand through a seductive campaign of perceived or real scarcity.

The luxury industry is the master of tugging at the customer's emotions and loosening up the purse strings. The entire business plan is based on luring the customer away from rational decisions based on functional qualities and measurable facts into the realm of the irrational. Contrary to mass-consumption strategies, the accent is never on price. The fact is that the fastest-rising costs for the luxury business are after-sale service costs, not rebates, discounts, and other types of price promotions, as they are for mass-consumption businesses. Of course, this requires consistency and rigor. Production is at times artificially lower than demand, inventory sales occur only at the end of a selling season or when introducing new models, and distribution is often directly controlled to ensure strict pricing. The company's business strategy is not about a short-term urgency to make more profits but a long-term desire to increase the brand equity and, consequently, the company's value. This approach has also been employed by mass-consumption companies that charge a higher price for their limited-edition models. It is a successful way for a company to gain credibility in the pricing of its entire product line.

Value is defined by the relationship between the benefits a product or service brings to its purchaser and the price paid. Decreasing the product's price usually increases its value. This is usually not the case for luxury products, since the price can set the level of expectation: Luxury companies should avoid underpricing their creations so they don't decrease their *perceived* value.

The toughest part of price is not establishing it but maintaining it. The given price must be accepted by the customers and respected by the retailers (in some countries, such as the United States, company control over retail prices is restricted, since it is illegal to fix prices). The true measure of success in business is whether a company can consistently convince its customers to pay a premium price.

* * *

THE CUSTOMER'S DESIRE sets the real price for a product or service, an often irrational phenomenon. In 1988, when Enzo Ferrari died, the price for new Ferraris skyrocketed, some of them reaching as much as four times the already high retail price. In 1992, the bubble burst and the market crashed (for Ferrari and all the dream cars), leaving scores of dismayed customers. In 1993, in an effort to regain customer trust, Ferrari launched a new model in the United States with full Hollywood flair. Three celebrities were proposed to host the event: Dustin Hoffman, Billy Crystal, and Sharon Stone. Sharon Stone was said not to like such public appearances, a dangerous shortcoming since the host was there to promote Ferrari's strong value by auctioning the car at the highest possible price. Yet with her ridiculously sexy performance in the then just-released film *Basic Instinct*, she was just too perfect to pass on. With a grand entrance onto the stage, she scanned the audience and leered: "I am very glad to be here tonight because Ferrari is the only thing on earth that has a faster reputation than I do." She paused, with a provocative smile to the stunned audience, and added, with a wallet-melting voice: "It is all right to be fast. Only, don't be cheap." The car sold 70 percent over the $120,000 sticker price and the event had the international media hopping. The remarkable match between the sexy and provocative actress and the equally sexy and provocative automobile meant Ferrari was back on track.

ESTABLISHING THE PRICE for emotional products or services is much less scientific than for mass-consumed products or services, since qualities are not as objective. The price that customers are willing to pay depends on their perception of the added value. There is a lot that the dreamketer can do to influence that perception. Consider art that appeals mostly to our emotions and how difficult it is to determine its price. What is certain is that just as auction houses have considerable influence in boosting the price of art, so can dreamketers help establish higher prices for their products and services.

DISTRIBUTION is a critical factor in the business of selling dreams. The easy emotional sway of the purchasing decision can translate into many opportunities for enhancing the customer's dream experience. Just as the large movie screen and Dolby sound power the action movie, so does the beautiful and charming saleswoman adjusting the customer's necktie at Hermès. The "store" sets the stage, creating a special state in which the customer can be caught up in the beauty of the product, and also in the ambiance, where dreaming and spending are there to tantalize.

A well-trained and organized sales force can perform miracles when it comes to swinging the customers' moods. Purchasing is motivated by impulsive reactions that can be highly influenced at the point of sale, since salespeople are in a position to magnify customers' perceived added value. Controlling distribution becomes critical in enhancing the added value. It is much easier to control the quality of production, which is centralized in a single factory or a small number of factories, than it is to control the quality of distribution, where employees must interact with the customers' many moods. Therefore, hiring the right people and thoroughly training them is fundamental. The sales force must be able to convey the excitement to very sophisticated and well-informed customers and satisfy their expectations, occasionally addressing even the most extreme egos. They must relay the aesthetic message that the creators and their collaborators have built into the products. A deep understanding of the emotional characteristics of the products and of the production process becomes essential. They too must have a visceral passion for what they are selling so they can better understand what motivates their customers. Often, the best salespeople are enthusiasts, such as former race car drivers or mechanics at Ferrari or Harley-Davidson, sailors at Swan, art or philosophy students at Rizzoli bookstores, or part-time models or young socialites at fashion houses and jewelry stores.

WHERE RETAIL STORES are located is another important way to inspire a certain buyers' mood. Just look at the long line of luxury stores on Fifth Avenue, Rodeo Drive, Via Montenapoleone, Via Condotti, Faubourg-Saint-Honoré, Old and New Bond Street, Sloane Street, Rue du Rhône, Königstrasse, and Gasa. These streets represent the most expensive real estate in the world, where "window shoppers" and "window wishers" can stroll, dream, and often buy, their moods peaked by the excitement of brushing up against celebrity shoppers. Home of the most famous and exciting luxury items in the world, these streets enjoy their own share of history. The prices for top retail properties is sharply on the rise, as supply is limited and demand continues to creep up. Yet it seems that the old-world strongholds of the term "luxury" are now being forced to pull in their sidewalks and make way for such "dream" companies as Nike, Disney, Warner Bros., Levi's, and Coca-Cola.

The distribution of products and services is undergoing substantial changes because of the Internet's overwhelming influence. However, while the Internet works well for mass-consumed items, it still seems more difficult to sell the multi-emotions of dream products through a computer modem and telephone jack.

While the Internet has exploded over the last five years, it still has barely influenced the business of selling dreams. At first glance, the Internet, with its two-dimensional presentation of products and services, seems unsuitable to promote the multidimensional and multisensorial world of dreams. The Internet has no soul. Its high-tech and cold screen is no substitute for the warmth that person-to-person interaction brings. While the Internet has proven to be a fantastic selling tool, when improperly used it can transform even the ultimate dream into a commodity. After all, most of the pleasure of purchasing dreams is in the purchasing experience itself: visiting beautiful stores, strolling and window-shopping those famous streets, eyeing glamorous people, speaking with a well-trained and personable sales force, touching breathtaking objects, seeing and being seen, and sharing all these emotions with others. It is still hard to imagine a customer asking her friends to join her in front of her computer screen for a day of shopping rather than a day out on whichever town, be it on New York's Fifth Avenue, Paris's Faubourg-Saint-Honoré, or Rome's Via Condotti. Harder still is imagining how Sotheby's, for example, will reproduce, over the Internet, the same excitement that boosts prices at its live auctions. Not to mention the fact that Sotheby's most wealthy customers (whose purchases make headlines) are more mature people not overly impressed by computers. While Internet auction companies are very hot right now and have astronomical price/earnings ratios (what about 42,000 times earnings for eBay versus an already generous market average of 26 times earnings?), they mainly sell inexpensive items. However, through the Internet, Sotheby's is beginning to attract new customers, like the younger generation, the Internet junkies.

Certainly, the Internet makes selling and buying more convenient by empowering customers like never before. It provides freedom (a major component of dreams) allowing customers to receive whatever they want, wherever and whenever they want it, without having to deal with any sales force. You could shop from your bathtub at any time of the day or night if that's what you want. The Internet eliminates the term "long distance," making it possible to view a desired product instantaneously from anywhere, be it a faraway villa in the Bahamas or a yacht off some distant coast. It makes purchasing immediate (a crucial factor in impulse buying): If, when watching TV, you see a movie featuring some actress looking outrageously beautiful in her new Ferragamo shoes, you can buy them immediately through the Internet. The Internet celebrates the individual since it exponentially expands one's capacities (knowledge, ubiquity, and individuality), eliminating any seller interference. It allows the individual to interact on her/his own terms: The products and services come to me, I do not have to go to them. It gives new meaning to the old adage "The customer is king." For the first time ever, the Internet has shattered the mass market into millions of individual customers all able to express their own personal choices. The Internet fuels customers with knowledge, freedom, and control, enabling them to forgo brainwashing from aggressive advertising or overly eloquent salespeople. Through the Internet, customers have real access to information about the products and services available to them. In the past, companies have profited from consumer misinformation, benefiting from the inability to compare prices in real time. Today, companies can't hide their products or services behind smoke and mirrors since customers have access to all knowledge. By making such information readily available to everyone, the Internet will kill mediocrity. Companies will also be hard-pressed to charge different prices worldwide since customers can tap even the most remote places on the globe with a click of the mouse. The Internet is accelerating the polarization of commodities-dream products. Those companies whose products are too close to commodities will see their prices "trend downward toward variable costs, and margins will be skinnier than an anorexic supermodel" (*Fortune,* December 1998). Only those companies able to seduce the customer with highly perceived emotional value will command premium prices.

The Internet activates the relationship between companies and their customers. Being an interactive system, it facilitates more customer involvement, sparking their curiosity and allowing them to be more creative in their purchasing experience, a critical factor when buying dream products and services. By interacting with a company, customers can better express their tastes and preferences and can take part in the life of the company; for example, they can "visit" the factory to better appreciate the creative impulse behind the product. In return, a company can learn much more about its customers and thus better fulfill their desires and preferences. Through the Internet, the company can also spin its own internal communication web and, coupling it with such tools as CD-ROMs, can further unite the entire organization by promoting the essence, the single passion, that defines the company.

The Internet is about to render traditional marketing strategies obsolete. Advertising and attractive pricing can carry you only so far. Now companies will have to formulate new methods of beguilement. They will not be about pushing or pulling the customers. What will matter is how you move them: touching their emotions so that they become impulsive in both their search for a company and their desire for its products and services. For example, the Ferrari site ferrari.com, with no advertising support, receives one million hits a day, placing it among the top 100 most visited sites in the world. Only passion can move people that way.

If properly used, the Internet can be remarkable in helping companies that are selling dreams, offering such precious advantages as unlimited inventory (because companies can show all their products without paying holding costs for every product), as well as improved customer counseling and before-sales service (because companies can increase the amount of information they provide to knowledge-hungry customers). While it still provides a less than fine-tuned representation of dream products due to today's limited technologies, the Internet can certainly help a customer already familiar with a company. After-sales service is also improved, since customers can contact the company more easily and conveniently from their homes or offices.

The Internet still suffers from technological limitations: Images, for example, often appear too slowly for users' nano-attention spans. These searchers waste no time waiting for complex pictures to download. While companies race to make their sites more exciting, presentation is still limited in color and movement. This may explain why the Internet has not yet conquered the business of selling dreams as it has other businesses. Its success depends on its ability to re-create dreams rather than report dreams in a newspaperlike printout of information. Today's sites are far from housing the emotional pull that customers find in stores. This will change as technology evolves and the number of images transmitted increases dramatically: Sites will look more like Hollywood productions than tabloids. If you compare the excitement of a Hollywood set, and how quickly it can be changed, with the setting of even the most luxurious store, you can imagine how exciting the Internet could be. Advances in virtual reality (a supreme example of a "technologically made" dream) will add a new dimension to today's Web sites. The Internet really could give new meaning to dreams! Since technology is what defines our age, the Internet may allow dream companies to be more *on-line* with the spirit of the time.

There will always be those customers who love shopping in stores. There will just be fewer of them. The Internet may not be as much fun as physically store-hopping, but it will be dramatically more interesting in terms of the increased number of products and services that you can browse at one time. While the Internet will not replace traditional retail shopping over the short term (the most optimistic believe it will reach 5 percent of total retail purchases in the next five years), it will fundamentally change the way customers purchase products and services. By testing the relative advantages that have made marketing tools successful until now—advertising, promotion, pricing, and distribution—it will force companies to find new ways to attract customers to their products and services. There will be equal access to the market for everyone from individuals to the largest companies. Customers, whoever they may be, will be able to evaluate every product and service; they will be able to compare quality and price objectively against the competition; and they will mouse-click infinite choices. Most likely, they will be less faithful than they've been in the past. Companies will no longer be able to rely on efficiency advantages and low prices, since they will be engaged in a constant on-line challenge. Companies lacking in creative excitement will be swallowed by the ever more consolidated commodity business, where only huge corporations will survive. The Internet will consecrate all those companies that can ignite customers' dreams. Dreamketing could quite possibly become the precious skill required for business success.

WHILE WORD OF MOUTH still proves very effective in attracting customers to stores, the increase in competition has forced companies to up their advertising budgets. Promoting dreams is every advertiser's wish in this glamorous, creative, highly emotional, and seductive business. It is obviously easier to fire up the emotional qualities of a sensual perfume, a seductive jewel, or an action movie than to make laundry detergent or noodle soup sexy.

The medium through which advertising is channeled is critical, since it determines how effectively the message is received. For fashion, such specialized magazines as *Vogue, Elle,* and *Harper's Bazaar* are most effective. Not only are they credible, but customers tend to read them when they are relaxed and most receptive.

Fashion and lifestyle magazines offer a more immediate launch for Pindaric flights of the imagination. Ron Galotti, former publisher at *Vanity Fair* and *Vogue,* believes the importance of lifestyle magazines stems from the fact that even if many of his readers are not buying from his most exclusive advertisers, they still represent a key audience. "The nonuser, the individual who cannot buy, is sometimes equally important to the user, if not more important, because if when I drive my Mercedes the guy doesn't think my car is so special, it doesn't have value because it's not about basic transportation, otherwise we'd all be driving Volkswagens. There's an equation that comes from advertising. Ralph [Lauren] needs to ensure that the person who will never have the lifestyle to enable him to touch his product will at least know what it is and feel aspirationally toward it. So, when I wear that Ralph Lauren badge or even a T-shirt, the other guy thinks positively about it. That's why people are so willing to spend what they do on an advertising budget, because they realize the importance of the statement."

Ron Galotti believes that magazines must do more to help their advertisers achieve their goals. His role as publisher is "to put in front of my advertisers new and innovative ways to think about media and the utilization of my media. For example, I came up with a power brand index and awareness analysis where we tried to affix very definable qualities to creating a power brand. I wanted to get underneath the shortcomings of a brand and look at the opportunities surrounding a brand. What we found was that awareness was not necessarily a factor for a brand to become a power brand. For example, one company we looked at was Elizabeth Arden. We found out that they had moderate awareness, but they had very high satisfaction in their user base, meaning those who had tried their products were very satisfied. Then we broke it down agewise and learned that, on an attribute basis, the people who used the brand felt good about using the Elizabeth Arden brand because they felt like they were part of a very special club. So, for me, what happens is rather than just taking their advertising and suggesting these nonsensical programs, based on the information from the study, I'm now in a position where I'm using real grassroots branding concepts. Now I can say I want a greater share of your business and if you spend more money with me, here's what I can give you."

Maximizing advertising reach is critical today in a world so crammed with communication. A company can grab an audience far more easily if it has a strong story to tell. What's so great about this business is that it ignites the dreams of the world at large. Its huge audience even consists of individuals who cannot afford to, but who still want to dream. The public-relations department must entice the media into drumming up stories about a company so its message can reach each aspiring dreamer. Editorials (articles not subsidized by a company) are always more credible than advertisements, especially when considering the level of customer sophistication. For example, whenever an automotive magazine writes a story about Ferrari, its sales automatically jump, because Ferrari happens to be a hot topic that car enthusiasts want to read about. Ferrari receives the most free press worldwide, which explains its record-high brand recognition.

Because companies in the business of dreams sell "the mood to enjoy life" rather than just a product or service, the dreamketer must constantly create new and different circumstances where the customer can slip into that perfect mood. An active public-relations department can help the dreamketer organize special events to which opinion leaders and celebrities flock. They, in turn, draw the media, which then fire off titillating stories about the company and its creations.

PETER ARNELL, whose advertising company, the Arnell Group, has been creative advisor to such companies as Chanel, DKNY, Tommy Hilfiger, the Guggenheim Museum, and Movado watches, agrees that what makes a company and its brand strong is to have a home, "because people love integrity and authenticity, they love to know there is a root. People do not like plastic trees. It is a natural thing: The deeper the roots, the bigger the tree. By buying into that company they feel a part of a tradition. Anyplace that has a home has a brand. Marlboro: We know where the cow lives. Nike's home is on Michael Jordan's court. Coco Chanel has a precise address in Paris. When people hear Coca-Cola they go for refreshments, which live very close to freedom; they see it as a brand that lives on a field without any traffic light, with grass, where they can have a moment separate from the rest of the Earth." The key to successfully promoting a brand, he believes, is "creating an address."

In the past, the creators themselves were the best promoters of their own products and services. For example, Salvatore Ferragamo would personally fit his shoes on many of his customers, taking their measurements and spending hours with them, not only to fill their demands, but also to educate them about the superior quality of his shoes. In Florence, Ferragamo bought one of the most beautiful palaces, Palazzo Feroni-Spini, where the aristocratic decor and Florentine splendor would welcome his famous customers while also transforming his footwear into something of a dream. Christian Dior opened his *maison* at 30 Avenue Montaigne in Paris, an elegant facility where he could display his beautiful creations. The most prestigious women would come from all over the world just to experience the charm of this famous couturier at work. A luxury company is often referred to in French as a *maison* (just as in England it might be called a "house"), reflecting the important association between an intimate place and a physical location where both employees and customers can identify the products and services. Palazzo Feroni-Spini and 30 Avenue Montaigne both house the human, familial, and authentic dimensions of these companies, wherein the creator and the company staff "infect" their customers with their passion, attention to details, and relentless dedication. Both Salvatore Ferragamo and Christian Dior have passed away, yet their legacies live on in their *maisons* of origin and tradition.

WHAT POWERS THE APPEAL FOR dream brands? A dream brand strikes the customer's imagination, conveying a clear message that transcends geographical and cultural differences. A dream brand can evolve while remaining true to itself. The more a market matures, as have the United States, Japan, and Western Europe, the more important brands become, since customers tend to base their purchasing decisions on the brands rather than on the products or services offered. Strong brands are what brings success to many luxury and icon-product companies. Think about Ferrari, Hermès, Ferragamo, Louis Vuitton, Gulfstream, Ralph Lauren, Nike, GUESS?, Coca-Cola, and the many others in their class. Their brand appeal commands a premium, which customers are willing to pay because they trust the companies. This premium represents the remuneration for the added value for the product or service, the financial risks, and present and future innovations. The strong emotional motivation behind the business of selling dreams emphasizes the important role that brands play. For example, the dream of social recognition is not attributed to a car or a bag, but to the Rolls-Royce car or to the Louis Vuitton bag. Customers buy brands, not products. The brand must legitimize the company, a crucial factor for companies satisfying ethereal emotions rather than tangible needs. There are a few key factors to brand management that these companies share: a history of very high quality standards in product originality and customer service; a mastering of tradition, a family feeling, mystery, glamour, inaccessibility; fanatical attention to details and coaxing the customer with a constant barrage of subliminal messages and seductive imagery; constant creative renewal, which keeps the customer hooked, and the absence of which could destroy the spirit of innovation, risk-taking, and important investments in R&D; harmony at all levels of the experience to make the dream more credible.

Dream brands are strong enough to stand the test of time. When a mass-consumption brand has lost its persuasiveness, there is little or no chance of reviving it. However, there are some success stories in this dream business in which brands have slid into obscurity, killing companies until aggressive entrepreneurs bought them and revitalized them. Gucci's recent and impressive turnaround is attributed to the fact that the company struggled under weak management, but had a strong brand name. Most dream brands prove more able to weather product failures than any consumer brand.

In a study conducted by Condé Nast's *Vogue* magazine in conjunction with Columbia University, it was determined that "power brands," brands with perceived strength, have been built through positioning. The study characterizes the customer as very intuitive and aware about what brands are supposed to do. For example, one attribute of the power brand is satisfaction. The automotive category ranks highest in satisfaction because the customer expects the car to satisfy a very specific need. Mercedes, for example, is the quintessential brand on the satisfaction chart, a company that does exactly what it promises. Aspiration is another qualifier on the power brand index. On the aspirational chart, for example, "*Vogue* has the number-one position because we feed the dreams."

A dreamketing strategy evolves around the brand. Since the products or services are merely accessories to the dream, the brand is the powerful source that inspires the customer's mood. Through their brands, dreamketers can nearly hypnotize the customer's purchasing power, establishing the trust so essential when dealing with emotions. The brand is critical in influencing customer perception. Just like acclaimed family names, outstanding brands need an origin, a history established by a recognized family member and the mission he or she stands for. Exceptional brands make companies attractive and become a shield against commodity pricing. Since the value of a company is determined by future earnings, the stronger the brand, the easier it is to secure those earnings. Thus, building a strong brand is critical to providing a company's long-term security.

HERE'S AN EXAMPLE of how creative packaging can build a strong brand. When it comes to wines, many experts agree that the Bordeaux region produces some of the best. Among these prestigious Bordeaux wines, the very best come from five famous châteaux, the *grands crus classés,* the first Bordeaux growth: Lafite-Rothschild, Latour, Margaux, Haut-Brion, and Mouton-Rothschild. While Mouton-Rothschild was the last to join the celebrated rank of first growth, it is often a favorite, and not only for the quality of its wine: As *The Wine Spectator* explained, *"Château Mouton-Rothschild is an auction anomaly. In strong vintages, it trades within a relatively small band with the other first growths, often leading but sometimes falling behind Latour (in 1970, for example) or Margaux (as in 1978). In off-vintages, though, Mouton is always the most expensive wine. This extra value can be chalked up to the label and its art rather than the quality of the wine."*

It is amazing to think that in the sophisticated world of great wines, an apparently frivolous feature such as the label can decide customer preference. Yet Mouton's labels offer more than simple information about the producer and its wine.

It all started when Philippe de Rothschild changed the entire business of wine. He chose to communicate his ideas and achievements in a most original and powerful way, and by doing so, his company sparked much attention, even before his wine was at the highest level of quality production (the wine was promoted to *grand cru classé* only in 1973). He wanted to make it very clear that he intended to bottle his wine at his own château (rather than by wholesalers-merchants, as was the case before) to gain control of the entire process, from grape growing, fermentation, and aging to bottling. Inspired by his own passion for art, Philippe de Rothschild asked chosen artists to create original designs to be printed on the upper part of the label (about 20 percent of its total surface). In exchange for their creations, the artists received five cases of wine of the current vintage as well as five additional cases, which they could select from the cellar, a tradition that continues to this day. Rothschild's idea was so successful that it became fashionable for famous painters to bless Mouton's labels. Among the most famous artists featured were Jean Cocteau in 1947, Georges Braque in 1955, Salvador Dalí in 1958, Henri Moore in 1964, Cesar in 1967, Joan Miró in 1969, Marc Chagall in 1970, Wassily Kandinsky in 1971, Pablo Picasso in 1973, Andy Warhol in 1975, John Huston in 1982, Saul Steinberg in 1983, and Francis Bacon in 1990. To respond to today's "globalization" of art and business, more international and foreign artists have been included, such as, in 1991, Setsuko from Japan, and, in 1992, Kirkeby from Denmark. However, the true strength of the collection comes from the less known (and less commercial) artists, whose only claim to fame may have come from their being selected to design the wine label. Their passion, however famous they may be, helped communicate Rothschild's personal fascination with his own time. The labels have become so famous that an exhibition dedicated to them has traveled the world.

Rothschild masterfully promoted his brand by labeling it with a cultural dimension that excited the artistic community as well as the customers and the wine experts. His idea did not emerge from some marketing ploy, but from an authentic desire to celebrate his passion for art and wine. Philippe de Rothschild had found a way to join the art on his label with the liquid art inside his bottle: Time passes, art and great wines are here to stay.

Château Rothschild is a perfect example of how many dreamketing instruments can influence the customer's perception of the added value. This is one of the best wines in the world, praised almost more for the beauty of its labels than for the outstanding contents of its bottle.

ONE OF A dreamketer's most delicate tasks is to position a brand. They must search for the ideal positioning, then try to establish their brand as near that as possible. A dreamketer should first determine the ultimate dream that his or her given product or service can ignite. For example, the ultimate dream of any fine wine is the immortality of an appreciation that will last forever. Château Rothschild has achieved brilliant positioning, since it likens its wine to the only man-made creation that is truly immortal: art. For a car, the ultimate dream is high speed or moving between places in no time. Ferrari's positioning in the automotive industry is unique because it defines this dream.

Perhaps this is why the Ferrari brand is so famous despite its scant advertising effort. Lodging that brand in the customer's dream is what will finally determine a company's success.

So what must the dreamketer really do? In 1834, Søren Kierkegaard wrote "The Diary of a Seducer," in which he pretends to have found a transcript of an introspective man eager to poetically live out his erotic experiences. While the title may sound provocative, Kierkegaard's character has the unusual quality of being a profound seducer, one who engages the reader not for the many young girls he seduces, but for the intensity with which he does it. The seducer chooses not to choose, dedicating his life to aesthetic enjoyment, where each moment becomes so intense that it is difficult to know whether he is seducing or being seduced. The art of Johannes, the seducer, is to promote himself as the object of desire and to encourage that desire by retreating. By so doing, he introduces a sense of uncertainty and ignites a passionate desire by developing in his chosen ones a feeling of anxiety and ambiguity. The erotic (which means the study of love, happiness, and emotional life in general) education takes place in two phases. The first, "the war of liberation," must awaken sensuality and the voices of passion; the second, "the war of conquest," must intensify anxiety and concentrate all attention upon the object of desire. He seduces by stimulating the ambivalence and training the fantasy. Far from being a superficial character, he is the source of meaningful inspiration. The following quotations from the "The Diary of a Seducer" might inspire anyone wishing to sell dreams.

On the customers' desires, their expectations, and how to capture their interest:

If you always know how to ***surprise,*** *you always win the game.*

She has a ***craving*** *for the* ***unusual.***

Reality *did* ***not*** *afford a sufficient* ***stimulus,*** *at most only a temporary one.*

I do not want to deprive myself of surprise. . . . No impatience, no greediness, everything should be ***enjoyed in leisurely draughts.***

On how to gain credibility with the customers:

She will ***believe*** *me, partly because I have confidence in my* ***art,*** *and partly because fundamentally there is* ***truth*** *in what I am doing.*

On how to convincingly communicate the message:

To confuse ***poetry*** *and* ***reality, truth*** *and* ***romance.***

With a keenly developed talent for discovering the interesting in life, he had known how to find it, and after finding, he constantly ***reproduced the experience*** *more or less* ***poetically.***

On what never to do to a customer:

She ***dreams*** *all the longer, provided that people are not so inconsiderate as to* ***arouse her too early.***

On the importance of choosing the right customers and listening to them:

It requires no art to seduce a girl but good fortune to find one ***worth seducing.***

I made myself as inconspicuous as possible in order to ***observe*** *her the better.*

The role of the dreamketer is to seduce, to entice the customer into intense desire for the company's creations. Seducing is much more than simply convincing: It is not about helping formulate a rational decision, but rather about provoking emotional locomotion. The craft of selling dreams, much like the seducer's, requires continual surprise through a poetical transformation of reality into a romance that takes people to a dream state. It is a conscious process that acknowledges the existence of ambiguity in dreams. The desire for dreams is often the expression of anxiety. Selling dreams requires directing this anxiety through an intertwining of incertitude, reserve, and mystery. This is what keeps the desire passionate and alive.

To succeed, dreamketers have to touch the customers' dreams. They must ensure that the product or service is emotionally charged by creating a design worthy of the company's original taste. They must construct a theatrical setting around the product or service, a home, an ambiance where objects of excellence are transformed into unforgettable experiences. They must assign a name to that setting: a credible and exciting brand that pulls the customers in and builds their expectations. They must relay a seductive message that confuses poetry with reality, truth with romance. Finally, they must find the customers worth seducing. This is the subject of our next chapter.

So when have the dreamketers accomplished their mission?

When history is over and the ***myth begins.***

4

The Customer: A Dreamer in Search of Surprise

IN *BREAKFAST AT TIFFANY'S*, Audrey Hepburn captured the excitement of entering this famous cornerstone of the American Dream. Her awe mirrored the sense of surprise and wonderment that so many feel when they ogle the dazzling Tiffany displays. With disarming distinction and grace, she portrayed the whimsical starry-eyed heroine, Holly Golightly. All the while, her subsequent rise to stardom epitomized the understated elegance that launched Tiffany from a mere jeweler to a company that could also make a "princess."

James Bond was the incarnation of a dream that could transform a beautiful set of gold cufflinks into laser guns and a silver pen into a bomb, a dream in which every adventure was rewarded with a toast of 1953 Dom Perignon and a token blonde. Good-looking, invincible, and swiftly successful with the opposite sex, Bond had become a modern-day knight with plenty of class and current technology. Be it his skillful driving of a 1967 DB4 Aston Martin or his sporty Rolex Oyster (both the car and the watch replete with rocket launchers and nuclear gizmos), the British secret agent became the irresistible and irreplaceable Bond by surrounding himself with objects of refined taste. Millions of viewers and wishful customers vicariously lived out their own Bond fantasies simply by purchasing those objects.

Al Pacino won an Oscar in 1993 for his portrayal of a blind, retired general in the movie *Scent of a Woman.* On the brink of committing suicide, Pacino's romantic character admitted there were only two reasons to go on living: "to breathe the beautiful scent of a woman, and to enjoy the indescribable pleasure of driving a Ferrari." Cut to the blind general tearing down city streets as he test-drives a Ferrari Mondial Convertible at blinding speeds, happy to hear the sound of the engine, feel the car's acceleration.

Salvatore Ferragamo dreamed of creating a shoe more beautiful, comfortable, and enduring than any other. Constantly challenged by the threat of bankruptcy, he never gave in. One day he received the phone call that would change everything. A movie, *The Ten Commandments,* was being shot in Hollywood, but a last-minute sick-call from the appointed shoe designer cleared the way for the young Ferragamo to provide the footwear for the actresses. From there, he worked his way to being the famous shoemaker in the era of great divas. Ava Gardner, Lauren Bacall, Greta Garbo, Anita Ekberg, Sophia Loren, Audrey Hepburn, and Anna Magnani were among the many actresses who became Ferragamo's faithful and inspiring customers. By carefully listening to their desires, Ferragamo, who quite literally began from the bottom up, eventually learned to see more than just beautiful arches.

* * *

THESE EXAMPLES, apart from revealing the glamour that surrounds the business of selling dreams, also show the very special relationship that exists between customers and the companies that create those dreams. Since this industry produces the most exciting products and services, it also tends to attract some of the most successful and admired people. While mass-consumption companies gain credibility by paying celebrities to endorse their products, companies that sell dreams can count many celebrities among their real customers. It almost becomes difficult to determine which image is enhanced by the association: that of the celebrity or that of the company. Did Dom Perignon become a status symbol because James Bond sipped it, or did James Bond become the classiest secret agent ever because he chose to sip the prized Dom Perignon? By creating the most outstanding products and services, companies can build a reciprocal relationship with the most valuable customers. What makes the business of selling dreams so outstanding is the fact that it is driven by the most outstanding (from a creative, financial, and image point of view) customers. After all, *a company is what its customers are.* Companies in this business are creative, famous, successful, and wealthy because most of their customers are creative, famous, successful, and wealthy. Any company, whatever its business, should strive to sell the best products and services possible to gain access to the best customers possible. The quality of the customers is the ultimate measure of business success: *Tell me how good your customers are and I will tell you how good your company is.*

* * *

A COMPANY SELLING DREAMS cannot lose sight of the real motivation behind the purchasing of its products. Most of these customers do not simply dream about wearing a Tiffany jewel or a pair of Ferragamo shoes, or about sipping a bottle of Dom Perignon or driving a Ferrari. They dream about becoming as elegant as Audrey Hepburn, as invincible as James Bond, as beautiful as Ferragamo's divas, or as hopelessly romantic as Al Pacino's character. The products—the Tiffany jewels, the Ferragamo shoes, the Dom Perignon, the Ferrari—are only the means of fulfilling these dreams. To succeed in this business, a company cannot simply produce unbelievable products and services, but must urge its customers to fulfill their dreams and become the people they aspire to be.

Art, dream products, and need-satisfying goods are three expressions of man's work, each with different motivations. While the purpose of art is to glorify the artist's emotions (it is not created just to be sold), the purpose of dream products and services is to glorify the customer's emotions (they have to be sold), and the purpose of need-satisfying goods is to meet the consumer's physiological needs. This statement proves the important role the customer plays in the business of selling dreams. For example, one could bottle water to quench one's thirst, then sell the water to every human being, certain that it will also satisfy their drinking needs. Little knowledge of the other human beings is required, since we all share this physiological need. To fulfill people's dreams, on the other hand, requires sensitivity and understanding of each human being, since we do not all necessarily have the same dreams. Understanding emotions entails a deeper soul-searching than understanding needs. While with art and need-satisfying goods, it is the intuition of the doer that counts, in fulfilling dreams, the perception of the receiver (the customer) is critical. After all, dreams are fleeting representations shaped in the customer's mind. As humbling as it may sound, this is a business overwhelmingly dependent upon the customers' whims.

THROUGHOUT HISTORY, this industry has shone through the visibility of its customers. Kings, queens, emperors, popes, dictators, merchants, bankers, and industrialists have always made the news for their particular appetite for the ultimate products and services. Maybe it is because making money is a relatively new notion (before the Industrial Revolution, fortunes were, for the most part, inherited) that rich people are mostly remembered for how they spent their fortunes rather than for the long, hard hours it took to amass them. Or maybe it is simply because in our dreams we fathom the pleasure of spending those fortunes rather than the hardship of building them.

ONE OF THE FIRST FAMOUS CUSTOMERS may have been Croesus,* last king of Lydia (reigned 560–546 B.C.). History's first great spender is responsible for inventing coins. Blessed with the problem of not knowing what to do with his surplus in gold and silver, Croesus conceived a bimetallic system of pure gold and silver coins, an invention that set the world on an all-time shopping spree. Wealthy customers were

*Croesus' great spending sprees made history when he built the temple to the goddess Artemis, one of the seven Wonders of the World, in about 550 B.C. The Artemesium was famous not only for its immensity, but also for the magnificent works of art adorning it, and the elaborate statue of Artemis, originally made of gold, ebony, silver, and black stone.

rarely known for their virtues. The legend of Midas may have first portrayed the image of greed that taints so many rich customers' reputations. According to the myth, his wish was granted as reward for rescuing Silenus, a satyr companion of the god Dionysus. Midas asked that all he touch turn to gold. Greed is rarely a smart counselor, and, facing starvation since all his food would also turn into precious gold, Midas repented and was luckily granted freedom from his curse. Rarely does wealth enjoy a good reputation, however; among the first such good reputations was that of Gaius Maecenas (70–8 B.C.), a Roman diplomat and counselor to the Roman emperor Augustus who was praised as the first philanthropist.* So fervent was his support of artists (such as the poets Virgil and Horace) that even today, those willing to let their altruism and love of the creative spirit untie their purse strings are referred to as "Maecenas." Another big spender was the famous American robber baron William K. Vanderbilt, who spent most of his wealth building houses.† The obsession that the self-made millionaire

*His patronage was, however, not always given out of sheer generosity, but often was exercised with the underlying political intention of glorifying Augustus' empire. Whatever the reasons for philanthropic support, art has often thrived when societies have invested heavily in cultural well-being. Take the wealthy Medici family in Florence, a driving force of the Italian Renaissance, just as Louis XIV, the *Roi Soleil,* was in establishing France's artistic splendor at the end of the seventeenth century. Even if the motivation behind personally endowing artists could be sometimes morally criticized, supporters of all types of artistic expression are crucial to society's cultural well-being. Creativity needs encouragement that is not only psychological!

†The "Marble House," his summer cottage in Newport, Rhode Island, cost him the equivalent of $365 million in today's dollars, an estimated $1 million per night, since he only slept there on summer weekends. Even by today's billionaire standards, this is steep (Bill Gates made headlines by building a main residence with state-of-the-art electronics for only $30 million).

Vanderbilt had with palaces was not born only of love for lavish living, but also from the desire to create the illusion of an old-world dynasty.

Few people today even come close to the frenzied spenders of the past, except perhaps Prince Jeffrey of Brunei and his royal family. By far the world's most lavish spender, the prince has made headlines for his peculiar taste. For example, he uses a 240-karat, $40 million pure diamond as a paperweight and owns a mega-yacht named *Tits* with two tenders: *Nipple One* and *Nipple Two.* The rich and famous will always be known for their excesses, and often one person's frolic is another's dead-serious dream. For example, Liz Taylor's beloved Maltese dog, Sugar, sleeps on the finest Pratesi linen sheets, which can go for upward of five thousand dollars; Melanie Griffith spends fourteen thousand dollars for a bottle of her favorite perfume; Kim Basinger only washes her hair in Evian; Madonna, the Material Girl, spends some five thousand dollars a month for her pet grooming and pet shrink. What most fuels the myth of this industry is the extravagant creativity that some of the customers display. For example, Dorothy Stevens insisted in her will that she be buried in her Ferrari 365 Gtb/4 Daytona, its engine running and headlights on as if to create the illusion of racing away from life while illuminating the darkness of death.

WHILE GLAMOROUS MILLIONAIRES represent only a very small fraction of this business's customers, they represent an *impressive* group of people, influencing others through their visibility and glamour. When Christian Dior was first launched, it made waves in the fashion industry, since it was the first time a company had started operations backed by a strong financial partner such as Boussac, one of the wealthiest European textile tycoons. Dior was free to concentrate on a strategy he believed would ensure success. Deciding that his *maison* should create a select number of very sophisticated dresses, he planned to sell them to the most elegant women in the world. He came up with a list of desirable customers, including ten Americans, ten Britons, ten Italians, and ten South Americans. Those selected were to be poised enough for his creations, but also admired enough to carry his message to the rest of the world. His search was nearly scientific, and it worked. The media went wild for stories about Dior's famous customers. Instantly, he had achieved worldwide recognition rarely seen before in any type of industry. Dior dresses were also promoted by a bevy of beautiful actresses—Marlene Dietrich, who was one of his first customers; Olivia de Havilland, who purchased more than two hundred of his dresses; Ava Gardner; and Brigitte Bardot, to whom Dior refused to donate a dress for one of her movies. To him, each customer was equally important and famous. Dior needed his famously beautiful patrons as much as they needed him. As Mrs. Randolph Hearst clearly stated: *"Dresses are better than a psychoanalyst! They create an image and help a woman to raise the opinion she has of herself."*

Successful, high-profile customers who proudly display a company's product have always proved to be the most credible and effective selling strategists. When Marilyn Monroe declared that the only thing she wore to bed was Chanel No. 5, the perfume soared to immediate success in America. The media always scramble to get the scoop to a public that just can't get enough of these famous lives.

Customers purchasing dreams also prove to be an *impressing* group of people: Their refinement works to impress a company's taste. Even if this industry links a vast, heterogeneous group of companies, producing the most disparate products, all have one similarity: a close relationship with their customers. Those customers represent an invaluable source of knowledge and taste. It all started with refined aristocrats who specifically instructed artisans to create beautiful objects. They were like artists filled with ideas but lacking manual skills. Since aristocrats refused to do any physical work, their self-imposed idleness prevented them from transforming their aesthetic visions into concrete objects. Artisans were therefore enlisted to bring their prized dreams to life. Today, artisans have been replaced by creators who conceive and design rather than simply execute. Likewise, because today's customers no longer reject the concept of work, they have less time to toil with aesthetic considerations. Though custom designing is not as common as before, it still represents a valuable source of inspiration. Customer relations may involve personal visits to the factory, personal presentation of prototypes and brainstorming about new concepts, direct retail offers, or written correspondence. Each company thrives on cultivating a close relationship with a group of core customers who actively offer their opinions to creators and artisans. For example, many directors review their new movies with a small, select audience before the final editing to get a reaction. There are also "historic customers" who have influenced the company's overall taste. Gianni Agnelli, a Ferrari customer long before he purchased the company, ordered cars built to his personal specifications. His were among the most beautiful Ferraris ever constructed, like the famous 365 P, a 1969 rear-engine three-seater across with central drive. Agnelli's models inspired future production of other stunning

Ferraris. Louis-François Cartier became so adept at following instructions from his queen and monarchs that Edward VII, king of England, declared Cartier "the jeweler of kings and the king of jewelers."

Customers are curious and well-rounded individuals constantly exploring their senses in order to expand their pleasure. Lou Noto's love for cigars is a great example of this 360-degree appreciation of the emotional experience.

"I like the look and the feel of a cigar as much as I like its taste. When that cigar is made right and it has that wonderful Connecticut wrapper on it, or a Sumatra wrapper, it has a sort of very, very subtle moistness to it, it has a very special feel in your hands when you touch it, it is not brittle, it is not soft, but it is just right, and that adds to my enjoyment of the cigar immensely. I mean, if the cigar does not taste right I throw it out. But given two cigars that taste the same I have double the enjoyment and twice the pleasure from the cigar that feels and looks right. When it comes to brands I am easy, eclectic. When I was a kid, I smoked White Owl—they used to be the sponsors of the Yankees. That was a terrible smoking experience. I can give you ten brands, any of which I could be very happy to smoke. Partagas Series 3d or the Lusitanias; Cohiba, the Esplendidos or the Robustos; the Epicurus 2 or 4—these are great experiences."

The customers' desires, aesthetic sensibility, and personal preferences have elevated this industry above the ranks of mass consumption. The challenge is to achieve growth while preserving this vital link with the customers and their creative support.

* * *

CUSTOMERS CAN also be considered an *impressionable* group of people, with their craving for recognition. What differentiates us from other animals is our sophisticated communication system, with its many symbols and nuances, languages and gestures. We create objects to express our feelings, thoughts, and emotions. The female cheetah hardly turns to miniskirts, lingerie, lipstick, or jewelry to enhance her natural charm, nor the male mandrill to automobiles, jets, and yachts to relay his sexual interest and power. Drive for recognition and "power trips" are not usually externalized by crowns, scepters, rings, or neckties in the animal kingdom.

The most refined customers may be drawn to dream products and services for their aesthetic and hedonistic emotions, but the vast majority purchase them for the symbolism. To these customers, products and services communicate social aspirations, a means of emulating celebrities, trend-setters, opinion leaders. Dream products and services let them escape from solitude and anonymity (*Homo socialis*'s most basic fear) by establishing their social presence. These customers may not stimulate creators with their product suggestions, but their generous contributions elate dreamketers, financial managers, and shareholders. Such customers are bound to increase in number with the acceleration of social mobility, and this industry will continue to supply "ego-boosters" for those in search of self-identity and self-assurance.

Their passionate desires, visibility, and influential taste are critical to shaping this industry, much more than in any other type of business. Though very heterogeneous in nature, these customers seem moved by two fundamental motivations: a strong *savoir être* for appreciating the beautiful things that life can offer and a strong *vouloir être,* a craving for recognition, status, or affirmation of their individuality. In the past, dream products and services were exclusively for the wealthy few who could afford to cultivate their *savoir être* through a life of aesthetic and hedonistic pleasures. Now that these products and services have become more accessible to a wider range of customers, *vouloir être* appears to be the main motivator behind the purchases. "Looking great" still seems to precede "feeling great."

Philip Warner, president and CEO of Asprey North America, believes that the famous English jewelry company has "two types of customers. One is the social elite born of 'The Establishment.' They are the aspiration builders for our second type of customers, the aspiration seekers, those who wish to be like them. 'By Royal Appointment' [having the royal family as customers] is an important title for Asprey. It offers the rest of our customers aspirational direction. Just as we needed Princess Di to shop with us because it motivated the rest of our customers who aspired to be like her."

The strength that makes companies in the business of selling dreams successful is based on the personal relationship they often develop with their customers. In the past, there were rich customers who would commission artisans, painters, sculptors, and creators to shape objects specifically to their demands and desires. Over the past twenty to thirty years, since dreams have become more available, the number of customers has multiplied, yet close customer relationships are still key. For Asprey's Warner, "What defines great customer relations is when somebody is genuinely pleased to receive correspondence or communication from us. That epitomizes it. It doesn't matter whether the person is spending ten thousand dollars or $1 million. If the relationship is very strong, it should be almost like a friendship, even though it is not a real friendship. We always need to keep the client-business bond strong."

DREAM PRODUCTS, be they luxury, icon products (Levi's jeans, Nike sneakers), films, status-enhancers (Wall Street brokers), ego-boosters (Viagra, physical or spiritual motivators), or well-being (vitamins, fitness) products, all share a fundamental characteristic: They strike the imagination and emotions of the buyer. Since it is the perception of the buyer, the customer, that makes the dream possible, understanding the customer explains the business. Let's look at what distinguishes the customer from a consumer.

In the need-satisfying business, **the consumer** is a statistic, a hypothetical figure symbolizing millions of other people. When buying something for its purely functional and utilitarian worth, the consumer completes an act of destruction, since the product is no more than discarded trash once it is finished. It is a destruction that is highly encouraged, since the more that is consumed the more the companies sell. Consumption implies a sense of waste, often associated with overabundance. Mechanical, in a sense, consumption rarely involves any feeling, much like the automation used to stamp out the same good. It is an uneventful act that means little to the consumer: Once the product is used for its practicality, it is thrown away (be it physically or in the sense that there is little remembrance of the act). Neither consumer nor product possesses any identity, due to the blurring effects of such massive quantities. The relationship between a company and a consumer is usually as distant as the act of consumption.

In the business of selling dreams, however, **the customer** is an identifiable person with a name, highly selective and distinct tastes, and desires. The customer usually purchases a product for reasons other than its simple "use." The product is not "consumed," therefore it is neither destroyed nor wasted, but rather represents the meaningful relationship between an owner's feelings and the special item. Even in the case of non-durable products, such as a meal at Daniel, a glass of Château Latour 1974, or a whiff of Guerlain Shalimar, customers preserve a "memory" of the experience, which has enriched their lives in some way. Both the customer and the object are specific "personalities" rather than an overabundance. Compare the sensual pleasure of, say, eating a hamburger in a fast-food joint with savoring a slice of Fouchon *fois gras,* chugging a soda versus sipping a glass of Château Pétrus 1961, or watching the movie *The Last of the Mohicans* versus a potato chips commercial. The "ownership" of a dream product or service entices the emotions, saluting the creator's imagination, the artisan's talented hands, and the customer's taste, be it over a lifetime, as in the case of a family jewel, or in the instant it takes an exceptional wine to wash over your senses.

This customer-consumer distinction helps clarify the company's business vision. Customers are more faithful and tend to spend more than consumers, since their emotional investment is higher. Because customers are so valuable, any company must focus on attracting and retaining as many customers as possible. After all, a company's total worth is equal to the sum of the purchasing power of its customers and their willingness to use it. Transforming otherwise common products into dreams is the best possible way to attract customers.

* * *

THIS DISTINCTION BETWEEN customers and consumers does not pretend to be a moral or value judgment. Consumption is extremely important to our social survival. What matters here is the individual's attitude toward a certain product or service. Being a consumer or a customer is a question of purchasing attitude. The same person could be both a consumer and a customer. One could be a consumer of luxury (remember Imelda Marcos with her five thousand pairs of Ferragamo shoes) or a customer of common goods (like Adam and Eve and the apple). While this distinction appears elitist and discriminatory, conceptually it is not. There are very poor people who are customers, since they appreciate, as the ultimate dream, what is perceived by others to be nothing more than a common good. There are also very rich people whose consumerism is bred of their own indifference—they have everything imaginable and nothing of importance. Today many more people can afford dream products and services than the exclusive and sophisticated few of the past. Technological advances have made dreams more affordable while dreamketers, through their emotional communication campaigns, have transformed many consumers into customers.

The customers' economic profile is about to change, not only because of the affordability of dreams, but also because people have more disposable income to spend on fulfilling their dreams. Today, the crumbling of socialist and communist credos has fueled the entrepreneurial spirit all around the world. Never in history have we lived in a society in which more people have the chance of being wealthy. In the past, wealth was either out of reach (becoming rich was only a birthright), or simply out of sight. Since world economies are growing faster than their populations, the number of rich people is increasing. Financial mobility is drastically accelerating the shift in earnings among the classes, and money is changing hands faster than ever before.

LET'S LOOK AT the customer's economic profile. At the very top are the few and very rich. While their number is marginal, they are highly visible because they tend to be imitated by the rest of the population.

The United States is home to the most billionaires, followed by Japan, Germany, and Switzerland. In 1995, the number of billionaires, with an average fortune of $2.7 billion, reached 865, up 72 percent from 1985. Real estate and retailing sectors account for nearly a quarter of these billionaires, followed by media, food and beverage, computers, entertainment, automobile, banking, cosmetics, construction, oil, shipping, and convenient marriages. Apparently sex and race are limiting factors. Of the 1,019 Americans who have been or currently are billionaires, only five were black and three were women.

CEOs represent a new breed of entrepreneurs whose revamped working spirit has extinguished their once bureaucratic mentality. According to *Forbes*'s list of America's highest-paid CEOs, the median paycheck for the eight hundred largest U.S. corporations in 1997 reached $2.3 million, including gains from exercising stock options. CEOs' earnings are growing not only in the United States, since stock options, originally a form of compensation reserved for American companies, are now spreading around the world. A study shows the average CEO compensation has gone from forty times the average pay of a factory worker back in the 1960s to today's three hundred times.

CEOs are not the only ones earning outrageous incomes.

Salaries in the sports and entertainment businesses are rising exponentially, with the price of celebrity never higher. Top Hollywood actors' salaries are up from $5 million a decade ago to $20 million today, just as directors, writers, producers, and others in the entertainment industry are also earning more. Evander Holyfield, world heavyweight boxing champ, enjoys career earnings of almost $200 million, Michael Jordan has earned $60 million a year, while Michael Schumacher, Ferrari's F-1 champion, earned more than $30 million in 1997. Not that everybody earns as much as CEOs, actors, and athletes, yet their visibility certainly feeds people's expectations. The more media coverage these glamorous and rich people get, the more everyone wants to emulate them. The age of possibility is changing the way people think. "You can do it" seems like today's motto. It no longer takes several generations to get rich. It can happen over the course of a few years. The "age of immediacy" has produced people like Bill Gates, who first made the *Forbes* list some ten years ago and now heads it with some $50 billion.

Most affluent customers, however, have more realistic incomes. All types of companies hope to win over this market segment, since it represents the largest concentration of spending power. Closely analyzed by marketing researchers, it indicates future spending patterns for the rest of the population. In the United States, the largest market in the world, the millionaire population, which was estimated at about 832,602 households in 1985, grew to include 1.2 million households in 1987. In 1983, you could become a member of the top 1 percent with a net worth of $1.3 million. In 1989, it took a net worth of $2.3 million to make the grade, a higher threshold reflecting the population explosion of U.S. millionaires. In the United States, the classification of merely "rich," that is, having a net worth exceeding $1.5 million, is quite democratic, since you only need to be in the top 10 percent to make the grade.

Affluence tends to be a family affair. Most affluent people are married (80 percent versus 55 percent of the total U.S. population) and very few are divorced (4 percent versus 10 percent: Nobody likes to lose a good thing!). Education is also an important factor. The higher the income level, with the exception of the $200,000-plus category, the higher the percentage of affluent individuals with four or more years of college education.

In the past, wealth was mainly inherited, but recent data published on inheritance revealed that less than half of the top 1 percent of U.S. wealth-holders received any inheritance at all. Furthermore, the sum of all inheritances for individuals in the top 1 percent amounted to only 9.8 percent of their collective wealth over their entire lifetimes. A majority of today's richest people are self-made entrepreneurs: 70 percent of those in the top 1 percent have reported being self-employed.

Wealth is age-related. Most millionaires are fifty or older. Only one in ten is younger than forty. However, wealth continues to seep into a younger age bracket (don't forget the wealthiest man on earth, Bill Gates, age forty). It is predicted that by the year 2000, the age group thirty-five to forty-four will inhabit the greatest number of households earning six-figure incomes.

No matter how these affluent people earn it, they tend to save far more than any other segment of the population. The life cycle proves to be a motive for spending or saving. Individuals save during the high earning years in order to spend during retirement. Today, the typical male retires at age sixty-four and can expect sixteen years of retirement. With an estimated

80 percent of the income of the top 1 percent saved and not consumed today, it proves that times have changed since the 1980s, when excessive greed and conspicuous spending equaled that of Gatsby.

THERE IS A RAPID TURNOVER within the rich group: 28 percent of the top 10 percent drop from this category within three years, which implies that, in the United States, half of the top 10 percent of the wealth-holders are replaced every six years by the *nouveaux riches* on their way up. This confirms the notion that America continues to be the land of opportunity and economic mobility, helped by a tax structure and an availability of risk capital that favors entrepreneurs. While Europe and Japan have a far more stable social structure, both societies are increasingly influenced by the American entrepreneurial spirit, favoring lower income taxes, smaller and less influential governments, and a wider availability of risk capital to finance new ventures. *Nouveaux riches* will continue to emerge within the highly entrepreneurial societies of tomorrow, bringing their desire for status and symbolic spending to the business of selling dreams.

Taxes are one of the most influential factors affecting the increase in wealth (not so much at the individual level as globally). The following table approximates some of the most significant taxes levied on the countries of the G7, and their highest rates (usually the rate paid by affluent customers):

	U.S.	Japan	Germany	France	Italy	U.K.	Canada
Income Tax (including surcharges)	39.60%	65.00%	53.00%	56.80%	51.00%	40.00%	52.94%
Capital Gains Tax	28.00%	50.00%	0.00%	16.00%	25.00%	40.00%	75.00%
Wealth Tax/Net Worth Tax	N/A	N/A	1.00%	1.50%	N/A	N/A	N/A
Social Security Taxes	7.65%	12.75%	DM11,747	18.00%	4.55%	2.00%	C$2122
Gift & Inheritance Tax	55.00%	70.00%	70.00%	40.00%	33.00%	40.00%	N/A
VAT/GST/Consumption Tax	N/A	3.00%	5–7%	5–20.6%	4–19%	17.50%	7.00%
Sales Taxes	various	N/A	N/A	N/A	N/A	N/A	7–12%

Note: This is only a cursory overview of the highest marginal tax rates for the most indicative types of tax. In specific calculations these rates may change, since different rates are applied to different items at different levels of income and may carry some maximum "cap." Tax rates are based on 1995 information. Tax laws may have changed in various jurisdictions.

It's hardly surprising that the United States, the country with the lowest income-tax rate, is home to the highest proportion of millionaires. Hong Kong is also seeing its affluent population explode thanks to a very progressive tax policy: no taxes on dividends and capital gains, 15 percent maximum on individual salaries, and 16 percent on corporate profits. Historically, European tax authorities have acted far more aggressively because of pressure from their governing socialist parties. Highest rates of income tax range from 40 percent in the U.K. to 58 percent in Sweden (a proper perspective on the total tax burden means considering both income taxes and consumption taxes).

Apart from taxation, governments rely on other tools that influence civic income and wealth. Changes in the money supply and interest rates, for example, can bring on the burden of inflation or deflation. Over the short term, increasing the money supply may bolster perceived wealth and *nominal incomes,* but it also triggers an escalation in prices, which often reduces *real income* over time.

As the price level rises, the purchasing power of the population declines. Inflation affects wealth much as taxation does. For example, the 2.7 percent increase in consumer prices in the United States during 1994 was equivalent to a 2.7 percent tax on savings and investments. Conversely, deflationary policies push down the price of assets such as shares, homes, or land. There is a direct correlation between interest rates and inflation. The change in expected inflation will cause the same change in nominal interest rates. In an ideal situation, when inflation is equal to zero, the real interest rate is determined solely by capital supply and demand.

Other forces work against emotional spending, including changes imposed by tax authorities regarding business expense deductions. In 1992 new legislation brought drastic changes to the business of entertainment in the United States. No longer were deductions on such business expenditures as country club fees or any type of social, sporting, or luncheon club membership dues permitted, and deductions for business meals and entertainment expenses were reduced.

Conversely, consumption credit availability feeds people's illusion of being wealthy by crediting them with instant spending power and easing any psychological hangups about spending (buy now, pay later). More of this will occur in the future as companies will offer their customers more creative forms of financing.

It's hard to say who is really rich and who is not, since this is a relative concept and varies not only over time but also from place to place. Statistics on wealth are usually computed in relation to the overall financial situation of a specific population; the top 25 percent of earners are considered affluent. This method cannot be generally applied around the world due to the vast divergence in GNP per capita. Companies should focus less on income and wealth distribution in relation to the rest of the population and more on **discretionary income,** defined as the proportion of revenues that can be spent freely on anything from education, leisure, and luxury items to any other pleasures that exceed the basic requirements for food, shelter, taxes, and other necessities. Discretionary income depends not only on total income, but also on the cost of living in a given place, which varies from country to country, and often within the same geographical region. While discretionary income is the best indicator of the spending power toward the purchase of dream products and services, there are other relevant factors. Besides the **saving factor,** there are other variables far trickier to assess, such as cultural and social attitudes that condemn luxury or hedonistic spending, religious norms that prevent consumption of alcohol or certain specific foods, and particular attitudes toward money. These variables may depend on subjective characteristics such as self-perception, lifestyle, personal preferences, and fears. Therefore, while wealth can be measured in an objective way, in terms of income, value of the home, bank balances, or portfolio investments, it is much more difficult to determine the potential market for dream products and services.

WHAT REALLY INFLUENCES emotional spending habits even more than one's financial status or the state of the economy is one's emotional makeup. Since purchasing is motivated not by physiological but by psychological needs, wealth in itself will not guarantee a purchase. Customers whose income would not classify them among the affluent often spend more freely and purchase luxury products and services more readily than millionaires. Affluence is often a state of mind, a style of living and spending. Some high-income earners lead a monastic life, deprived of any type of luxury, while many other individuals, although not wealthy, manage to pursue a luxurious lifestyle, either by overextending their credit lines or by spending their hard-earned cash on grand appearances or simply on having a good time. In a sense, being attracted to products and services with high emotional content defines affluent buyers more than their income bracket. When asked if his restaurant was considered one of luxury, the Swiss chef Fredy Girardet Calvinistically retorted that many of his customers were nonaffluent people who came to celebrate very special occasions or to enjoy a great meal. Obviously, Girardet's populist comment does not consider that low-income people can hardly dish out two hundred dollars for a spread. Yet here's another example of the powers of persuasion that a brilliant dreamketer can wield to convince many to spend beyond their financial means.

Customers must crave that very special experience—it can't come too easily. What makes dreams so exciting is the fact that you never know what adventure the night will bring; similarly, dream products or services mustn't be too predictable and common or the customer will grow weary or bored. Look at champagne: Sales peaked in 1985 at 216 million bottles, when champagne flowed like beer on tap. Because champagne became too accessible, its appeal as the celebratory drink for special occasions vanished and its market collapsed: Only 144 million bottles were sold in 1997, with prices cascading as much as 65 percent. Sales will soar once again with so many corks expected to pop for the Big Millennium Bash. But champagne may never again gush as romantically as it once did unless dreamketers can uncork the aristocratic sex appeal that distinguishes this bubbly drink from all the bottles of beer out there.

While there is usually a clear link between income and wealth and the purchase of dream products (especially luxury), other important cultural, psychological, and economic factors are likely to influence the purchasing decision. The tendency to spend is also affected by elements of an individual's background, such as religion (almost every religion heralds frugal living), custom, nationality (French and Italians spend more on fine food than anybody else), sex (less than 2.7 percent of Ferrari customers are women), and profession (lawyers buy expensive watches to better measure the time they charge). Switzerland is the largest market per capita for Ferrari cars, with 220 units sold in 1997, almost ten times Italian and thirteen times U.S. penetration rates. For Rolex and most luxury watch producers, Italy is the largest market in the world. Japan tops the market for leather products from Gucci, Ferragamo, Hermès, and Louis Vuitton. China appears to be tipping back unusually high amounts of Hennessy cognac and other luxury spirits. Americans cash in the highest box-office grosses for the movie industry. Cultural norms, environmental regulations, traditions, and religions can deeply affect customer preference.

BEHAVIOR IS NOT always easy to interpret. For all the advantages and privileges it carries, affluence often instills contradictory impulses: the fear of losing the privileges or the burning desire to achieve them, guilt *vis-à-vis* the less fortunate or envy toward the more fortunate, frustration at not being able to reach the top or arrogance at having done so, the desire to prove oneself and to compete with others or a disdain for such widespread superficiality. The motivation behind the purchase can vary substantially, ranging from the ambition to reach a social status, to a desire to impress or even humiliate some people, to a way of hiding physical and mental weaknesses, to the pursuit of sheer pleasure, to a compensation for emotional stress. For example, from birth we are taught that society reveres those who are successful while loneliness is the emblem of social rejection for those who fail. Therefore, some people express their desire to be socially accepted through objects symbolizing success. To others, it can be the quest for aesthetic excitement or, occasionally, the means of overcoming boredom that leads them to purchase emotional products. Even giving a pleasurable gift to a loved one or buying the favors of others can be the motivators. Building self-esteem, going wild, or simply keeping up with today's spending trends are other factors.

Whatever the motivation, spending responds to man's complex and ever-changing psychology. Physiological needs are internally motivated, therefore easier to detect and interpret: A baby cries because it feels pain in its empty stomach, indicating the need for food. Psychological desires are harder to understand and are usually motivated by external stimuli: Seeing a beautiful woman can arouse passion. Mario Buccellati describes the similar attraction a customer feels for a special Buccellati jewel: "It's like asking what does a young lady look for in a man and vice versa? There has to be a natural attraction unlike with some jewels that you would see in more commercially oriented companies, in which seasonal or direct fashion trends influence the displays. A Buccellati piece may sit in an assortment for a long time until the right person walks through the door and is smitten by it. Just like in a courting relationship, we must find the right piece for the right person. We are essentially matchmakers."

THIS IS the business of selling dreams. Success comes to those who can ensure that their customers can dream, or at least reach a special state of mind slightly detached from reality, free of obligation to be pleased and reassured. A company can lure its customers into such a special state only if it understands the customer's salient psychological traits. For example, the jeweler Edward Asprey describes how "our Asprey customer is in search of the unique or the unusual. They are people who, in their lives or business, have been involved with quality and service and want to translate that into their purchase of highly emotional products. Particularly those people who have made a lot of money and understand the value of quality and service. They are people who enjoy culture and want to learn to appreciate craftsmanship. What attracts them to us could be a number of reasons: It could be the English aspect, which carries a certain history and tradition, quality, and design. Or it could be that Asprey is really unlike any other place. We have always claimed to be able to turn a customer's dream into a reality. Not just provide something there for them to see, but to actually work with them and create something they have dreamt of, something that was unattainable."

* * *

CUSTOMERS TODAY are usually very active, be it at work, at play, with their family, or socially. Becoming affluent nowadays, in an ever more competitive and success-driven society, requires a surplus of energy and the determination to forge ahead professionally. These are characteristics that surface not only in the way affluent people work, but also in how they enjoy their leisure and social time. Their tempo of activity is akin to that of children, with similar intensity and dedication. Just like children, their attention spans are short and they tend to tire of things and quickly search for new stimuli. These customers want to interact with people who have a story to tell. They listen only to those salespeople who can excite their imaginations and enhance the value of a product. Their professional and private occupations acquaint them with many people, increasing their chances to influence or to be influenced in their lifestyles (making word of mouth a very effective mode of communication). Their articulate, opinionated, and passionate manner makes them strong communicators, able to sway the purchasing trends of others, even shape the mainstream. Of course, if they are ever dissatisfied, their product boycotts are never a thing of silent disapproval.

The higher their income bracket, the more homogeneous these customers seem to be. The country of origin, the household size, the ethnic group, and the religious beliefs seem less important, since these very rich have a lifestyle that transcends country boundaries and ethnic cultures. Travel brings them an international blending of ethnic or cultural preferences. This may explain why companies in the business of selling dreams have usually been able to export their original products and services to foreign countries more easily than mass-production companies, which struggle to adapt them to local conditions and consumer habits. Affluent customers can better appreciate foreign stimuli, as they are more receptive to the message, the culture, or the aesthetic values behind emotional products.

These customers are also well informed. Being competitively informed is one way to achieve social and business edification. Their hunger to learn could sometimes be the consequence of a fear of being left behind rather than a sheer pursuit of intellectual excellence. Their curiosity makes them discriminating customers who know about a product even before they decide to purchase it. The more expensive the purchase, the higher their involvement and emotional investment. For example, an intimate dinner at Alain Ducasse in Paris requires a slightly different purchasing strategy from dropping into the local McDonald's. Product design, quality, maintenance, construction, and, in this age of environmental conscientiousness, how environmentally friendly or safe the product is are essential points that they want to know. This explains the impressive growth of trade and lifestyle magazines, like the *Robb Report* and *Forbes FYI,* that offer "the good life" and high-end product coverage.

Sometimes their quest for information exceeds product quality alone. They want to know everything about the company's management, its social and environmental policies, its customer base and social positioning, and any philanthropic contributions. They tend to seek companies that share their values or their ambitions. For example, the celebrity guest list at a first-class restaurant might be more savory to them than the quality food or service.

CUSTOMERS WANT TO BE in control of the purchase, usually resenting unsolicited marketing techniques such as mass advertising or aggressive salespeople. It takes a very sophisticated public-relations team as well as a finely tuned sales force to establish the perfect purchasing mood. Since jewelers are the ultimate charmers, we asked Asprey's Philip Warner whom he relies on to woo customers. "The ideal store manager has two sides," he replied: "the back-end side, which refers to someone's understanding the retail principles, and the front-end side, which refers to the person's ability to appeal to the clients and relate to them. Our customers prefer to see a familiar face. Asprey's retail success is based on the fact that many salespeople have been working at Asprey for thirty years or more. We have a very low turnover. Our entire business of selling is about relationship selling. For customers to get up into certain price brackets of spending they need to trust the salesperson. Especially for new products or products whose value is difficult to ascertain, customers want to trust us that they are getting good value. Trust takes time and builds a frank relationship. As we spend more time with a client and gain more trust, they in return spend more with us." When emotions are concerned, a personal relationship is key. For example, Dior went to extremes to gain the duchess of Windsor as a client. He even hired away an Hermès saleswoman who had dressed the duchess in the past just so the duchess could feel comfortable around a familiar face. This is a business of trust simply because of the customers' high emotional (and often financial) investment. In a sense, their desires are laid bare, and this requires delicate and sensitive handling. Customers are generally wary, since they are constantly solicited for their obvious spending power. These customers always appreciate personal recognition from someone who genuinely knows their individual tastes and special requirements. They also want to feel they belong to an elite clan. In this business, some successful companies are set up like clubs, with everything focused on customer relations.

STRONG BRAND LOYALTY is the crux of this business. Once customers feel strongly for a brand, they stick with it. This is the key to the repeat purchases that so many of these companies enjoy. While average repeat business in the auto industry is around 15 percent of total sales, it is almost 40 percent for luxury automobiles, and as high as 60 percent for Ferrari. The "collector's mentality" often means these customers may purchase several models of watches, jewels, pens, or automobiles. For example, what made the movie *Titanic* so successful was the number of young girls who went back over and over again to relive the love story. Keeping customers happy is no small feat, especially today. Customer retention is a telltale sign of how healthy a company is.

IT'S ONE THING TO TALK ABOUT these character traits; it's another to know where these customers are hiding out. They shun a sales force that insists too strongly and often seek privacy. Companies must reach them personally. Since dream products and services are usually purchased while in a particular mindset, a company must connect with its customers at the most appropriate moment.

Reaching the customer at home is one of the best ways for a message to be heard. It spreads to the rest of the family—an important factor, since the significant decision to purchase emotional products and services is often made after consulting other family members. At home, customers are usually more relaxed and more receptive to anything that promotes fun, pleasure, and self-fulfillment. Special mailing services, ZIP code–directed magazines, interactive television, E-mail, and particularly the Internet make this easier than before.

With the exception of inherited wealth, fortunes are made by those who spend long and intensive hours at work. The challenge is to win their attention away from work activities while they're shackled to the desk. However, sometimes a message from out of the blue grabs them. Articles (rather than advertisements) in specialized trade magazines, exclusively designed for lawyers, doctors, and so forth can offer an introduction to your company's world. Magazine editorials (a source of free promotion) are an important source of legitimate product endorsement, as are the "advertorials," the part-editorial part-advertisement arrangements between the company and magazine to show a mutual commitment to the product.

On vacation we all dream of playing and relaxing. In effect, we become more receptive. The advantage here is that affluent customers tend to play often. In the United States, only 49 percent of the total population are members of any sort of private club, while 73 percent of the wealthy population hold club memberships. Here, leisure and sports magazines or well-positioned retail stores are a strong bet.

HAVING A BETTER PERCEPTION of who your customers are—of their preferences, spending behavior, background, social role, and professional status—still does not clarify why dream products and services have such a powerful draw. Intense feelings often prompt these customers to do the proper research, which may reduce their purchase risks in the long run. The risk level depends on the given product or service. The more the customer has invested in the purchase, the higher the perceived risk. Generally, the higher the risk is, the more attracted customers are, sort of a vertigo effect. The risk is often proportionate to the desire to be surprised. Hedonistic and symbolic products are riskier than functional ones. If you buy a Timex, you risk being late for an important meeting if the watch doesn't perform well. If you buy a Patek Philippe *phases lunaires complication* because you love its design and mechanical complexity, you risk discovering that someday you might not love the watch as you did, or that it didn't measure up to your expectations. Here, the risk grows, because it's harder to influence taste than repair a watch. Finally, if you buy a gold Audemars Piguet Royal Oak because you want to impress members at your country club, your risks soar should you find that your watch is no longer *in vogue* because the gold is too flashy: How can you change the taste of an entire country club?

Customers communicate through emotionally charged products and services. Culture affects not only our most noble activities, such as the arts or sciences, but also our daily lives, as a "lens" through which we perceive the phenomena of our surrounding reality. It also blueprints human behavior, directing social action and productive activities. Culture categorizes the world (in terms of class, status, sex, age, occupation), while such material possessions as a Swan sailboat, a pair of GUESS? jeans, or activities like going to see the movie *Titanic* or playing golf at the Golf Club at Purchase all work to substantiate these categories. For example, expensive clothes can suggest a certain upper-class "refinement." Cultural categories are not fixed. The more mobile a society, the freer individuals are to select a cultural category. Companies influence customer choice through the cultural meaning they ascribe to their products and services, be it through the design and technology chosen by creators and engineers or through the marketer's metaphoric and seductive fantasies.

One axiom of symbolic interaction is that culture sways the individual's behavior in a given society. While culture itself is shaped by history, institutions, languages, religions, science, art, and any other expression of human thinking or action, human conduct is directed by *symbols of influence,* which are generated and disseminated by "specialists," highly creative individuals such as artists, designers, writers, musicians, actors, engineers, politicians, professors, and managers—in short, social leaders. These specialists, through creative innovation, constantly introduce or adopt new products and services, thus directing social taste. For example, Audrey Hepburn made Tiffany; James Dean and Marlon Brando made Levi's jeans; Gianni Agnelli launched Ferrari; the Emperor Augustus established Capri as the ultimate Roman resort; Brigitte Bardot launched Saint Tropez, Michael Mann's *Miami Vice* Miami, and the Aga Khan the Emerald Coast; King Edward VII made the Ritz; Michael Jordan made Nike; Churchill made Monte Cristo cigars; Bill Clinton made Cohiba.

WHEN IT COMES TO material possessions, we tend to make assumptions about others based on what they own or purchase. Self-image is largely determined by how others see us. Though these superficial presuppositions can prejudice us, they also represent, bad or good, the key to a nonverbal method of communication that fuels a pleasure of self-expression based on our personal possessions. From childhood, we learn that certain products can affect our social role-playing. As a result, our possessions become an annex of ourselves. If these products correspond to our own self-image, then dreamketers must promote products that suit our individual images. For example, blue jeans (whose name has even changed from "denims"), originally considered the uniform of poverty-stricken miners, have become the symbol of free-spirited democracy; the Alfa Romeo Spider symbolized the young generation's love for romance; sneakers now symbolize a sports-crazed youth; Chanel's *tailleurs* once defined a new liberation for independent women; Hermès ties were the badges of Wall Street bankers; Viagra is now the "vitamin" for swinging septuagenarians.

Clothing is one way people communicate, influencing others in terms of judgment about status, personality, ethnicity, lifestyle characteristics, attractiveness, attitudes toward social issues, and even intimate preferences. People even go as far as behaving differently toward others depending on the clothes they wear. A woman in a tight Dolce & Gabbana miniskirt, fishnets, and stilettos is more likely to be "read" by a typical "macho stud" as a neon sign for sexuality than a woman done up in monachal garb.

Recognizing status starts in young children and grows as social condition and sex become more important. Studies have shown middle-class children are quicker to recognize social distinction than working-class children. Other studies show boys exhibiting greater interest than girls in possessions and achievements, while girls appear more interested in family and social relationships. Some psychologists say that the stronger attention to status differentials by boys is necessary in motivating them to invest the time, money, and the effort necessary to achieve success in their career. Do we believe that?

* * *

CONSUMPTION does not happen in a vacuum. Products and services are woven into society, important in "setting the stage" for the many social roles we must play. Evaluating a single person's role often depends on the suitability and quality of the role's accompanying symbols. For example, the proper Wall Street dress code includes a blue suit (Brooks Brothers, for lack of a personal tailor), an Hermès tie, and such appendages as a Mont Blanc pen and a Hewlett-Packard 12C calculator. The same business meeting in Los Angeles among Hollywood executives calls for a much more laid-back look: Nike sneakers, a "Comic Relief" T-shirt, and two Motorola StarTAC cell phones. Gold worn by a man (a ring, a chain, a bracelet, or even a front tooth) is, in some cultures or social environments, a sign of social success, while elsewhere, it may be frowned upon as the drippings (or droppings) of *nouveau riche* or bad taste.

An individual can play several different roles simultaneously. For example, a man can be a husband, a father, a boss, and a tennis player. The behavior is largely based upon role playing. Depending on the presence or absence of culturally linked product symbols, role playing can either be facilitated or inhibited. For example, if a boss consistently showed up at the office dressed as a tennis player, his or her credibility would be, at best, questionable. Even though the person is the same, playing the role of the boss requires a certain level of authority and work responsibility, which is inhibited by product cues.

No doubt products play a crucial role in satisfying needs and communicating in an *a posteriori* manner: After becoming a Wall Street broker, a college dropout will discard torn jeans for a dark blue Brooks Brothers suit and an Hermès tie just like everyone else around him. But products can also play an *a priori* role by stimulating a behavioral pattern: By wearing a dark blue Brooks Brothers suit and an Hermès tie, a college dropout talks himself into becoming a credible Wall Street broker (just as the cowl makes the monk).

Products and services carrying strong symbolism are "read" by others to determine an individual's place in society. The opposite is also true, since individuals do manipulate these symbols to carve out their social identity. Symbolic cues can also affect psychosomatic perceptions. For example, when asked by a *Forbes* reporter why he bought a motorcycle that leaked oil, vibrated badly, and was hard to handle due to its excessive weight, a Harley-Davidson customer responded: "Because you get laid!"

SOTHEBY'S STOCKS one of the largest product ranges. From the most classical expressions of art such as Greek and Roman antiques and Islamic, Chinese, and Japanese works of art, to contemporary art, to books, manuscripts, photographs, comic books, jewelry, wines, watches, automobiles. . . . As Diana Brooks puts it, "We sell dreams. We sell history." At Sotheby's, the business strategy that ties this amazing diversity together is not a common thread among the products but rather among its customers. "I think there is a common thread among collectors. What they share in common regardless of what it is they collect is that they have a particular eye, with an appreciation and understanding of a particular aesthetic. They have an unbelievable passion and thirst for knowledge. They have focus to develop a strong knowledge about the field they are interested in. One of our best collectors, Leonard Lauder, for example, has a great emotional attachment to his works of art and a passion, a pleasure that he derives from the hunt, the search. It is not simply about ownership. There are all those other emotions."

Customers define this industry and direct its business strategy. Customers are why the business of selling dreams is so successful. Their tastes, visibility, glamour, leadership, passions, determination, and purchasing power boost this industry's creativity and economic might. In an era in which the "customer is king," this industry can easily claim to have many "kings" as customers. If it is true that a company is worth the sum of its customers' spending power, then this industry is potentially the largest in the world.

At age eighty-two, Cecil Shonenberg is still a very faithful Ferrari North America customer. He has owned more than twenty-five Ferraris over his lifetime and still owns seven, three of which are the same model, in assorted colors. Mr. Shonenberg has already placed his deposit down to purchase the new model that will be introduced next year. He has one particular request, however. He wants to see the new car before anyone else. He understands that Ferrari is very secretive about its new models, but he explains that he would like to see the car now because by the time it will be delivered to him in the next few months, the disease he is suffering from, macular degeneration, will have rendered him blind. By then, he will not be able to see or drive, but he will still be able to dream about the beauty of his Ferrari while somebody chauffeurs him around in it.

Mr. Shonenberg is one of those special individuals who prove how hopelessly passionate customers can be and how fortunate companies in this business are to know people like them.

* * *

THE GOAL OF EACH COMPANY, no matter what its business, should be to transform consumers into customers. Since need-satisfying products are dwindling into a commodities business, to strengthen their brands, companies must tighten their client relations. Pure function and "take a number and be seated" will no longer do. To succeed in today's wildly competitive business arena, companies must give their clients a meaningful experience worthy of a memory. Companies must consider their clients' personalities, tastes, and desires. In return, companies must earn their regard as trustworthy, reliable, and exciting partners. After all, their customers' pleasure, not their own egos, is what is supposed to inspire a company to work so hard!

A COMPANY IS ITS CUSTOMERS. For a real self-evaluation, a company should take a sample of its customers to understand who they are and what their dreams are. Are the customers passionate individuals with a deep knowledge of the product or are they very efficient consumers who are more concerned with cost than with emotional quality? How positively do they reinforce the brand's image? Does this image translate into a precise customer? A brand, after all, is an identity that a company awards its customers, enabling them to be the individuals they aspire to be. At the same time, the identity that the brand is associated with is reinforced by the customers. All strong brands were, at one point, personified by a leading customer who became the idol with whom other customers could identify: Marlon Brando defiantly poised on his Harley-Davidson; James Dean leaning against the corral fence in his tattered Levi's; Tom Cruise scanning the skies with his impenetrable Ray-Bans. The dreamketer must choose and educate the customers so they reinforce the image of the brand. For example, in the late 1980s, Ferrari was mainly attracting people interested in the status symbol and the glamour rather than the design and technological beauty. Those customers who the company believed were buying its Ferraris for all the "wrong" reasons were also the least faithful. Their interest was mostly superficial and most easily swayed by mood swings and changes in fashion or the economic climate. No longer recognizing itself in some of its customers, Ferrari decided to boldly promote the company's racing heritage by introducing track events and launching the Ferrari Challenge, a racing series for owner-drivers eager to learn more about their cars' performance. Customer profiles rapidly changed and Ferrari attracted enthusiasts who drove their automobiles much more than the speculators of the late 1980s (thus increasing the spare parts and service business). These "Ferraristi" helped reinforce the brand's strong message (timing was perfect, since motor racing over the past five years has become one of the fastest-growing sports).

SUCCESS in this very competitive business comes to those companies able to choose their customers. Each company will always have different types of customers, like those who best relate to what the company stands for, the core customers, and those who only follow fashion trends or want to experiment, the marginal customers. Through communication and customer relations, a company can maximize the number of core customers and learn how to enlist them in the company's evolution without risking the company's identity.

EVEN IF GOLF SEEMS to be outstroking all other sports lately, many of the exclusive U.S. clubs are still very parochial. Golf is a game that supposedly encourages conversation, but the truth is that these conversations are usually bracketed by the ethnic and religious parameters that keep club members to themselves. So, when launching his Golf Club at Purchase, Masahiko Kasuga decided to create an international club. He began by assembling the most outstanding group of international golf enthusiasts for his Board of Governance, people who, in return, enlisted some of their most distinguished friends. Because Mr. Kasuga ensured their privacy, the high-profile members could escape media hype and enjoy the challenging course designed by Jack Nicklaus on a most majestic piece of upstate New York real estate. And, just to stay true to the passion for golf that his club heralds, Mr. Kasuga enforced one rule above all others: No business is to transpire on club premises.

THE INDUSTRIAL REVOLUTION brought fundamental changes in how things were produced. A group of relentless industrialists imposed their wills and ideas to completely alter the way products and services were consumed. Now we are witnessing a customer revolution that represents a fundamental change in how things are purchased and enjoyed. This customer revolution is driven by millions of customers who want to impose their taste and desires in order to change the way companies produce and sell. Unlike consumers of the past, who were very receptive and easily swayed by companies' promotions and advertising claims, customers today are much more assertive and know what they want.

They are much more **entrepreneurial** in their choices and more willing to experiment. Change does not scare them as it did their parents' generation. Change challenges and stimulates them. They **want newness;** they want technical sophistication. This is the techno generation, empowered and in charge of its own destiny, a generation that genuinely believes in its own ability to modify Nature and extend life. They want to live more **intensely,** packing more experiences into their lifetimes. To this age, intensity is another way (and the surest way) to prolong life.* Technological successes have pumped the members of this generation with self-assurance. They are not afraid to exalt their **individuality.** They want to adapt what they buy to fit their own personality rather than jam their personality into what they buy. They yearn to be part of the creative process—to choose their own colors, shapes, models, and accessories. They demand products and services that are tailored to their own desires. They are **in control** of the purchasing experience, not to be persuaded by the sale force. They are more **knowledgeable** and not at all impressed by bombastic advertising. They know how to find information and how to use it to their advantage. They are aware of the value of money: They save when buying

*We live more intensely when we increase the amount of experiences in a period of time. An average person can feel an experience in a time period as short as one tenth of a second. If we could train ourselves to feel an experience in a shorter time period, say, one hundredth of a second, it would be like prolonging life by tenfold. Imagine an average life span of eight hundred years.

necessities so they can spend on fulfilling their desires. They are **passionate.** They live to be moved. They are **younger,** in both age and in spirit. They want to feel young, have fun, play. Like kids, they are very impatient and seek immediate gratification. Yet, when products grow too accessible, their interest fades like a firework. They are **mercurial,** constantly attracted and distracted by the multitude of offerings.

Companies can no longer expect customers to be the faithful patrons of the past. Retaining them will be more difficult, since the badges of admiration and respect have grown tarnished (even the British royal family has lost its reverence!). It will require more creativity and larger investments in R&D to constantly innovate. Companies will have to tease, surprise, and amuse. As in the past, they will have to work with powerful images. Customers, after all, purchase products or services to satisfy their individual role-playing dreams, in which they become heroes. Even in the age of scientific information, images that strike their emotions are still more important than rational data. It's not the 0–60 acceleration that counts (it's possible to find a Japanese motorcycle quicker than a Harley-Davidson), it's about being as rebellious as Marlon Brando; it's not the UV protection that matters (Ray-Ban marketing does not particularly focus on that), it's the fighter-pilot persona Tom Cruise portrayed. Customers who are hero-seekers may be changing, yet inspiring dreams hardly ever do (they moved Mount Olympus the same way they still move Hollywood).

A dreamketer will have to seriously upgrade to modern technology in order to win over individuals and know each individual: his/her taste, likes, dislikes, physical and emotional characteristics, sense of humor, earning and spending potential, purchasing shares spent with the company. Inputting all that information, the dreamketer can work to tailor-make individual dreams. The dreamketer will have to know individuals the minute they walk through the door.

THIS AGE OF POSSIBILITY, with its constant technological revolutions, has reduced the cost of satisfying basic needs and increased the discretionary income available to the masses. The big screen, the television screen, the computer screen, all with their hypnotic fantasies of glitz and glamour, have the masses dreaming about how to spend that additional income. Today, many more people can role-play in their lives and many more roles are available to each individual to play. Social mobility and population migrations are reshaping the way people live and dream. The way people identify themselves is changing, since religious, racial, ethnic, national, social, and other forms of traditional distinction are petering out. The entrepreneur has marched onto communism's crumbled path, as more and more countries all over the world are fueled by the spirit of the American Dream. Everything is possible, provided you work hard and smart. Enjoying success is no longer frowned upon, especially if you earned it the hard way.

Dream products and services are no longer burdened by the negative and superficial connotations that have weighted them down for centuries. They now express our creativity, curiosity, and desire to feel and progress. At the very least, they are society's safety valve, a material and direct method for people to express their emotions, play their roles, affirm their identities, and celebrate their successes. The future of this business looks very bright, given the enormous number of potential customers. There are some 6 billion consumers in the world, and most of them are dreaming of becoming customers!

A company is truly only worth the sum of its customers' spending power. The ultimate goal of a company should be to transform consumers into customers. This is becoming more and more difficult since customers have grown extremely sophisticated. Customer surveys are not enough to inspire new products. They merely provide information that all companies can easily access. A company must find a visionary who can lead the way to creating an original and distinct taste. This is the creator, the heartbeat of this industry of dreams.

5

The Dream-Makers: The Creators

MAKING DREAMS COME TRUE requires one important quality: creativity—not the abstraction often touted in companies' mission statements, but a presence easily recognizable in each product or service a company offers. Dreams are born of a creative effort that can stir customers' emotions. Exciting our emotions in today's innovation-obsessed world is challenging. Transforming otherwise common objects and services into dreams means sparking the customers' imagination through constant surprise. This requires a *continuous, original,* and *purposeful* creative process. *Continuous* refers to how creativity must be the company's fundamental *modus operandi.* It cannot be limited to a few individuals or a department at work on a specific project. Since creativity implies the risk of exploring new ideas and setting new trends, a company must be culturally committed to creativity, from its designers to its shareholders. That Chanel, after more than sixty years of working in fashion and perfumes, can still excite its customers and the media with every new season's collection means the company is successful at renewing the Chanel spirit through rigorous and planned creative work. The term *original* refers to "possessing an origin," a *raison d'être* that is not purely based on imitating what other companies do or what the market trends say to do. To connect with its customers' emotions, a company must develop its own aesthetic direction. For example, Patek Philippe,* unlike most watch companies, does not manufacture quartz watches (possibly today's most precise technology in timekeeping), because the Swiss company believes that the beauty of its watches is in the originality of its movements rather than simply in their precision. After all, its customers dream about a timeless object, not only about a timekeeping instrument.

The term *purposeful* reflects a company's commitment to its creative process, because the quest for aesthetic excellence should precede the pursuit of commercial success. Creativity requires freedom from commercial or production constraints. With several ways to make money, a company must select the one that best reinforces its aesthetic integrity. Having a purpose proves the most direct way for a company to develop a fine and recognizable taste. It is also the surest way to build the long-term credibility of its brand. When New York's Museum of Modern Art made the unprecedented decision to organize an exhibition on an automobile manufacturer, it invited Ferrari. The museum had recognized Ferrari's "purity of purpose" and celebrated the fact that Ferrari was developing technologies and designs to win

*Patek Philippe is, with Girard-Perregaux, Blancpain, and Jaeger–Le Coultre, one of the few companies that still manufactures its own movements. The majority of luxury watch companies purchase the movements, limiting themselves to the creation of the case, thus becoming jewelers instead of watchmakers.

races, rather than solely for the purpose of selling more cars.

This continuous, original, and purposeful creative process is only possible if someone knowledgeable and powerful enough is there to impose creative culture on the entire organization. This person is the creator.

CREATIVITY WAS, at first, considered a religious concept, an act reserved only for God. Today, the term has trickled down to include human activities in a somewhat diluted take on the divine interpretation. While God shaped the universe out of spatial and temporal nothingness, human creativity must make use of pre-existing elements in order to obtain a new and unique rearrangement. Even the most radically innovative work is inspired* by a preceding reality. When, in 1907, Pablo Picasso painted *Les Demoiselles d'Avignon,* he broke with the artistic conventions of his time by distorting women in an interpretation of reality never seen before. Yet the famous painting† would never have been accomplished had Picasso not been influenced by painters like Cézanne (1839–1906), Matisse

*In Greek mythology, it was believed that original ideas were breathed into people by the Muses—hence the term "inspiration," which describes the act of suddenly generating a new idea. Interestingly, its opposite, "expiration," means "to die."

†The painting, which describes five prostitutes in the parlor of a brothel, takes its title from Avignon Street in the red-light district in Barcelona. It was revolutionary because it severed the connection between reality and what was represented by the painter, as Picasso placed his intellectualized concept before his immediate vision. The *Demoiselles* are not a faithful reproduction of the five prostitutes, but, to suit Picasso's purpose, they were portrayed as grotesquely distorted in order to repel the spectator. This may reflect young Picasso's strong concern about contracting venereal diseases in a period of his life when he actively frequented brothels.

(1869–1954), Manet (1832–1883), and Derain (1880–1954), or by Iberian and African art.

In his memoirs, Dior, one of the most celebrated fashion creators, modestly stated: *"Nothing is ever invented, since one always starts from something,"* implying that creation always finds its inspiration in the encompassing cultural and historical environment. One must first imitate in order to later surpass. Christian Dior would not have been a creative legend if it weren't for the artists he encountered throughout his life, such as Max Jacob, Igor Stravinsky, Jean Cocteau, and Pablo Picasso. His contemporaries in fashion were also a great source of inspiration and motivation. Associating with such eminent people as Molyneux, Balenciaga, Madame Gres, Chanel, Schiaparelli, Lanvin, and Pierre Cardin was, no doubt, extremely important to Dior's personal evolution. Such a stimulating and emulating environment had transformed the son of a producer of cow manure (by definition the vilest of all products) into one of the foremost creator of haute couture and perfumes.

Creativity is man's way of re-examining and reorganizing his environment into a new order, magically linking the past and the future with the power of the imagination. This requires a *subject*, an *object*, and a *medium*. The *subject* is the creator—the painter, the poet, the musician, the director, the designer, or the couturier who will invest his or her emotions, energies, and convictions in order to bring about the change. The *object* is what inspires the creation, the cause the subject draws upon, usually Nature, the subject's environment, or another human being. The *medium* is the "body" of the creation, the means through which the creation is transformed from an idea into a concrete entity such as canvas and paint, words, tones, a sequence of frames, precious stones, fabrics, or even automobiles.

One of the most complex issues connected with creativity is evaluating creative work. Look at how the same works of art are judged differently over time.* While in art, other people's opinions ought not influence the artist, when creators want to market their imagination they must take into account the customers' approval or reprobation. The real challenge for the creators is to find a balance between their own creative impulses and their companies' commercial needs. Thus, their work cannot be evaluated by aesthetic and cultural considerations alone, but must also comply with business necessities. Since dream products and services are to be sold, they must strike a *harmony* between the creator, the director, the designer or craftsmen's aesthetic vision, and the customer's desires. A fashion collection best exemplifies the fine balance between the creator's desire to make a statement and the company's commercial requirements. Michael Kors, the American designer hired by the French *maison* Celine, believes that "good fashion always represents the time we live in: It is the ultimate barometer. Fashion, to me, is a form of sociology, since it should always be interpretive of a culture. It should be a combination of precious and practical, yet if clothes do not make women feel more beautiful, I see no point in them at all." While a painting or a sculpture can be evaluated in absolute

*For example, Johann Sebastian Bach's music was ignored for more than fifty years after his death. Bach was not recognized and appreciated as a genius until after the criteria of judgment had changed in the musical community. During his lifetime, the work of the Dutch painter Jan Lievens was much preferred to that of Rembrandt, his contemporary. Yet today Rembrandt is considered one of the greatest painters in history, while few even remember who Jan Lievens was. Critics' judgment of Bach's music and Rembrandt's painting has changed over the years, yet their work has remained the same.

terms, a dress must be judged by whether it makes the customer feel attractive. Fashion becomes an instrument of physical enhancement. Dresses cannot be created as museum relics, but must be made for the customers' enjoyment. "Through cut, fabric, proportion, and color I can emphasize a woman's good points and minimize the bad." Mr. Kors finds inspiration for his collections in assimilating his vision with the desires of "real women." A new collection usually begins with a flash, a sudden idea that sets the mood for a particular theme.

What follows the initial flash is an exploratory period in which chaos and instability cut paths for anything imaginable—photos in old books, garments found in a flea market, a piece of cloth found in a remote town on a trip to a foreign land, images from the television, a magazine, anywhere that the tiniest details can catch the eye. It is a haphazard process in which coincidence, accident, and surprise move the pens to create a deliberate dizzying of perspective. Often, creativity means spanning the distance between two polar opposites strung out clearly in the creator's mind: the starting point and the conclusion. Creativity must respect certain business requirements, making time a limiting factor: time for delays, for change of heart, for finding new inspiration, time to anticipate competition. Fashion is often an aesthetic exercise in compressing time. As Michael Kors says, "The fact that six months of work culminates in a fourteen-minute show is the hardest part of the process."

When selling dreams, a company must be able to evaluate its creative output. It cannot judge itself on financial statements and market penetration alone, but must also consider how strongly its brand can emotionally affect its customers. If its products and services are admired and prized by the media for their aesthetic and cultural contribution, then the brand is succeeding in forging the company's credibility. For example, the indie film *The English Patient,* with its nine Oscars and international acclaim, established Miramax far more than another of its more commercial films that might have earned more at the box office. For a proper self-evaluation, a company must consider its commercial and financial goals as well as the aesthetic quality of its creations. Products and services must be beautiful, please the senses, and fulfill customer desire, while also respecting cost considerations (so that the company can generate profits). But, because compromise usually does not bring about beauty, companies must reduce their tendency to restrain creativity. Through technological advances, companies can curtail the many cost and production constraints imposed on their creators. And, through the work of dreamketers, they can educate customer taste, freeing creators from aesthetically dubious requests. Dream companies should measure their progress based on the freedom of their creative energies.

Creative people, whether they are artists or creators, surface in particularly large numbers during certain periods of history and in given geographical areas. According to Silvano Arieti, one of the foremost contributors to the study of creativity, this uneven distribution suggests that special environmental circumstances determine the emergence of creativity, rather than solely biological factors.* He mentions some of the

*Plato and Descartes both believed certain ideas to be innate or *a priori,* meaning they are already mapped out on man's subconscious even before birth. Such British Empiricists as Locke and Hume maintained that man is born with a "tabula rasa" or blank slate for a mind, and ideas are *a posteriori* because knowledge is only acquired through life experiences. Today, many agree that creativity is a combination of both, the synthesis of genetic qualities and knowledge acquired through extensive learning.

sociocultural *creativogenic* factors that promote creativity: the availability of cultural means (art, museums, universities, media), the most crucial factor; openness to different and even contrasting cultural stimuli; free access to cultural media for all without discrimination; tolerance for diverging views; and any activities that stimulate creativity. These criteria do not solely apply to countries but are also valid for companies, which can foster a more creative environment by increasing exposure to cultural means and encouraging freedom of thought.

Alfred Louis Kroeber, one of America's pioneers in cultural anthropology, agreed that so-called creative geniuses are not randomly scattered throughout history, but are clustered together into definite configurations, such as the classic Greek period, the Italian Renaissance,* the Enlightenment of the seventeenth and eighteenth centuries, and the period of German Romanticism. These periods prove that creativity does not occur at random, but is stimulated by environmental factors, such as cultural influences and economic, military, religious, and political conditions. If highly creative individuals are "manufacturers" of their cultures, then reciprocally their societies also stimulate their achievements. Culture is the "spread knowledge" that acts as the framework for the development of individual creativity, spinning out a network through which ideas can flow. Creativity constantly enlarges the cultural boundaries of society. Culture does not automatically make great people, it

*A quotation from Orson Welles: "In Italy for three hundred years under the Borgia there have been wars, terror, criminality, and bloodshed. But they have produced Michelangelo, Leonardo, the Renaissance. In Switzerland they lived in fraternal love and had five hundred years of peace and democracy. And what have they produced? The cuckoo clock."

only offers those who meet the conditions the chance of becoming great.

On the whole, the environment seems to play a greater role than heredity in the emergence of "geniuses." The sociocultural availability of appropriate role models* raises the odds that any given generation will contain an eminent genius. Admiration and the competitive will to surpass others and oneself is a strong force in personal development: Growing up in times of exceptional intellectual or aesthetic stimulation may, in itself, be conducive to overall creative development. The geniuses who are active during these periods owe something to their less well-known precursors. Isaac Newton expressed his gratitude from the zenith of his own fame: *"If I have seen farther than other men, it is by standing on the shoulders of giants."*

In the business of selling dreams, there are several examples of cultural clustering, one of them being the luxury industry, which is mainly geographically centered in France and Italy. These two countries enjoy the largest concentration of art, museums, and cultural events that have fostered societies open to aesthetic experimentation. Hollywood is another famous example of a geographical concentration of creative talent. In both examples, impressive networks of artists, creators, designers, and craftsmen are organized in flexible companies of the most diverse sizes, all offering the critical support, elasticity, creativity, and cultural infrastructure wherein the business of selling dreams can flourish.

*Creative geniuses cluster into particular cultural configurations due to the effect of "emulation," a concept that is not new (Roman historian Velleius Paterculus had already mentioned this notion as early as 80 B.C.). The availability of creative role models, past and present, may very well be essential to the development of creative geniuses.

I asked Sydney Pollack, director of such films as *Three Days of the Condor, Out of Africa, Absence of Malice,* and *The Firm,* to explain why so much creative talent is concentrated in Hollywood.

"America, in its earliest days, was looking for a lingua franca to immigrants," he said. "Because it was born of a country whose culture was derived from an odd stew, a recipe of all other cultures thrown in, it had no past, it had no culture, and it had no history. The early film pioneers were immigrants, mostly Russians and Jewish, who were looking to speak to masses of people almost independent of language or culture. So they took the motion picture concept and began to make movies that worked worldwide, and still today American movies work worldwide. It is very difficult to get an Italian or French or Russian film to be as successful on a worldwide basis as an American film (the complaint of many countries who are concerned about the survival of their own filmmaking cultures). They gathered in California because of the sunshine. At first films started very slowly, with all daylight shooting outside; the studios came later. This was the dream factory that would become Hollywood.

"Hollywood used to promote the dream that everything was possible and [individuals] of the most common and meager beginnings could become some of the most romantic and powerful people. It seemed there was no barrier, except your own determination and skill, to what you could achieve in your life"—possibly a simplistic concept, Pollack agreed, but it was one that "translates easily and captures the imagination of young people around the world. The American concept was always the individual, the power of the individual. Because it was a new country compared to the majority [of countries that] had hundreds and thousands of years of history and tradition, it was inventing itself.

"All of us were gut-influenced by the Europeans, especially the Italians and French—Antonioni and Fellini and all the early Italian and French [directors] who in the late fifties and early sixties turned Hollywood on its head by re-examining what we thought were rules of cinema. But still, the overriding influences were the Hollywood films I saw as a young man, the films of William Wyler, Elia Kazan, George Stevens, Fred Zinnemann, John Ford—classic American directors. Those are the films I remembered most vividly that offered me a dream."

Another important factor in the development of creativity is the exposure to different and contrasting cultural stimuli. One reason ancient Greece earned such cultural prominence was due to its open acceptance of different cultures (Persia's, Egypt's) and its receptivity to many of their elements. Some historians blame the decline of the Greek civilization on a law enforced by the great Pericles forbidding foreigners to live in Athens. Over the years, Italy has been one of the most prolifically artistic countries in the world, yet also one of the most frequently invaded and most politically unstable. Such foreign populations as the Greeks, the Visigoths, the Normans, the Huns, the Arabs, the Spaniards, the French, the Austrians, and the Germans have all trampled the boundaries at one time or another over the course of Italian history. These numerous invasions (or "improvements," as they are called in Sicily, where each culture that blew through brought new temples or monuments or mosaics), accompanied by Italy's many political upheavals, have woven together a complex and rich civilization. If exposure to other cultures is a major factor in fostering creativity, the world may be slipping into a privileged position by virtue of the migratory explosions and exchange of opinions via the media over the last fifty years. Creativity is becoming global, inviting many more countries to participate. For example, let's look once again at the fashion industry, a priceless barometer of creativity in business. While fashion was practically a French prerogative after the war (Christian Dior, Yves Saint Laurent, Courrèges, Ungaro), the 1970s brought a wave of Italian designers (Valentino, Armani, Versace, Fendi, Prada), and the last ten years have seen an overwhelming influence of American designers (Ralph Lauren, Tom Ford, Michael Kors). Even Hollywood is no longer alone in making movies, as several cinematography centers in England, Denmark, Italy, India, China, and Japan are now producing successful films.

CONTRARY TO COMMON BELIEF, creativity is not an attribute reserved only for great minds or geniuses. It belongs to every human being. We are all born with creativity. Just look at the behavior of every child, who, with a keen sense of discovery, can play with anything within reach. Creativity is born of a genetic knack for observation and perception. Yet, because everyone's genetic makeup is different, each of us perceives things in a slightly different manner, offering various interpretations of what our senses identify. Creating does not require an exceptional thought process, like "illumination" from the gods or "inspiration" from the Muses. Creative thinking does not differ much from ordinary thinking, which is based on a certain continuum in which old knowledge is applied to generate new. In other words, the inspiration that compelled Michelangelo to paint the Sistine Chapel came from the same thought process we use to compile a grocery list. This is not meant to diminish the importance of creativity in life. It is after all our only means of forging our own destiny. Armed with persistence, creativity becomes a formidable power: *the power to change one's dreams into reality.* Creativity is what can propel a company to success. It is also a gift that can be destroyed, often crushed by social or organizational conformity, making it, quite possibly, *the most squandered resource* of all.

Creativity is not simply the doings of genetics but can be substantially influenced by culture. It is not reserved for geniuses only, it is the prerogative of every one of us. Therefore, creativity can be enhanced within an organization provided that at the helm there is a visionary with clear and distinct ideas. This is the creator. Creators are individuals with a profound knowledge of the company's product or service. They make the final aesthetic decisions. For example, in fashion, the creator is the leading designer who directs all the other designers—Armani, Ralph Lauren, or Tom Ford. In the movie industry, directors such as Michael Mann, Jim Cameron, and Sydney Pollack are creators who have such leverage with production companies that they can impose their taste with little compromise. In the automobile business, they are called the "car guys." They determine what the new models will be; they are precisely the people missing at a company like Nissan, or, for example, the kinds of people who could help a company as grand as GM shift back into its original gear. The creator's vision is critical in ensuring that R&D money is well spent. Since R&D expenditures are rapidly soaring to ensure that companies can stay ahead of the competition, creators must come up with constant innovations, knowing what to produce and how, and must keep their companies from squandering money on the development of inappropriate products. A creator helps get it right the first time. Creators are leaders who can take a company toward originality and distinction. They are the matchmakers, just as Michael Jordan was to basketball, Michael Schumacher is to racing, Gabriel Batistuta or Lido Vieri is to soccer, or John Elway is to football. Just like these sports champs, creators must thrill their fans/customers. It's almost like hero worship: Customers praise the creators through every item they purchase and collect.

CREATORS FILL a very important role. Their taste and aesthetic sense bring beauty to otherwise common objects or experiences, enriching our everyday life. Most important, their cultural leadership and artistic sensitivity help industry and society maximize their creative resources.* Creators lead and in-

*While creativity fluctuates with respect to different historical periods and across various geographical areas, it can also fluctuate over the course of a single lifetime. For the average person, the highest levels of creativity generally occur during childhood, often fading away in adolescence when social pressures dictate intransigence for young original thinkers who have ideas of their own. In complying with society's norms, youths succumb to the overemphasis placed on preventing mistakes. Threats, destructive criticism, and coercive peer pressure are just some of the ugly forces at work to enforce social uniformity. Unfortunately, the taboos and the preconceptions ingrained in a given culture hinder the search for novel interpretations of reality, not to mention the stress of monotony, inherent in many jobs, which stifles mental activity and creativity. "Brainstorming" is one of the methods used to access the creative outlets located in the brain's two hemispheres: The judicial component analyzes, compares, and chooses, while the creative component visualizes, foresees, and generates ideas. Most people are endowed with both capacities, yet over the years, our creative mind is stifled by an increasing tendency to simply judge, and in doing so, to reject many possibly valid ideas. Brainstorming eliminates the inhibiting consequences of premature judgment, self-discouragement, and timidity.

spire their collaborators and their companies to infuse emotion into their work and adopt a more eclectic and artistic approach to business.

CREATORS STRADDLE the world between artist* and entrepreneur. The distinction between artist and creator is often blurred, since both individuals are guided by intense and irrational emotions that override rational motivations. With their vivid passion and relentless work, both share a thorough understanding of the final product. Both strongly believe that they know how to dream, conceptualize, and transform raw materials into beautiful objects. Their hard work results in an aesthetic experience that stirs an emotional response in us. The difference, when it exists, is in the motivation behind the creative effort. While one romantically believes that an artist's

*The Renaissance introduced the distinction between mechanical arts, undertaken by artisans, and *belle arti* (beautiful arts), the work of artists. We speak of art as the combination of distinct intellectual, emotional, and manual qualities in a work that would not otherwise have existed in nature, even if nature often acts as a source of inspiration. Although subjective and impulsive, art still requires respect for strict procedures and the development of a specific knowledge. Art is the creative act of producing a work that is appreciated for its aesthetic values, be it art with a practical purpose, like utilitarian art, or art devoid of anything utilitarian and driven by idealistic considerations, like fine arts (visual or performing). It is the artist who creates works of art, while it is the artisan (from the Italian *artigiano,* derived from Latin *artitus,* meaning "learned in an art") who executes the work rather than invents it. It was with Velázquez that this distinction was made and artists acquired their present status of excellence and nobility. Creators are those who infuse aesthetic values into useful objects or services, thus bestowing beauty on even the most common aspects of daily life.

creative energy is not driven by financial pressure,* creators are sensitive to business rewards. Their entrepreneurial spirit compels them to organize their creative gifts into an income-generating activity. A creator could be described as a materialistic artist, or more kindly, as one who has chosen to merge his idealistic aspirations with business activities: a "businessartist" (as opposed to a businessman). In other words, while the artist aspires to idealistic goals, the creator seeks utilitarian ones. An aura of purity and nobility still seems to linger around the artist who hasn't "sold out." After all, an artist's ultimate ambition is winning historic permanence rather than hitting the *Forbes* 400 list.

For both the artist and the creator, the message is essentially in their product, whereas in the mass industry the message is issued from the marketing department. While true artists need no instant approval, since they are usually ahead of their time, creators, on the other hand, relate closely to their customers, often finding inspiration in their wishes. While the artist works on **intuition,** generated by his or her own spirit or soul, the creator's work comes more from a **perception,** emanating from an interpretation of the customer's desires.

*This demarcation is only theoretical, because art has always been sold and therefore economics have obviously played a role (the Church being for centuries one of the most enthusiastic subsidizers of the art market). Occasionally, artists were business-minded, like Rubens (1577–1640), who became very wealthy, while others were not so business savvy, like Rembrandt (1606–1669) who, unfortunately, went bankrupt. Other creative activities organized as businesses were cathedral building and the many *botteghe* (workshops) of the Renaissance. Dalí (1904–1989) displayed great marketing techniques when he shrugged off all "artistic ideals" to single-handedly segment his customers' market by selling his originals to the very wealthy, reproductions to the middle class, and lithographs to those aspiring to appear wealthy.

The artist's setup is different from the creator's. While artists usually work alone or in very small groups, creators are always surrounded by craftsmen and technicians who help transform their ideas into the final product or service. This implies a cooperative creativity in which complementary skills and motivations join to generate the final product.

There is also a different degree of freedom in the artist's and creator's work. An artist is less constrained, given the individualistic nature of interpreting a personal vision of the world. Creators, on the other hand, must meet many business demands and incorporate their collaborators' ideas and suggestions. Theirs is a more collective approach to more concrete products and services. In several instances, the creators are inspired by the artists. For example, the Art Deco furniture, jewelry, and architecture of the 1920s and 1930s is directly derived from the experimentation of such cubist artists as Braque (1882–1963), Picasso, and Juan Gris (1887–1927). Quite often, creators translate abstract forms born of an artist's intuition into new designs and styles.

Creators are usually very cultivated individuals acutely sensitive to their environment, and, like artists, they weave society's ideas, trends, and tastes into their work.

The biggest difference between a creator and an entrepreneur is in the way they approach business. A creator's desire to produce something beautiful *precedes* the need for financial reward, while entrepreneurs are driven by the need to maximize profit and the company's value. To creators, earning an income is a means of financing their passion. Entrepreneurs can be very successful without any personal knowledge of how to make a product. Creators choose their profession with their heart, developing a specific style or product knowledge at art or engineering schools, by working for other creators, or simply by developing a passionate understanding of the products. Entrepreneurs, on the other hand, learn it at business schools or by running companies. Creators infuse emotion and feeling into their work, more so than the entrepreneur might.

Creators cover a broader business spectrum. By bringing emotions into play, they have made work a more natural extension of life. Calling what artists do "work" may sound awkward, because it is their life before it is their money-earning activity, just as creators' emotional involvement expands the reach of their work, making it more stimulating, enriching, and fun. Creating is fulfilling and enjoyable. In highly creative environments it is hard to know what's work or play. Just look at Hollywood, where you never know if people are enjoying the social scene in a restaurant or on a golf course or at a private party or if they are "working the room." The boundaries between living and working fade away and people become freer to express themselves. While, in the past, only a lucky few felt this freedom, today's computer revolution has swept away some of the drudgery of daily chores, freeing more of us to our creativity.

MICHAEL MANN, the film and television director/producer responsible for bringing Pacino and De Niro together onscreen in *Heat* and the creator of the groundbreaking *Miami Vice,* comments on what it is to be a creator. "Creators make dreams happen. First of all, you're starting with something that you have a fanatical, obsessive belief in—in my case, it's the rightness of the movie. The movie is not made with any skepticism or cynicism." In praising his colleague James Cameron, the director of *Titanic,* Mann adds: "This is the full incarnation of his cinematic dreams. He lived and breathed *Titanic*. Right or wrong, whether you're critical of the movie or not critical of the movie, or whether you endorse the movie, or embrace the movie, this man truly believed in this picture that he was making, he was a true believer, a fanatic to the point that when the studio told him, 'We, the studio, who own this negative, are ordering you to cease principal photography, stop shooting and come home,' he said, 'No, no, I'm going to stay here in Mexico and I'm going to keep shooting.' That's when they took away his 12 percent back-end fees so that he was bereft of money, that's how truly this man believed in the picture. Now that's what produces a product like *Titanic*—it doesn't come from any marketing analysis. It's from the soul of one true believer, and if he's right (and this guy was, in spades), then it manifests itself in something like *Titanic* or, *Titanic* being such a huge exception, something even a fraction of *Titanic*."

The creator builds a dream by connecting with deep yet simple emotions, common to a wide group of people. As Mann explains, "For example, Cameron creates an opportunity for tremendous identification with the Leonardo DiCaprio character who becomes the wish fulfillment of every young woman. He's wonderful to look at, he's unpretentious, he's encouraging Kate Winslet to be who she truly is inside herself, and on top of everything else, he's willing to lay down his life for her. He's a protector, and at the same time he's recognizing the inner qualities of her and he's fulfilling every adolescent girl's and young woman's dream. This is one reason for its success. Another reason is the simple fact that the film takes you into a place you have not been before and it does so with such verisimilitude that you lose yourself in the world of it. A creator is able to transport you, be it through a movie, a dress, or a jewel, into a feeling of being in a state of otherness, a place other than in your life."

A director should not succumb to the compromises imposed by investors. As Mann says, "In what I do, if you compromise you not only don't fulfill yourself but, historically, you are not terribly successful. It's the uncompromising creators who have the really big successes. Jim Cameron compromised not one iota on that film and he had struggles and battles and wars with those people that you could not believe. You cannot compromise if you want to succeed. It's a very romantic notion, but it happens to be true. This is how huge successes are made. The mediocre successes come from people who have certain tastes and make certain compromises, but the huge successes come from no compromise.

"The creator/director is crucial in this business. There is a common belief that films are made by people who run the studios. The truth is that, in Hollywood, studios own the product, market it, and distribute it, yet they don't determine the content, they never have. They can decide, okay, we're going to do three comedies, and four action adventures, and one spectacle, but whether it's a complete flop or is any good, they can only determine the genre categories and subgenre categories, but that's about the extent of their influence. Hollywood product is determined by the people who write and direct the movies. *Titanic,* oddly enough, is not a product of Hollywood, it is a product of Jim Cameron. If somebody else had said to you five years ago, let's make a movie about the sinking of the *Titanic,* everybody in Hollywood would have said, are you out of your mind? How can you tell a story about the *Titanic,* we know how it ends, it goes down. Where's the story? So Cameron was only able to make *Titanic* in the beginning because he's Jim Cameron and he's had success before with other projects in which he was an obsessive true believer. Hollywood didn't make *Titanic,* a movie generating $1.4 billion on theatrical alone. One guy did, Jim Cameron."

What is it that sparks your desire to make a movie and the conviction to ask financiers to invest and risk millions of dollars on your ideas? As Mann states emphatically, "When I make a movie, I have to love it personally, that's an absolute requirement. I have to absolutely be enthralled with it. I know I will not make it a success if I don't love it, because the arduousness of making that picture and the multiplicity of decision-making is so huge that you can only endure it and ride it and triumph with it if you truly, in every pore of your being, believe in it. To think you could do it skeptically is the height of foolishness. Sometimes I have ideas I decide to put on ice, or that I may decide to do later, or not at all because I'm interested in making movies that lots of people go see.

"I don't go in believing I can predict what people want to see. I don't know what does make people want to go see a movie. In myself, I know that if I really love something and I'm turned on by it that usually so is everybody else. It's certainly happened the last three or four things I've done, and half of the television I've done."

Listening to Mann, I had to think that was one modest way of saying Miami, for example, was not the same city before his hit, *Miami Vice.* In fact, many believe that Miami started to breathe when *Miami Vice* came to town. Now it's a fantastic city, alive with a real-estate boom and a real life of its own. I wondered, "When you were doing *Miami Vice,* did you have a sense that you could make a city with a movie?"

"Absolutely, and not only did I know, everybody who worked

on it knew. We knew it, and when you know it, you know it. Down to the guy scouting locations, and the expert casting. We all knew it was exciting. Why? Because it was exciting to us in such a strong way and it had some other things that experience tells you are going to work. We were in a new environment, people hadn't seen it before. We were in the Casablanca for the whole of Latin America and the whole of the drug trade, in the northern banking capital for the whole of Latin America. And a wonderful twilight zone kind of place, which Casablanca was, which Las Vegas was in the '50s, '60s, '70s, early '80s, where there's a suspension of normal life, where things have a certain truthfulness because they're actually devoid of meaning, where transience is liberating in a way that's both horrific and euphoric at the same time. That's like being in a dream, in a place where drama is going to happen that is completely engaging. That was Miami, the way it was. And there was a certain true synergy because whatever became an icon for the show, suddenly took off. I put Wellcraft offshore racing boats on a show; their sales increased 1200 percent in one year. We decided to take a look at Gusmano Cesaretti's photography and I said this photography is so terrific, let's do a calendar; it was the biggest-selling calendar in the U.S.A. for 1986. We got all this great music on the show; it occurs to me, why don't we do a soundtrack album; well, there hadn't been a television series that sold records since *Peter Gunn* in 1956, and all of a sudden we've got a number-one album. *USA Today* in those first two years of the show, every Friday, dedicated a full page to the *Miami Vice* episode tonight, who was in it, the music, everything. It was all about desire.

"In terms of merchandising, we were very careful about the commercialization. Everybody offered us a *Miami Vice* men's wardrobe line, women's wardrobe, and millions of dollars in advances for a percentage of wholesale from Sears. We turned it all down, everything from that to *Miami Vice* lunchboxes and sandals. We passed on 90 percent of it. If there was something very select and good, we did it. We designed a crew jacket, really cool, and we decided to mass-market those and we sold about fifty thousand of them. But it had to be something really cool, it had to be something very special, it couldn't just be commerce, for two reasons. For one, my taste and general inclinations wouldn't have personally felt right if we had just kind of marketed it every way we could. Secondly, there was a certain commercial enlightenment to it because we were protecting a bigger asset, which was the name of the show. That if we had suddenly released a barrage of junk out there, you would cheapen the brand name."

Michael Mann is living proof that creators must be conscientious businesspeople, but above all, they must be true to their own identity. Successful creators are not the blind followers of market dictums. To build their company's taste, they strive for original aesthetic experimentation through firm commitment, knowledge, self-assurance, and the romantic belief that they should never compromise. Marketing analyses do not make great successes, creators do. With steadfast conviction, they lead their collaborators through the hardship and doubt. At times their success can have influence far beyond the realm of business, just as Michael Mann managed to change the image of an entire city with his hit TV show.

WHEN IT COMES to stimulating a customer's dream, merging business sense with an artistic appreciation is a complex yet crucial part of this industry's production. It's up to the creator to select a very special team that can help realize these dreams. Every creator has conceptualized, designed, and built the final product with his mind, his heart, and his own hands long before asking anybody else to do it. Armed with full understanding of the creative and production processes, he knows exactly what is required of himself and his employees. This lets the creator direct the artistic (and sometimes undisciplined) egos that make up the creative force in this industry. Anywhere else in industry, only gifted engineers possess product knowledge even remotely close to that of a creator. However, unlike creators, product engineers seldom lead their company or decide on future product lines, nor do they bother much with conjuring up aesthetic enhancements for their technologies. When a creator can bring originality and perseverance to his company, then his organization will listen and so will his customers. No matter how humble their beginnings, these creators rise up to become cultural leaders.

SUCCESSFUL CREATORS ARE all on a quest for perfection that urges them to stretch the outer limits of inspiration. Coco Chanel, for example, felt compelled to test her creations beyond the norm. Her lifelong love for the heightened style of theater and costume design was a passion shared by other famous *couturiers,* such as Christian Dior, Yves Saint Laurent, and Valentino Garavani. On stage, the dress acquires a highly decorative and cultural meaning, stripped of any function: It does not merely cover the actor, but somehow becomes its own character in the drama. In the theater, these creators could explore new interpretations and present them in the most culturally astute world, that of the arts.

Enzo Ferrari dedicated his entire life to motor racing, a very expensive passion that proved a constant financial drain. Yet, to Ferrari, racing was the relentless search for maximum performance. It was the only possible way to build the world's ultimate automobile. Every time Enzo Ferrari was asked which, of all the beautiful automobiles he had built, was the one he considered perfect, he'd answer perfunctorily: *"The one I am yet to build."* Enzo Ferrari understood that the search for perfection never ends. It is precisely what keeps the creative mind sharp and alive.

Salvatore Ferragamo's exposure to Hollywood meant experimenting with many different styles, from the Babylonian-Egyptian-Hebraic periods all the way to the modern. Yet, for Ferragamo, the perfect shoe was not defined by different styles and looks alone. He believed, above all, that a shoe should be beautiful *and* comfortable. This conviction led Ferragamo to enroll in UCLA, where he studied anatomy to better appreciate the foot's complexity.

Creators stretch their work by experimenting with extremes, be they fashion shows, theater, racing, trade shows, film festivals, sports, or any other type of event in which the need for change and newness is forced. This helps build a proactive organization prone to explore and ready to anticipate changes even when commercial successes do not call for such action.

ANOTHER FACET of the creators' personality is an intense curiosity, which is fed by a wealth of sensory imagery. They ask unusual questions and seek out unusual problems in a continuous process of destruction-construction. By shattering the pieces of what already exists, they reorganize reality in a different manner. It is a process often plagued with fears and suffering. Observation combined with curiosity, investigation, input from the five senses, and inspiration all spur the discovery of something new. Sensory exploration is particularly important for creators, who constantly explore their environment. We all possess sophisticated sensory systems, but curiosity compels creators to probe the many different angles of perception that the rest of us may be exposed to but fail to fully sense and feel.

Usually the larger a company grows, the more averse it becomes to risk. Even in the highly creative world of luxury, the largest companies are less willing to take the financial risks that accompany a creator's exploration of new aesthetic possibilities. For example, larger luxury companies like Ferragamo and Hermès offer their conservative take on fashion and let smaller fashion houses like Dolce & Gabbana propose new, shocking collections. The more customers, the more difficult it is for a company to please everyone by going to extremes. Risk-taking can, however, be very rewarding. Tom Ford, in revolutionizing Gucci's taste, has generated so much excitement and media attention that the company has seen its sales multiply sixfold in only four years. Once design-defunct, the born-again Gucci has attracted a new generation of customers and Ford has become the "hottest" designer in the business.

* * *

TASTE ALLOWS ARTISTS AND CREATORS to capture and emulate the many expressions of beauty through their own creative effort. Taste is uniform in all of us, since it refers to common faculties of the mind where aesthetic judgments originate. However, the degree of taste can differ for two reasons: a greater degree of natural sensitivity or longer and closer attention to the object. The greater the curiosity and interest (which determine the intensity with which one stores information) and the time devoted to the observation of beautiful objects, the easier it is to recognize patterns and develop methods of appreciation. Since there are no criteria for duplicating beauty, but only a principle of harmony, taste cannot be asserted through theory, but rather through empirical analysis. People of taste have accumulated a vast aesthetic "memory," the product of continual observation and the foundation for their judgment.

Creators need a great deal of taste in order to chart the aesthetic direction of their company. They must either directly design the products or services, or indirectly guide the designers by choosing from the many ideas proposed. With their taste, leading creators shape the "spirit of the time." When admiring the work of Carl Fabergé (1846–1920), René Lalique, Pierre Frey (1903–1994), Aimé Guerlain, Sergio Pininfarina, or Abraham-Louis Breguet (1747–1823), one can go beyond the jewel, the crystal, the fabric, the perfume, the automobile, or the watch to appreciate the aesthetic and technological expressions of their time. Their creations have survived the whims of fashion as timeless reminders of years ago. This magic link comes when creators connect with their surroundings. To be effective, the creator must balance social norms with individual appreciation to create products that customers can assimilate and enjoy. Creators, while responding to their milieu, must be courageous and divergent thinkers and doers who can originate interpretations of existing cultures and spawn new trends. Creativity can therefore be defined as a special form of leadership: Creators are cultural leaders.

For example, Chanel did not just create beautiful dresses, she also redefined the woman's role in society. To Chanel, a woman was not only the passive object of desire stereotyped by contemporary creators. To her, it was a woman's duty to gain status in society by exceeding the traditional roles of wife and mother to enter into political and business circles. She liberated women from uncomfortable and imposing clothes by redressing them in simple, casual elegance that allowed them to perform more freely in their new roles. Chanel's fashion codes crystallized her beliefs. While most creators will be remembered for their style (Molyneux for his understated elegance, Dior for his splendor), Chanel will be celebrated for having done a great deal more than just dress women up in society.

Creators must spread "taste" in society. Ralph Lauren is the American designer who has brought aristocratic elegance to volume clothing. Mr. Lauren believes that "dreams are about real things. You cannot sell a dream without a product. I sell what I believe is quality: quality of life, quality of living, quality of the product. The product has to be good. If I am making clothes, if I am making shoes, I try to capture the mood of what I believe in."

With a father who was an artist and had little money, Lauren hungered for this quality as a youth. "Dreams become intensified when you cannot own something. If you do not have the money, clothes becomes important to you because as a young man you want to make a nice impression with girls or with your friends. Your desire to work and to establish your own taste is intensified because it becomes more important to you."

The first American to become an international authority on taste and elegance, Ralph Lauren was inspired by certain celebrity elegance. He grew up admiring the duke of Windsor, Fred Astaire, Cary Grant. "I knew Audrey Hepburn. She had a wonderful personal style, she knew what looked well on her. She understood the essence of it. What her body was like and what would make her look the best. She always knew what was appropriate for the right time. Gianni Agnelli is just like her."

Unable to find the look and the quality he liked, he set out to create his own line of clothing, starting first with ties. "I had visions of style and then went on to make suits and shirts and made the kind of things that I felt had the taste level I liked. The taste level was not the downtown look; it was not the hot disco look. It was the world-class look, an international taste. Whatever prompted me to develop that taste, I am not sure. But what I loved was the elegance and quality. Americans always thought about 'mass.' In other words, buy a car if it has new fins, great, when it gets to be two years old, throw it out. Europeans were always more conscious of longevity, the tradition, keeping it going. Americans were always in and out. My sense was that I loved old things, I also loved saddles, older cars, old leather, shoes that look old with age but yet had great quality, so that if you polished them they looked beautiful. When I started, nobody knew who I was and I went on and designed ties and they were beautiful ties and they were handmade and the fabric was beautiful and unusual and different for the moment, but they were timeless and special. You are aiming at a certain customer and that customer speaks your language and there are other customers who do not speak your language. They like a brand because that brand says something else to them. It says conservative or it says fashion. I try to make my own fashion something that you want to look at. But at the same time it is still classic and it is not ordinary. It is hard to define because it is a different eye, it is a different feel. I find that no matter what country people come from, there are people who love what I do, that I look at what they are wearing and that they are exactly my style. They do not necessarily wear my clothes but they have the same taste.

"Some people like trendy things. If you look at the market, you look at designers, you look at MTV, what kids are wearing, they like the 'in' things of the moment and then they change. My taste, somehow I like things when they get older, things that age well. Just like I think a woman or a man with gray hair doesn't need to dye their hair black because they look better as is. My sense is a long-term classic sensibility."

Just like Michael Mann, Ralph Lauren is another creator who believes that "you should not have to compromise. I think there should be a balance between what you believe in and your advanced thinking, because you are always pushing forward. Sometimes the consumer is not at the same level as you are. They may like shirts with logos and I might say I do not like as many logos. Then you make it both ways: some suits with logos, some without. The world is constantly changing, and if you are giving in to the consumer and trying to please the consumer all the time, you are making a mistake, because basically you've gotten where you are because you had an idea. The idea is to constantly trust yourself, trust your innovation, and constantly move forward as you see fit and not try to say, 'That sold very well last year, so I am going to make the same thing again this year.' You have to keep going and trust that you are moving correctly. The most important thing is consistency in the point of view. I am not looking like Armani today and somebody else tomorrow. I look like Ralph Lauren. And my goal is to constantly move in fashion and move in style without giving up what I am. This is a subtle movement. In every industry that I admire, be it the automobile or the clothing, there is always a constant change but they want to make the statement of who they are. When they start to be somebody else that is when they are in trouble. You have to pay attention to what is happening out there, but you also have to use your own sensibility of who you are. You constantly have to let your customers know who you are and what you mean in your communication. I want to be individual but also be in tune with the times. I have done a new collection of Polo Sport and now I am going into active sports, more technical sports. I am constantly moving and developing the brand, the image, the taste, and trying to make the quality better and better. If I change that, I think that I would lose my business."

Keeping up with the times is one of Lauren's main concerns.

"There is always a new movement coming along in the tradition of companies. It is important to preserve your lineage and tradition in your line, but the world changes around you and you have to stay with it. I started to make a Polo Sport line, now I am making really technical sportswear because I feel that that is the same customer. That is my customer. Your customer [that is, the Ferrari customer] is similar to my customer: He is wealthy, does not want to look flashy, and does not need to go two hundred miles per hour, but he wants distinction, he wants to be part of sexiness, so you have to continue with that sexiness and, at the same time, be sensitive. You have to be advanced today but also simple."

RALPH LAUREN has been extremely successful at overcoming a common belief: Americans are all about change and cannot express a lasting taste. With a conservative approach to fashion, he has brought the lasting elegance of international celebrities to a larger crowd. While consistently expressing the essence of his aesthetic beliefs, he has stayed current with the times and constantly strengthened the value of his brand. Ralph Lauren best expresses the most demanding challenge every creator must face: the balance between following and leading. The customer is moving ever more quickly. Creators must stay with them and follow their customers' desires to experiment with new trends and new technologies. But, most important, creators must also lead their customers to them and be there at the end of the customers' search with a product that answers their desires. This means educating the customer to look in the creator's direction and recognize his/her taste and aesthetic style.

CREATIVITY IS synonymous with change and, sometimes, even with provocation. Historically, creativity has often been perceived as a threat, first destroying a reality before the new one can be reconstructed (as Einstein did in the case of physics or Marx in philosophy). Change upsets the norms and disturbs what had been accepted as the only true wisdom. Creators need the courage to change in order to develop their own original ideas, without being as revolutionary and provocative as artists, at times, can be. When Christian Dior first introduced his collection back in 1947, with an unprecedented theatrical presentation, critics worldwide dismissed it as a disgraceful and unacceptable flaunting of luxury in a world still shaken and war-torn. (While ordinary clothes were still being rationed, Dior would extravagantly use as much as fifty yards of the most luxurious material for his dresses.) However, the "new look" became a hit, promising every woman from every social rung the dream of playing the *grande dame.* While this was shocking to many, Dior had rediscovered the purpose of fashion: celebrating life, even in times of darkness. His magnificent dresses, long gowns, and ample skirts had courageously reinstated a certain splendor that the war had shattered. It was as if he had understood that no matter what, the desire to dream and live is our most powerful impulse. With perfect timing, Dior's "new look" had arrived just when fashion was still wallowing and ready for some sort of resurrection. Dior's major achievement was to reinstate Paris as the haute couture capital of the world, a deed that won him the *Légion d'Honneur* from the French government in 1950.

CREATORS USUALLY POSSESS a certain *eclectic* erudition. Studies on the creative personality have proved the importance of vast interests, a breadth of perspective, a need for novelty, diversity, and complexity. A very creative person is often one who is exceptionally versatile and quick to grasp a wide range of ideas. This explains why some of the most famous artists and creators have lived and flourished in culturally stimulating environments, where their interests and visions can extend beyond one simple subject (for example, the creativity of the

Renaissance Man,* who could apply notions and principles from one field to another). Versatility is a psychological trait closely tied to intelligence.

ONE OF THE MOST ECLECTIC CREATORS was René Lalique (1864–1945), a "poet-artisan," the inventor of "modern jewelry," and a successful industrialist who pioneered complex glass-making techniques that revolutionized the use of the material. Lalique began his creative career as a jeweler, particularly interested in innovative pieces inspired by nature and the symbolist movement. He believed a jewel's artistic content was far more precious than its monetary value. Lalique therefore replaced the traditionally used rare and expensive gems with materials conveying a greater symbolic potential: gold treated with enamel to enhance its colors; opals and moonstones for their symbolic allegorical messages; ivory and rock crystal for their splendid organic composition. Lalique also incorporated glass into jewelry, playing with colors and forms. Perhaps it was out of despair for the early death of his wife in 1909 that he abandoned jewelry to work exclusively in glass. His work was re-

*Leonardo da Vinci is considered one of the most outstanding geniuses. His ability to excel in several apparently unrelated fields is what earned him such high regard. Apart from having been one of the greatest painters of the Renaissance, Leonardo was also a sculptor, inventor, architect, physicist, biologist, engineer, writer, philosopher, and even musician. The Italian genius developed such a wide scope of knowledge because during the Renaissance, artists strove to study several different disciplines simultaneously. Gianni Versace used to say he lived his life from a tower where he could constantly peer out at the world all around him. His travels took him to new cultures where, for example, he saw a swatch of cloth in a desert town in India that would later translate into one of his most powerful collections ever.

markable, achieving aesthetic excellence by juxtaposing conservative forms with innovative technical procedures, manual artistry with machine technology. Lalique had successfully balanced eclectic creativity and artistic sensibility with business acumen. His company produced very limited series of pieces, using blown-glass and lost-wax techniques. He created unique decorations for churches, boats, trains, and automobiles, but he also manufactured a most diversified line of glass products, including all types of bottles, vases, bowls, tableware, toiletry accessories, and lighting fixtures. Creativity, as Lalique and many other creators have demonstrated, can expand horizontally into what are traditionally considered unrelated fields. Creators, with their continual cultural and aesthetic experimentation, can help companies view things with a more horizontal business vision.

CREATIVITY ONLY COMES ABOUT through hard work.* By testing ideas that may be considered absurd at first, by aban-

*With this hard-work ethic, documented in many successful accounts of creative talent, comes heightened productivity over time. Mozart (1756–1791) had well over six hundred compositions to his credit before his untimely death at thirty-five; Schubert (1797–1828) composed more than five hundred works before succumbing to typhus at thirty-one; Picasso executed more than twenty thousand works; Thomas Edison (1847–1931) held 1,093 patents. There is some truth in Thomas Edison's famous saying: *"Genius is one percent inspiration and 99 percent perspiration."* For example, Napoleon's (1769–1821) reputation as a military leader is no doubt due to the fact that he fought and won more battles than any other general in history. Pasteur (1822–1895) believed that, in the field of observation, chance only favors the prepared mind.

doning widely accepted concepts, or by examining them and reworking them, the creative mind can apply a problem-solving approach, while opening up new channels of thought in order to gain knowledge and enhance judgment. The more knowledge and experience, the better. Creativity is directly proportionate to achievement. If not continually exercised, creativity withers and dies. Creative individuals are driven to observe, to use their intuitive instincts, to seek out the new through imagination, and to strive to discover a different angle of approach as if it were a riddle to solve. Very likely, there is a direct correlation between the quantity of work and the creative output. As creative work is often guided by the exploration of unknown possibilities and persistent trial and error, increasing the number of such occasions multiplies the chances of success. Extended knowledge, accumulated through relentless research and direct experience, helps one to better recognize opportunities.

Listening to Gusmano Cesaretti speak about Michael Mann's work ethic best describes this concept: "He's totally dedicated to his work. He easily can spend fifteen to twenty hours a day in his office dealing with his script and with production, forgetting what time it is. I constantly have to remind him of his appointments. What I really like is that he pushes me to the limit. He is so demanding about his work, it gives me so much energy that my creative juices start pumping, like I'm getting high—it's like a drug being creative. I want to get more interesting stuff for him. He trusts me. It takes a lot—he's very loyal and he takes care of me. I would feel horrible not being able to give Michael what he wants. Michael is a true artist. As for me, when I start a project, I tell my wife, 'Good-bye, I'll see you when it's finished.' I can't make any commitments besides my work. My commitment is with Michael. Everyone that works with Michael is like this. We are special people—we don't just work for the money."

ON THE OTHER HAND, *far niente* (to do nothing) is the opposite of hard work. Laziness is, however, also a fact of life and, curiously enough, may contribute to the creative process. While *far niente* is considered to be an Italian national sport (in a most derogatory sense), it is rather amazing how this behavior has influenced the vast creative activities of this Mediterranean country. "Doing nothing" is a contradiction by definition, since doing is precisely the expression of activity, of an action guided by a goal or simply by the need to expel excess energy. To be idle, as opposed to working, is what we have been taught not to do. Throughout history, idleness has been condemned as a sin by most religions (especially the Protestant) and by moral doctrines. It is man's duty to work all his life in order to deserve his salvation (*ora et labora,* pray and work). Idleness is often earmarked as the single most preponderant cause of failure. Yet some types of idleness have been accepted in many civilizations, be it meditation in Buddhism or the stimulation of dreams in Greek culture. To recognize, however, that *far niente* is not exactly idleness, we turn to a study done by UNESCO in which it was established that 49 percent of all worldwide works of art happen to be concentrated in a single country: Italy.

Far niente is not idleness *per se,* which implies an aimless sense of being lost without direction, but rather, it is a need to be alone with oneself, an expression of freedom, contemplation, and solitude, or a time to relax and recuperate after intense work. It is a time for detachment and stepping out of life's rut to better appreciate one's own fantastic resources.*

FINALLY, LET'S CONCLUDE this look at creative characteristics with one element that can really make the difference between success and failure: luck. Aristotle believed luck to be God's gift to man, hidden away from human perception. To some people, luck is the only thing necessary for success in life, while to others, its influence merely accelerates or slows (in the case of bad luck) success.

One day, Salvatore Ferragamo was very late for his flight from Los Angeles to New York. Having rushed all the way to the airport to take that flight, he finally arrived at the check-in counter, breathless. The steward, who had come to lend a hand, told him that he still had time to board the flight. Suddenly, Ferragamo decided to stay, much to the surprise of the steward, who insisted, but to no avail. After having spent so much time and energy to finally "make it," Salvatore Ferragamo decided he would not board the airplane, but instead

*Take a set of twins who choose to dedicate their lives to the pursuit of knowledge. One leaves home to travel the world, convinced that by living as many experiences as he can, he will acquire vast knowledge. The second stays home, shut away in his bedroom, where he turns his search inward to discover the source of knowledge within him. After many years and many experiences, twin number one returns home, an old man now. He finds his beloved twin in the bedroom where he had left him so many years before. Exuberantly, he recounts his worldly tales. After listening, his brother smiles calmly. From within the four walls of his room he has found what he did not need to search outside himself to know: Knowledge and imagination really come from within. Though he had never traveled anywhere, his mind had journeyed into the infinite world of dreams, where his imagination proved omniscient.

would wait for the next one. That decision indeed saved the future of the Ferragamo business. The airplane, which Ferragamo willingly missed, crashed during its flight. There were no survivors.

A CREATOR'S CONTRIBUTION goes way beyond his or her work. Tough competition and the media's never-ending need for celebrity stories more than company fact sheets have turned creators into the true stars who help brands become credible. No longer can they win the public through their creative work alone; today they must also be charismatic, extravagant, and glamorous. For example, Bernard Arnault has masterfully revamped his LVMH's fashion houses by hiring two creators, one as enticing as the other is provocative: John Galliano at Christian Dior and Alexander McQueen at Givenchy.

Creators are cultural leaders. Their efforts present the world of business with an aesthetic vision that is otherwise locked in the realm of art. Their creations spread beauty over a much wider range of products and services. Creators are often inspired and energized by the excitement surrounding the business: the beauty and glamour of the products and services, the famous, successful, and challenging customers, the visibility of the media all engender a "hype" that is conducive to creativity. Their greatest contribution includes pushing the boundaries of knowledge in the business world. Whereas traditional business schools prepare managers to rationalize and solve business problems by reducing the working environment to an organized, predictable, and well-structured model, creators challenge their companies to strive in unpredictable, always changing, and apparently unrelated experiences.

At times, creators struggle with irrationality. In their work, they must constantly expose their feelings to external judgment, perhaps accounting for the delicate emotional makeup of many creators and creative individuals. Investing love, jealousy, fear, hatred, and even a sort of madness into their work, it appears they let a kind of folly permeate their entire lives. Their curiosity, emotional intensity, and fanaticism for perfection propel them to introduce new ideas, often clashing with society's ingrained fear of change. Often in history, creative people have been associated with madness. However, there is a fundamental difference between the two: Madness refers to someone living outside of any reality, while the genius is someone who can change reality. Creators are often considered a bit odd because of their many idiosyncrasies, moods, or egocentric ticks, but theirs should be termed a healthy folly.* After all, as Baudelaire (1821–1867) advised: *"Strangeness is the essential flavor in any beauty."*

*There are some instances in which one could speak of real folly in the creative process, given that certain types of mental disorders might contribute to the highest levels of creative productivity. For example, in their 1988 book *The Key to Genius: Manic-Depression and the Creative Life,* D. Jablow Hershman and Julian Lieb provide a convincing account of the role of manic depression in the creative lives of Newton, Beethoven, Dickens, and van Gogh. It is possible that such mental states contribute to a heightened motivation for engaging in creative cognition. Novelist Virginia Woolf (1882–1941) often used the experiences of her depressions in her writing. This intermingling of genius and folly is not a recent theory: Even Seneca (4 B.C.–A.D. 65) claimed, that *"there is no great genius without some touch of madness."* Beethoven claimed that one thing alone prevented him from committing suicide upon learning that he was going deaf: music. Too many masterworks still waited in his mind to be transcribed to paper. Art has, at times, been used as a means of alleviating mental disabilities ("raw art"). In psychiatric hospitals, patients with mental disorders are asked to paint because it is considered a therapeutic exercise that could help restore a certain mental balance.

What is generally referred to as folly when speaking of the creative process is a quality that, in ordinary business, is often called vision. When Jules Verne wrote of mysterious submarine adventures and underwater worlds, or imagined trips to the moon, many thought him more crazy than visionary for his futuristic foreshadowing. One of the most brilliant essays ever written regarding society's dismissal of original thinking is *The Praise of Folly,* written in 1509 by Erasmus of Rotterdam (1466–1536). In it, Erasmus attacks the intolerance of the Catholic Church by praising folly as the resolute will and strength required to contest the Church and its narrow beliefs. The following quotations best express Erasmus' lucid and modern thoughts about the importance of challenging acquired knowledge:

> *Me* is life's best and happiest moments that I give back to the individual. If the mortals would decide to part from Wisdom and live incessantly with me, instead of the boredom of growing old, they would know the enjoyment of always being young.*

> *If we love children . . . is it not because there is, in them, the seduction of Folly? . . . Where does the charm of the children come from, if not from me who saves them from reason, and, at the same time, from worry? . . . The more man pushes me away, the more he lives less and less.*

> *What distinguishes the crazy from the sage is that the first is guided by passions, while the latter is guided by reason.*

**Me* refers to Folly.

In the universe, the least miserable are the closest to animality and stupidity.

Who cares if he died, since he never lived.

Creativity is an exercise in risk-taking. The fear of wandering outside the boundaries of what is right and safe will never provoke creativity. Unfortunately, the fear of failure is deeply rooted in most cultures. From an early age, we are taught to be right, not wrong, because society and especially business organizations have little time for errors. Yet errors are important learning experiences that contribute to any lasting success. There is an intense emotional involvement in creative work because risks not only affect the financial outcome, but also threaten the individual. Like artists, creative people often fear the critics and the public, who may not appreciate or recognize their talent in time. The ego factor weighs heavily, because creative people are so involved in their work that any minor observation or criticism is received as a direct and personal insult. Organizations are excellent at stifling creativity. The last decade of intense re-engineering and streamlining has somewhat shrunk bureaucracy in the corporate world, yet still the maximization of creative resources is a distant dream save for a handful of dream companies. Creators can change this. With their mix of business acumen and artistic characteristics, they bring aesthetic experimentation and artistic creativity to the world of business. Their position of power within the organization can help companies promote the search for aesthetic excellence along with the maximization of profits. Their knowledge of the product and production systems can direct the creative efforts of the craftsmen, designers, and engineers and can lead the company to invest in technologies that maximize creative freedom by reducing production constraints. They can also insist that the search for quality and aesthetic integrity not succumb to the short-term profit push that most financial people and shareholders usually favor. Creators shape a company's personality through their original products and services and their search for innovation and taste. Most important, they instill the confidence needed to be attuned to the market, without giving in to it by forfeiting the company's identity. Over a lifetime, these creators dedicate passion and attention to developing product and service knowledge far more refined than that of their customers. No market studies or customer questionnaires can match their ingrained sense of what is best for a company.

Creators are the soul of the company. Even a company with no creators on its team would benefit greatly by inviting creators to bring their eclecticism and culture to the boardroom.

Creators alone cannot make dreams. They need team support from highly creative collaborators such as artists, designers, craftsmen, and other cultural people who can transform their visions into "commercial" products and services.

6

Redefining Excellence

CREATORS ALONE CANNOT create dreams. They can envision them. They can provide inspiration and direction, but dreams do not come from one single person. Dreams are not made of a single product. Dreams are an emotional experience. Many ancillary activities must take place to transform a product into an emotional experience. All those activities cannot be performed by a single individual, no matter how gifted that individual may be. For an artist, once the masterpiece is finished, the work is over. For a company in the business of selling dreams, however, the creator's masterpiece represents only one part of the equation. The masterpiece has to be accurately reproduced in several units in order to make the business worthwhile: It takes a team of gifted and knowledgeable people to transform a specimen into a production line. Then comes financing, commercialization, and technical support, just as in any other business. To become a dream the emotional experience has to be harmonious at all levels, lest the customer wake up or the dream become a nightmare. Creators must therefore seek a creative coalition not only at the production level but in every aspect of the business—communication, distribution, postsales service, even financial departments. Every single department must provide creative support and obsessive attention to details in order to continually reinforce the dream. Customers have become sophisticated and well-informed (from the Internet flows a dysentery of comparative product information). They are quick to distinguish a dream from advertising dribble. Only outstanding products and services with convincing emotional qualities can become dreams. It takes each collaborator in the organization working, as if in an orchestra, under the maestro, the creator. But, as in the orchestra, each member must express his or her own ideas and creativity in order to give an outstanding performance. Getting back to the example of the restaurant, the lobster alone will never transform dining into a dream, nor will the menu, the wine cellar, the decor or the celebrities. Dining becomes a dream when the chef and each of his or her collaborators work together consistently and harmoniously.

Dream products and services begin as the nascent idea of an aesthetic visionary: the creator. Business success follows only if this creator can build a team of highly skilled collaborators who share the desire to generate profits without compromising the company's taste.

WHAT A COMPANY PRODUCES is certainly key in determining the creativity factor within an organization. As already seen, the highest levels of creativity exist in art production, where painters, sculptors, poets, and musicians respond to the least amount of constraint, therefore freeing their inspiration. Obviously, a painter is required to be more creative than an accountant (that is, an accountant who goes strictly by the books) and will work far more at being creative (which, in itself, requires plenty of work) than an accountant. Clearly, not all products stimulate the same amount of creative output. If the utmost expression of creativity can be found in the arts, then business creativity is more likely to surface in the industry in which products tend to possess more artistic content. Isn't it reasonable then that the industry producing the strongest creative expression is composed of those companies responsible for manufacturing dreams? In these companies, an important investment goes toward attracting, training, and motivating skilled personnel who can, through their *savoir faire* and aesthetic predisposition, generate the high added value that distinguishes this business. This tradition, inherited from the artisan organization, represents a continual learning process that lasts a lifetime and leads to an intrinsic understanding of the craft and the acquisition of clear aesthetic values. Training is a crucial part of the learning process and builds organizations that thrive in highly stimulating and creative environments, rich with gifted designers, engineers, experts, and craftsmen who constantly experiment in creating beautiful objects. What was once the "master" in craft organizations has been replaced by today's creator. Inspired by the creators, collaborators at all levels of the organization tend to spend more time on the specifics of aesthetic experimentation, on the look, feel, touch, and color of the product. The aesthetic search does not stop with the creator, but spreads to all levels of the organization as a shared culture. In such an organization, the marketing department has less weight in product decisions, focusing more on building and expressing the dream experience. Curiosity urges a company to explore beyond the immediacy of market parameters. For example, Ferrari decided to custom-make luggage able to fit its automobiles' uniquely shaped trunk and to withstand tough racing and hard driving conditions (hot temperatures and stiff suspension that slaps the luggage about), without adding to the car's weight. This is how a new line of accessories is born, not from market research, but from purposeful thinking.

In an organization that sells dream products, creativity is not an isolated accomplishment, but a steady climate of curiosity that is regulated by the company's aesthetic values. Unlike most mass-consumption companies, organizations in the "dream business" can open up to aesthetic experimentation rather than concentrating solely on the functional characteristics of their products and services. Creativity becomes the communion between the collaborators' own curiosity and intuition and the company's proprietary cultural knowledge and aesthetic appreciation. Built up over the years, it all crystallizes in the company's "memory." This "memory" represents the company's driving force, a most valuable source of energy to orient and inspire the original effort of each collaborator. The "memory" expresses the company's taste, which people can then recognize in each object or service produced. It conjures up an emotional integration of *savoir faire,* technology, designs, colors, shapes, tastes, textures, and materials, representing the company's major artery into which flows the creativity of every collaborator. The core of this memory can be found in the company's archives. Be it the 350,000 documents of Cartier, the 6,000 dyes of Puiforcat tableware, the 25,000 models of Ferragamo shoes, the 1,000 watches in Girard-Perregaux's collection, the many films in the Disney archives or Pfizer's laboratories filled with millions of compounds, each company frequently searches these treasured archives for new ideas to spin off. They are a priceless source of inspiration from which "creative" brains can build instead of starting from scratch each time they set out to achieve something innovative. A company's style emerges from the archives, which help to tame the occasional overexuberance of a young designer or engineer bent on creating some way-out design or advanced technology. Archives can also counteract a new CEO's wild desire to leave his own indelible mark on a company's history. Archives help reduce the risk of launching short-lived products and services in the fast-paced turnaround of today's business by giving the experiment a launch pad.

To create dream products and services, a company must develop a taste that lives on even after the creator is gone. The taste, distinguishable in the products or services the company has sold over the years, must inspire each collaborator to create objects and services worthy of customers' dreams. By respecting rigorous aesthetic guidelines, an organization can achieve profits and growth through a sort of "benevolent cycle" (as opposed to a vicious one) in which creativity is the axis. The more a company produces creative products and services, the more it attracts creative people, and the more the organization's overall creativity can surge.

Dream products and services emerge from an ideology of originality in all areas: design, technological solutions, the process of fabrication, and execution. Originality needs a certain degree of freedom. Creativity must not be stifled by overly stringent cost controls or rigid product standardization. The degree of freedom is usually what distinguishes companies working to create dreams.

*Savoir faire** (know-how) or craft, which is the combination of inherited talents and learned practical skills, endows an individual with a unique ability not easily accessible to those who do not naturally possess it. Technology, on the other hand, is formalized knowledge, a rational application of production activities. Technology can be learned and employed with little inherent skill and calls for no emotional involvement, whereas craft† requires learning and emotional devotion. Most important, unlike technology, which is owned by a company or by anyone who can use it, *savoir faire* is usually reserved for a gifted individual. This influences one of this industry's most important characteristics: the concentration of production around well-defined geographical areas where such individuals can be found.

While mass industry can move production bases practically anywhere in the world, since training workers is not an issue, companies creating dreams, on the other hand, usually thrive in selected areas where the cultural *savoir faire* has been passed down from generation to generation. *Savoir faire* is what truly

*The French expression *savoir faire* seems to have a more artistic connotation than the English "know-how," which has a more mechanical sound to it. It's like *la soupe du jour,* which always tastes better than "the soup of the day."

†As far back as Plato, the art of "doing" was thought to produce a "work of art" as long as *tekne* or technique was infused with *episteme,* which Plato did not call science, but rather a force without which the work of art would be left to chance. Tolman called it "desire," Freud called it "pulsation," Adler and Spengler "willpower." Whatever the term, this emotional involvement, the result of a period of waiting, expectation, and hope, is the engine of creative spirit.

generates the added value, so those individuals possessing it are very valuable to a company. They are freer, since organizations do not control them, but offer them the chance to create, to express their skills and passion. If they work in an organization, it is because they enjoy it rather than depend upon it. Very creative organizations flourish because of this freedom from constriction.

After the Industrial Revolution,* *savoir faire* gave way to machines churning out a uniform quality more effectively and consistently. *Savoir faire* has, however, endured in highly creative companies in which the exceptional artistic content could not be readily replicated by machines. *Savoir faire* is critical in the creation of dream products and services, since it determines their emotional content. Their value comes from the crystallization of *savoir faire,* which occurs when the precious time, soul, knowledge, and talent of artistic people are transferred into the product.

The following examples prove this point.

*After the Industrial Revolution, mass production squelched craft production with the help of such major cultural and artistic movements as constructionism, futurism, cubism, the technical and popular art of Fernand Léger (1881–1955), the functionalism of Le Corbusier (1887–1965), and particularly the Bauhaus. These movements exemplified the intellectual background of mass-production ideologies with their interest in rationality, simplification of processes, and essentialism of forms. Not until the 1950s did scores of new artists, such as J. Tinguely, Cesar, and more recently, W. Vostell and G. Brecht, and intellectuals like A. H. Maslow, Friedman, McGregor, Herzberg, and Hughes, propose an ideological alternative that praised human involvement in the performing of quality work. The strict hierarchical structure of mass consumption had failed to involve the worker and was unable to offer intellectually or emotionally stimulating jobs because it was, in effect, a system where any emotional input upset the norm.

Perhaps one of the most coveted jobs in the industry of making dreams is that of a test driver at Ferrari. Ferrari cars are extensively tested, from regular roads to the most extreme conditions (from the heat of the Saudi Arabian deserts to the ice of the Antarctic) as well as at the company's two racetracks. Test drivers rack up more than one hundred thousand kilometers a year on any range of road conditions, usually at high speeds and sometimes at very high speeds to test the cars' limits (this job's thrill doesn't come without potential fines and, unfortunately, occasional accidents). Several variables determine an automobile's driving characteristics, ranging from chassis rigidity, weight distribution, aerodynamics, suspension setting, towing, camber, tires, balance of each of the four wheels in braking, and the engine's power and response, all to be adapted to given road conditions. With so many variables at work, the test driver must have more than just experience to be sensitive enough to even the subtlest behavioral nuances of the automobile. It usually takes several months of hard work to develop the optimum driving characteristics of a new model and the best compromise between performance, comfort, and adaptability to different road conditions. The test driver must also ensure that each new model evinces the driving characteristics that make a Ferrari such an emotional machine.

Dario Benuzzi is Ferrari's chief test driver. He joined the company as a mechanic in 1971. His great passion for sports cars and his desire to learn have made him one of the best drivers in the world. He is not only whiplash fast (today, at age fifty, he still clocks lap times similar to those of young F-1 champions), but also intensely accurate (he can determine the pressure of the tires by the way the car drives). He crafts the driving characteristics of every new model, the very soul of each Ferrari. He must ensure that the advanced technologies constantly increase driving comfort but do not emasculate the new model nor the emotions that grab so many passionate Ferrari drivers. Benuzzi knows better than anyone that while German luxury car manufacturers eliminate road feedback to achieve maximum riding comfort, it is that very distinct "feeling of the road" that charges through the Ferrari customer in a rush of emotions and adrenaline. Benuzzi's knowledge, extraordinary sensitivity, and passion for race cars is Ferrari's best guarantee that each of its new models will carry the unmistakable characteristics that have distinguished the Ferraris for more than fifty years. The people of Maranello have grown accustomed to seeing his Ferraris dart by on roads around the factory. No longer surprised, they know it's just Dario enjoying another hard day at "the office."

I asked Gusmano Cesaretti, the associate producer of numerous films for Michael Mann, what his creative process consists of.

"I started out as a photographer. Michael discovered my work in a magazine. I did a documentary of the gangs in East L.A. and he saw the black-and-white images and called me in the middle of the night and said, 'My name is Michael Mann. I liked your work and I'd like you take pictures for me.' When he was doing the film *The Jericho Mile* that took place in jail, he invited me to photograph the cell and the jail. He said, 'Look at everything and photograph everything you like.' That's how we met. At first I thought he was crazy. I gave him fifty prints in black and white, and that was in 1979. Every project that he's done since, he's asked me to get involved. I'm an emotional artist. Michael is very intellectual. It's a great combination because it's very complementary. I bring warmth, color, and texture to his wishes. I bring life to people. I find interesting characters to add to the films. I have a good sense of design and I get involved with wardrobe, makeup, and hair. If it doesn't work, I tell Michael. Michael and I respect each other.

"Basically, I'm like Michael's eyes when he's away. For instance, when we did the film *Heat,* Michael said to me, 'I want you to discover Los Angeles in a way you've never seen it before.' I started cruising at night and different times of the day, trying to look at places in Los Angeles which are very familiar to me like it was the first time I had seen L.A. I got in my car, played some interesting music, and starting driving around the streets and alleys. I would stop and see the way lights create a shadow, reflections on the glass, on water, and on the streets. I set up all these details and I create a pallet of color for Michael to decide for himself.

"At the beginning of the film, I read the script, and then it takes me two weeks to get into it, then I start thinking how I see the film, how can I give Michael something interesting that is applicable to the script and the story. Then we go location scouting with a technical scout. Michael takes the camera and we start clicking the way Michael would shoot it with the camera. I put together a book and create it before we start shooting, by selecting images and photographs, cutting out things from magazines and books, and creating a color photo storyboard of the whole film. I copy and color-Xerox things like handbags, sunglasses, and say that maybe this character could look good with these glasses or this pair of shoes or a jacket. It's seven huge panels that I put together before shooting, scene by scene. I place it on the wall and Michael walks in alone with his scripts and his notes. Michael goes through it and takes what he doesn't like out.

"The key members of the crew get copies of the scene-by-scene photo storyboards because it's a reference of what we are going to do. Michael and I shoot the movie in still film before we do it in motion picture."

At seventy-three years of age, Juan Garcia is still going strong as a chief cigar roller in his very labor-intensive job. Each tobacco plant must be tended by hand every day for a four-month period. But Juan, who was born in western Cuba, in the Pinar del Rio region, is proud just knowing his tobacco leaves are the finest in the world. "From October to January the crops mature, then once the green tobacco leaves are harvested, we string them up on poles in the barn." He points, with hands tanned and weathered just like the leaves after they've dried for a sixty-day period. "We bunch them together, press them flat, lay them out, and from April to July they ferment naturally. No chemicals"—he wags his gnarled finger insistently—"means lower acidity, tar, and nicotine than cigarettes. The leaves are sorted by size and all cigars are hand-rolled. It takes nine months of hard work apprenticing before you can become a professional roller like me. All production ends in November, then I can relax." He smiles proudly, his front teeth stained from his own passion for the finest cigars, which he enjoys for free. He nudges me. "It took me only six months, my father taught me since I was small like the young tobacco plants. I've lived around these fields all my life so I know how the soil and weather must be, I know the exact temperature so the leaves ferment just right. I know which leaves I have to discard, and my nose will tell me which leaves will blend the perfect cigar. But most of all, I know how to roll the best cigar. I can roll 130 a day. I may look old, but when you've done as many as I have, experience still lets me outroll even the youngest and greenest.

You may think life is no more than rolling one cigar after another, but it's not so dull, we have our ways." A smile creeps over him. "We rollers, we're better read than most school kids today. As we roll, we are read to, educated. It used to be novels; today, we get more of Castro's philosophy."

These three skilled individuals share a *savoir faire* that really determines the added value for which customers are willing to pay so dearly. Benuzzi, Cesaretti, and Garcia all actively participate in the creative process. Their passion, skill, and understanding of their companies' spirit help transform the creators' vision and ideas into sellable products. Their imagination and dedication are the silent signets of their companies' greatness. Their access to the best materials and most advanced production processes certainly helps. What would a sports car be without light or composite materials, or cigars without the finest tobacco, or jewelry without the precious stones and metals, perfumes without essential oils, fashion without colorful silks or exotic fabrics, wine without selected grapes, shoes and luggage without the finest leathers, movies without special effects? It's like asking what a painter would do without color. When creating dream products, as in any artistic expression, materials are the natural means by which man can compose his ideas, imagination, and concepts. Therefore, the pursuit of and experimentation with the most sophisticated, the oldest and newest, the most precious and purest materials, is essential in this industry's quest for perfection. Often the quality of these materials determines the value of the creation, challenging the artist, creator, or craftsman to develop new *savoir faires* in order to overcome the inherent difficulties in transforming them, or new designs to best express their natural beauty. These materials are not only the celebration of nature's richness, they are also man's tribute to the beauty of his natural environment.

These richly aesthetic products and services all come from the creator's inspiration, the passionate and dedicated individuals who are hired as collaborators, the promotion of the emotional experiences, the risk-taking, as well as the rich materials and sophisticated production processes. These aesthetic values must be something the entire organization strives to enforce. Making dreams creates a certain "dream team."

CREATING EXCELLENCE requires fanatical dedication. In 1759, the philosopher Hume wrote a meditation, entitled *Passions,* calling passions slow and restive compared to the imagination, which is rapid and agile. He noted that while an idea can quickly change in one's mind, a single passion can remain fixed in one's personality for many years. Passions grow stronger with knowledge and when faced with opposition: *"The effort to which the mind is subjected to overcome a hurdle stirs the mind and vivifies the passion."* Uncertainty also intensifies passion, while security and certainty only weaken it (creating dreams involves facing the uncertainty of customer approval). After all, a passion is not born of an entity but of a nonentity, not of a presence but of an absence. Passion is the outcome of a deficiency.

Today, these passions may appear to be the far-flung emotions of a romantic past. We live in an era in which passions are more difficult to express. Life today seems driven by convenience and efficiency rather than by the impulse of emotions. Ours is a throwaway society in which everything is discarded as waste and no one can grow attached to anything. Everything can be replaced, even one's heart. Today is the era of scientific discovery. Mystery belongs only to the past. Passion now seems to take shape in various forms of alienation, such as alcohol, drugs, and violence. Most strikingly, passions seem to have lost their previous nobility. Wars of liberation have been replaced by terrorism; love letters take the form of E-mail; Rigoletto becomes Rambo; sportsmen become steroid-shooting professional athletes; craftsmen are displaced by the factory line and taverns by fast-food joints.

Much like human senses, passions can weaken over time and become dormant if not stimulated. The excess of consumerism and the advertising invasion have also robbed passions of their substance. Today, even while Rhett Butler and Scarlett O'Hara share the kiss of a lifetime, the television suddenly cuts away to a mouthwash commercial in which wife and husband greet each other awkwardly after a long night's sleep, and love only seems rekindled after a good gargle. Passion is blighted by the long sword of commercialization, a strong example of modern marketing. No longer cherished deep in the heart and soul of the individual, passions are now stocked on local supermarket shelves in a pathetic effort to strengthen rapid consumer spending and companies' overall financial performances. Far from gaining any new credibility, this new pseudoromanticism only further alienates the consumer. Passions suffer, continuing to lose their ingenuity to the overrationalization of scientific research: Love is not love anymore. Love is a high sperm count in a frozen test tube. Passions are confused by our society's contradictions that swing from lax permissiveness (X-rated movies, slaughter-style television, kiddy porn and prostitution, crack cocaine, and four-year-olds bringing guns to their nursery school Show-N-Tell) to the most castrating prohibitionism: no smoking, no drinking, no sex, speed limit 55, fat-free, no noise, no wake until at last we wonder if there's still a sun behind that obscuring signpost.

Passions are a compulsive force born deep in our psyche, so we are not about to become an apathetic society deprived of any passionate impulse. We are simply adapting to a *prêt-à-consommer* society wherein customers can emotionally experiment not only in romantic flights of fancy, but even in their daily life. One reason why customers are so drawn to dream products is that they ignite their passions and stimulate their sensory systems at multiple levels (no love of your life or war of liberation required). In business, life is fairly antiseptic, with little or no talk of our passions and emotions, but here, our senses are what fundamentally inspire and govern this industry of selling dreams.

SENSES* (from the Latin *sentire,* to feel) are the vital ability to bring the environment inside us so we can relate to it. They offer the chance to live and feel the palpitation of time. They keep life from fading away, linking us to the past in ways far more dynamic than any rational memory. A sight, a sound, a smell, a texture, or a taste can bring to life, in the most resonant ways, moments of

*Senses, contrary to some religious or poetic accusations, are not reserved for pleasure-seeking. Their fundamental mission is a very functional one: to help man survive in the constantly evolving and often adverse environment. A most obvious example is pain, which is an alarm system provided by our senses (a blinding light, a deafening sound, an asphyxiating odor, a burn or a strong pressure on the skin, the bitter taste of poison) to alert us to danger. Sensory systems are not immutable, but continuously evolve to surmount the challenges of the environment, through a slow genetic adaptation, which Darwin termed "evolution." The environment determines which senses are important to the species.

pleasure or pain that are long gone. The French poet Rimbaud (1854–1891) believed that in order for artists to attain truth in life they must be confronted with "every form of love, of suffering, of madness." This is only possible by means of "a long, immense, planned disordering of all the senses." For Rimbaud, as for other philosophers and psychologists, the senses* were the most essential channels through which man could "perceive" the totality of life, by going beyond the rigid interpretations of reason.

Dream products and services manifest the perceptions of the customers' senses. The more senses they can stimulate, the more intense the dream becomes.

* * *

*The following chart shows which senses are involved in the appreciation of a few products, such as jewels, perfumes, fashion, wines, and sports automobiles. The purpose here is to explore the kind of sensory system that the object stimulates, the qualities that the customer should discover, and the aesthetic values the creator must be able to express. The goal should be to enhance the customers' experience by stimulating the maximum number of senses possible.

luxury product	**sensory system**	**critical quality**	**value**
Jewels	v, t, h	luminosity	visual force
Perfumes	s, v, t	richness of fragrance	harmony of smell
Fashion	t, v, h	softness of tissue	softness to the touch
Wine	ta, s, v	fullness of body	richness of taste
Sports automobiles	v, h, s, t	immediacy of response	intensity of motion
Movies	v, h	expressive imagery	intensity of emotions

v = vision; h = hearing; s = smell; t = touch; ta = taste.

The more intensively a product or service stimulates the sensory system, the more senses it reaches, thus the greater the quality of the experience. Intensity depends on the level of refinement that the creator achieves. Take jewelry. The stone's natural luminosity can be enhanced by the way it is cut, set, and mounted. The better the overall production quality, the greater the num-

Of all the senses, vision most attracts us to dream products and services, simply because we see before we hear, smell, touch, or taste.

Jewels best exemplify the objects that stimulate our visual sense. With precious stones, four properties determine value: Rarity tells us how scarce a resource it is; hardness refers to the cohesiveness of the minerals or the strength of the chemical bond (an important determinant, since the harder the stone, the more clean-cut the surface edges); chemical resistance preserves the stone's brilliance over time; beauty, though it is subjective, is based on rather objective criteria expressed in the stone's optical characteristics.* Optical beauty refers to an inner

---

ber of senses stimulated. Embellishing a jewel means focusing on characteristics other than the purely visual, such as "wearability" (for example, the way a necklace hangs around the neck). This opens up the enjoyment of the jewelry not only to include its visual appearance but also the pleasure of wearing it (touch). When all components, including the weight of the jewelry, are perfectly integrated into its powerful "presence," more senses, such as touch, are aroused.

*The term "optical characteristics" refers here to the properties of light. When a ray of light hits a surface that separates two different media, such as air and a mineral, part is *reflected* and sent back into the first medium, part is *refracted,* entering the second medium, and part is *absorbed.* Depending on the nature of the mineral, one or another part can prevail. From these three properties of light, a stone develops its individual characteristics. What gives a stone *luster* is the amount of reflected light and the sensation of warmth or coldness that it produces. The type of luster depends not only on the nature of the stone, but also on the degree to which the surface has been polished, which is greater the harder the material. The refraction of light determines the *dispersion.* When a beam of light enters the stone, it breaks up into multicolored rays, with different angles of refraction. The dispersion produces the play of light that gives precious stones their magical luminosity. Finally, the absorption of the light determines the *color* of the stone because a substance assumes a color depending on the mixture of light rays not absorbed (for example, a ruby appears red because it absorbs part of the green radiation).

perfection, an internal order produced by the regular arrangement of atoms continuously and identically replicated. In other words, a precious stone is naturally beautiful in essence, but in its natural form, it does not convey all of its beauty. It takes man's creativity to transform a precious stone into a symbol of eternity. In the past, a stone was presented as a cabochon, a simple rounded form. It is believed that facet-cutting stones and arranging them into jewels didn't begin until the mid-fourteenth century. Apparently very little has changed this process, since many of the facet-cutting tools are just as primitive today.

Because it requires such patience and precision, less valuable stones are cut where they are extracted (Sri Lanka, India, Thailand, Brazil, or Colombia), where labor is cheaper than in the main cutting centers of Antwerp, Amsterdam, New York, Tel Aviv, Bombay, and Cape Town, where the most valuable stones are cut. As the stone's value is determined by its luminosity and weight, when cutting the stone, the craftsman must minimize weight loss (a brilliant-cut stone weighs around 40 percent as much as the original rough stone), while making sure the best coloration is visible from the tablet face (the larger face on the uppermost part of the stone).

Mario Buccellati, president and CEO of Buccellati North America, believes that jewelers are an extinct species. "There are technicians and there are artists. I think that in the traditional interpretation of what a jeweler is to be is someone who mixes all the classical aspects of art and creativity with the science of jewelry making. I think that by the attrition of our general marketplace, we are the last ones left standing who truly interpret artistic design and rendering and realize them in unique pieces of art.

"Buccellati's *raison d'être* is our constant striving for the perfect combination of art and science to bring out the character in any given stone and incorporate it in an interpretive design of beauty. It takes a boundless imagination, the deepest and richest know-how in manufacturing, and a tireless attention to details in the execution. All of which comes only from the most rigorous training process. We use what would best be described as a feudal system where you have an apprentice and a journeyman and a master at any given specialty and discipline within our manufacturing process.

"For example, one of the many processes that is integrated into our type of production is engraving, which is the treatment of any surface of metal by carving or scratching in an organized fashion to create a certain texture or a certain effect on light. The simplest forms of engraving are straight lines. It takes years for an individual to engrave a straight line. Then when you start to mix in all the other techniques it might be five to six years of us investing in an individual before that individual can become the master engraver and really work on any of our objects. It's a long investment before we can even see the fruits of that person's labor.

"What is today known as the Buccellati style of intricate engraving was pretty much invented and created by my grandfather back at the turn of the century. It is now constantly being refined and evolving, but in general it is still faithful to his original idea. The generations that have followed are keepers of the flame in one respect and also are continuously refining and subtly experimenting with variations that will continue to broaden the appeal of Buccellati.

"We are always in search of beautiful and unique pearls and stones and materials that we can combine into our work. Many times these individual pieces of material, be they stones or pearls, will inspire certain designs as integral pieces. On the other hand, when these stones are not looked at that way, we are always looking at classical themes from nature, architecture, to inspiration from arts of all periods, in which these themes are interpreted to create a harmonious item. It takes looking at an item from a concept point of view and never compromising to make it a reality."

But how does one manage the dichotomy between exceptional quality and cost?

"That's what keeps us going. We have an ongoing business, a vertically integrated business—we manufacture, we distribute and we retail. We do this on three different continents, and soon to be four, and we have been doing it for almost a hundred years. Being able to stay almost in a Renaissance manner, to match the highest possible forms of art and management of the marketplace, is what enables a company like ours to exist and go on. That is the magic formula. Our key is we never compromise. I think the concept of compromise is the road to aesthetic ruination. People can survive beautifully and perhaps even better than we do from a financial point of view by compromising, but we are faithful to what has brought us here and we are faithful to keeping the flame. So, as far as a compromise is concerned, we will never dilute our style, our image, and our brand. We'll always look to grow it, never dilute it.

"From a product point of view this means keeping true to the core. We are jewelers and silversmiths. We are not ceramic makers, we are not glassblowers, we are not tailors, we are not leather people. It's very simple to go out and say, 'Okay, company X, we licensed you to make scarves for us.' We could do very well, but quite honestly, we are jewelers and silversmiths. We can grow and expand and evolve in the appropriate and cautious manner in those areas, but we really don't have any reason to go outside of that. That's what enables us to maintain the integrity that we do.

"Just to mention a few names, Cartier and Bulgari, who are absolute financial phenomena, and I'm not saying this to downplay their financial success, they have broadened their markets, broadened their appeal, expanded dramatically, but lost some of their cachet. This is strictly an issue of policy, nothing more. We have a phrase here in the U.S., 'to sell out'; you can sell out and make a beautiful living and live very comfortably, but at the same time you are not what you were. We have a tremendous amount of brand equity available to leverage without expansion and dilution."

Buccellati has flourished for more than three generations precisely because of its aesthetic integrity, constant experimentation, and the strict training of its collaborators. The trademark engraving, so distinctly Buccellati, rests in the hands of the skilled craftsmen who can interpret the creator's vision.

SMELL* may be our most primitive sense, born of our animal origins when it was all we had to guide us through an uncon-

*While we humans have, on average, 5 million olfactory cells, a sheepdog has as many as 220 million. Had we not lost so much smelling sensitivity, today we might be able to sniff out any number of intimate facts about our business associates as they spew financial projections during, say, a tedious business meeting: who is sexually repressed and who is receptive, who has power, who is afraid, and any other tidbits that could provide a detailed profile of each individual. Our sense of smell evolves over time. Children prefer simple scents. Adults are more attracted to perfumes with sexual contents. Smell is a sexist sense, given that females usually score higher than males in sensing odors. Like other senses, smell is a combination of genetic traits (albinos have a poor sense of smell) and the result of consciousness. Because it is not purely genetic, smell can be enhanced through training.

scious life deprived of reason and speech. In practically every species from the most primitive reptiles to the most advanced primates, the olfactory system is located in what is known as the reptilian part of the brain. Here lies the nervous system that directs such unconscious muscular activity as heartbeat, breathing, pupil dilation, and the most essential social interaction skills, including sexuality and genital excitement (thus the close neurophysiological relationship between our sense of smell and sexual activities, a phenomenon dating back to our earliest evolutionary state). Our sense of smell possesses an intrinsic beauty: It enlivens precious memories, no matter how long past. A whiff or impromptu scent can immediately recreate past pleasures and transform blurred images into vivid reminiscence. This is an invaluable quality. After all, a human being is no more than a "memory bank."

Professionals working in the scent industry can heighten their perception of odors through training, learning to recognize the components of various aromas and even the most sophisticated scents. Becoming a "perfumer"* requires an innate sensitivity to smells, but also an astute knowledge of the characteristics and combination of various scents (scents can change

*Perfumers travel searching for the best ingredients and new fragrances. For example, they scour France (roses, jasmine, lavender, violet), Italy (iris, orange, lemon), Turkey (damask rose), Bulgaria (damask rose), Morocco (oak moss that produces one of the highest *absolutes* of perfumery), India (sandalwood), Sri Lanka (barks, kernels, roots, and plants), China (ginger), Reunion (vanilla), Comoro Island (ylang-ylang), South America (patchouli). And, just like our other senses, smell is also influenced by our cultural environment, explaining the diversity in perfume preferences around the world. Scents are grouped into seven categories: citrus, floral, fern, chypre, woody, oriental, and leather. Each group is then subdivided under seemingly infinite variations.

based on the ingredients they are combined with and perfume can vary depending on the skin it is applied to).*

The perfume sector has evolved dramatically. While old traditions still remain, the extensive introduction of advanced computerized systems and new technologies has revolutionized the way perfumes are made. If, in the past, perfumes would commercially linger for decades, today their life cycle is cut short by the yearly introduction of new fragrances. New technologies have led perfumers to discover more than two thousand new scents from which they can compose new formulas. Though computers are used extensively, new perfumes still rely on the human factor, that is, the "nose," to decide the final formula. Nature also plays an important role. A flower's scent can change depending on its soil or the environment's climatic conditions. Whereas flowers contribute with their soft and gentle femininity, it is the animal† notes that infuse power and deep sensuality into a perfume.

*For example, the tantalizing jasmine from Grasse (the town near Nice, France, world famous for its naturally grown herbs and flowers used in perfumes), the key ingredient in Chanel No. 5, sells for more than $12,000 a pound, an important premium compared to $900 for Moroccan jasmine, or $680 for Indian jasmine. The way the harvest is organized is also critical, since it determines how well the flower's scent is preserved (flowers are usually harvested at dawn).

†Animal essences include the suave and very sensual musk, produced by the musk deer living in the Himalayas and Siberia; ambergris, mainly found off the shores of Portugal, is a warm and subtle essence with oceanic tones that the sperm whale naturally excretes into the sea; a strong and warm essence produced by the civet cat, a small animal living in Ethiopia; and castoreum, a leathery substance obtained from Russian and Canadian beavers. Today, animal scents are often replaced by synthetics in observation of the growing number of animal protection regulations (Great Britain has banned animal essences altogether).

* * *

WHEN I VISITED a perfume plant, I was struck by the juxtaposition of cold metallic machinery and computerized systems with the delicate wafting of evanescent flowers. In the alchemist's shop, once "the organ," a table resembling the musical instrument, housed all the scents necessary to create perfumes. Today, the organ has been replaced by laboratories filled with molecular-analyzing computers able to sniff out thousand of complex new scents. Perfume operations combine both old and new technologies. For example, one of the oldest methods of creating perfume is through distillation, in which odorous molecules are separated out through evaporation by means of an alembic. Distillation is still a popular method today. During the Middle Ages, distillation was merely used to collect the water distilled from flowers and plants. During the Renaissance, it was discovered that the residue oil, not the distilled water, embodied the quintessence of the plants' scents. Since not all flowers respond to this method, other techniques were developed. *Enfleurage,* for example, was first used by the Egyptians. It consists of laying out freshly picked flowers on glass frames coated with a layer of odorless fat. The flowers are regularly replaced until the fat is impregnated with the flower's essence. In 1880, a new method was developed to extract fragrances from plants with only faint aromas, such as dry materials, bark, or roots. The process, called volatile solvent extraction, works like distillation. The aromatic materials are placed over perforated trays inside extractors to allow the solvent to suck away the odorous molecules. This extraction produces a perfumed fat, the *pommade,* which is processed until a waxy material, the *concrete,* is obtained and then purified with alcohol to produce the *absolute,* the essence from which the perfume is created.

Synthetic scents have revolutionized the manufacturing of perfumes and ignited the industry's growth. Synthetic oils are not only cheaper, they are also free of any uncertainty in terms of crop outcomes, so the supply is guaranteed and readily available (unlike current difficulties in importing oak moss and lavender from the former Yugoslavia or resinous fragrances from Somalia). However, synthetic reproduction is not easy. The chemical oil must come as close as possible to the natural counterpart (an essential oil extracted from a flower or plant may include as many as six hundred components, some in trace amounts measured in as parts per million). From this, a score of new scents that do not exist in nature are created. No conflict exists between natural and synthetic scents, since each has its own properties and olfactory characteristics. Natural oils are more discreet and complex in structure, somewhat like the human makeup, which may explain their sensual appeal. With a subtle richness and faint odor, natural oils are predominantly used to "round out" and "soften" the harshness of man-made materials. Some customers prefer natural fragrances, believing they are healthier for the skin. Yet, with such growth in the perfume business, purely natural fragrances can no longer meet the demand.

MUCH IN THE SAME WAY we can smell something only when it starts to evaporate, we can taste* things only as they be-

*We taste through some 10,000 buds. Judging by this fact alone, you could say we are animals of poor taste, if compared to a cow, with some 25,000 buds, or a rabbit, with its 17,000 buds. Those 25,000 taste buds allow that cow to turn

gin to dissolve into liquids with the help of our saliva. Foods are usually smelled before they enter the mouth. This, in itself, is enough to make one salivate, which, in turn, triggers the process of dissolving the food for easier digestion. Taste is usually the combination of the four basic perceptions (sweet, sour, salt, and bitter) plus one or two secondary ones. There is, however, more than just pure flavor in the taste of food.* Color, shape, presentation, smell, texture, temperature, and "bite" (spiciness) also come into play. That's why chefs try to titillate as many senses as possible.

I ask Daniel Boulud, owner of the prized New York restau-

---

what we may consider the same boring fodder into one great meal. If we can assume this observation is correct (nobody has yet interviewed a cow), one big question comes up. Where exactly is the essence of a great meal: in the succulent dishes prepared by a creative chef or in the taste buds that Nature has provided us? The answer falls somewhere in the middle, since, like all of our other senses, taste is partly genetic and partly enhanced through years dedicated to eating and training.

*Each culture considers different foods to be aphrodisiacs. In the Far East, the rhinoceros's horn and the tiger's testicles are prized for their supposed aphrodisiac properties (these two unfortunate animals now top the highly endangered species list as a result). Europeans, who, today, are considered to be more civilized and more respectful of fellow animals (bull testicle soup is a custom of the past), attribute those sexual enhancing properties only to the innocuous truffle. Potency has never been a cheap quality, and truffles sell for as much as one thousand dollars per kilo (still less than an average trip to the plastic surgeon), not too shabby for a potato (truffles belong to the tuberous or potato family). But truffles are potatoes with a rather impressive pedigree. Greeks believed truffles were the upshot of thunder. Mighty Napoleon was believed to have conceived his only legitimate son after feasting on truffles. Truffles, unlike common potatoes, are hard to find. Production is limited to Perigord, in southwest France, famous for its black truffles, and Alba in Piedmont, or Tuscany in Italy, where white truffles grow.

rant Daniel and the new Café Boulud, who has worked with some of the best chefs, such as George Blanc, Roger Verger, and Michel Gerard, what it takes to be a great chef.

"You need a hearty gastronomic education, joined by a perseverance in researching the produce quality, the precision and consistency of various recipes and preparations. You must develop a very sensible palate, which can judge quickly, you need to smell, see, feel, and hear. You need to be very emotional and sensitive, yet also disciplined and rigorous. And you must be very ambitious, so you can gain access to quality and master it."

When designing a new menu, Daniel is inspired by the pro-

Most recently, the crazed demand and steep prices have stimulated the production of cultivated truffles. It is difficult to determine whether truffles really have an aphrodisiac property, yet, in some ways, they are linked to elements of sexuality. They carry twice as much androstenone (a male pig hormone) as is found in a male pig, and androstenone is involved in the reproductive activities of the swine (thus it is not startling that sows have been the preferred truffle hunters for centuries). There is a close chemical similarity between pig pheromone and human male hormone, which may explain why man finds truffles so arousing.

Sexual arousal is not the only thing that declares a meal outstanding. The exhilaration of a death wish can also make a meal something to die for. The *fugu* or blowfish is a favorite Japanese dish, better known for its poison than for its taste. The preparation of this deadly fish requires very special care in the cleaning of its fillets so that its poison is thoroughly removed. So demanding is the preparation that, in Japan, it is considered an art. The slightest oversight on the chef's part and the courageous diner is dead even before he can get to dessert or, for that matter, pay his bill. That is precisely the lure of this frightening dish: the chance to actually taste death. The most respected *fugu* chefs are those who leave the slightest trace of poisonous taste, just enough to titillate the lips with death, without (literally) losing the customer. Eating *fugu* may be considered a perversely aesthetic experience: heightening the senses through the fear of death.

duce. "Each time I work on a new menu, I take the list of all produce from the upcoming season and I start to think about possible combinations. For me, the produce defines the inspiration. At times, I am also inspired by a particular taste I want to reproduce. For example, in the spring we like making a refreshing iced soup consisting of a bouillabaisse base yet softer and more refined in taste than the usual fishy one. Thus, we use lobster and bind it with seasonal cranberry beans to accentuate the flavor and give it a velvety texture. This mélange of flavors produces the equilibrium.

"I am also inspired by cuisine of the past: recipes from the seventeenth or eighteenth centuries nourish my inspiration. When I design a new dish, the importance is a harmony of taste, the marriage of textures. There are several levels to savoring, which you can discover while eating a dish. I search for freshness and a variety of tastes that marry well, yet nothing so shocking as to be overwhelming. Creation usually takes place in the kitchen, very spontaneously. The best dishes are usually the most spontaneous. The most extraordinary moment comes from that spontaneity and the uncertainty of the intuition, the pleasure of tasting something I have never savored before. I constantly think about experimentation, so much so that in the new kitchen in the new restaurant I will create a small research laboratory and have a chef who only does research, the study of recipes and their preparation."

It is the team that makes a restaurant great. "When I build a team, I always look for young people who are willing to go through sacrifices and tough training because their ambition is to become the best. They must have the passion and a surplus of patience. The great restaurant is not only the product of the chef who is the visionary responsible for creating it, but also the team spirit. I give freedom to the individuals, be they in the kitchen or out on the dining-room floor. I want each individual to be their own style of person. I will never try to stereotype them into a service style. They, of course, need to follow the same service rules, communication rules, and harmony in the functioning of the service and be as precise as possible. I let the chefs express themselves because it is very important for them to feel their own creativity and know that they are a great asset to the company. Even the *garçon,* responsible for making the coffee, must feel proud of his work. It is the many small details that, when linked together, make a great restaurant. At Daniel, each person feels they have participated in the restaurant's success. My fear is whether we will be able to be as successful in twenty years without compromising quality.

"The wine cellar is also crucial, since certain foods, when coupled with a particular wine, make an unforgettable experience. Wine is indispensable to good cooking because it elevates flavors to a new level. You taste a particular food, savoring the flavor of the dish, then, by drinking a good wine, you can reinvigorate the dish. Wine is extraordinary in taste, not to mention the fact that its acidity helps us digest food."

A knowledgeable and creative team makes a great restaurant or any dream experience. Creators coach their collaborators, building an excitement that fuels them to push hard and sacrifice. The creator trains them to perfect their craft and hone their taste. With the precision to recognize those slightest details that add so much depth to the overall emotional experience and the freedom to let them experiment, the creator is the patron of creativity.

* * *

WINE* combines our olfactory sense with our sense of taste. Quite simply, wine is the juice of grapes, nothing but rain recovered from the ground by the plant that bears grapes, the vine. As the vine grows older, its roots penetrate deeper into the ground in search of a steady water supply, acquiring new substances from the richer and more diverse soils. The vine therefore improves with age, reaching its prime production time between twelve and forty years. To produce their prized fruit, vines need large quantities of light and water, a warm climate, relatively humid air, and significant care to protect them from nature's capricious ways. Here, quality is undoubtedly related to quantity: The greatest wine can only be produced by substantially limited crops, achieved by pruning back the vine.

THE MOST IMPORTANT FACTOR in determining a wine's quality is the ripeness of its grapes. As the grape ripens, its acidity decreases and its sugar increases. The grape should ideally be picked when acidity and sugar reach a balance. The grape

*Dating back to before history was even recorded, wine first appeared as early as 6000 B.C., in Mesopotamia. From there, it flowed into Egypt and Greece, then Rome, up through Italy, and eventually into France, Spain, and Portugal after 1000 B.C. Noah, our biblical flood victim, has traditionally been called the first wine grower and, apparently was an avid imbiber. During the Middle Ages, grape selections and various styles of wine that exist even today were first introduced. The Church, with its keen appreciation for what is good in life, held wine to be among the most sacred splendors. Among its many cathedrals, monasteries, and religious orders, the Church also created and owned most of the greatest vineyards in Europe. Wine was a major fixture not only in religion (Christ changed water into wine and wine represents the blood of Christ), but also in daily life, where it was deemed the celebrated drink of social and family events. Wine finally reached a larger audience in the later seventeenth century with the invention of the glass bottle.

juice turns miraculously into wine through a natural process of fermentation. Left to nature, all wine would be dry, with the sugar converting into alcohol. However, it is possible to stop fermentation before all of the sugar is converted (adding sulfur, filtering to remove yeast, and so forth), which enables the winemaker to decide which type of wine to produce: red (red grapes fermented with the skins that give the color), white (white or red grapes fermented without the skins), rosé (red grapes only initially fermented with the skins), sweet, dry, or sparkling (white wine that is bottled before fermentation is completed).

WINE IS THE COMPLEX SYNTHESIS of materials the vine has drawn from its surrounding natural environment, like acids and sugars, minerals and pigments, phenols and tannins, and even the elements the grapes have absorbed from the oak barrel. Wood is an agent of change. The most sophisticated oaks, like the slow-growing Troncais, strongly influence wine's aroma and flavor. This synthesis has a life of its own and requires patience and plenty of time to evolve into a harmonious wholeness of breed, body, and maturity, the ultimate expression of wine's nobility. Wine's catharsis continues even after the precious liquid is enshrined in its bottle, as infinitesimal amounts of oxygen enkindle its maturity. To reach greatness, wine therefore needs life's most fundamental and precious elements: time, light, and air.*

Weather threatens winemaking with its uncertainty. The cli-

*How fitting that one of France's greatest scientists, Louis Pasteur, should discover in 1863 oxygen's influence on wine: Too much contact with the air encourages the growth of vinegar bacteria, while the most minimal amounts of air cause the wine to mature.

matic conditions from bud-break to harvest are what determine the final quality of the vintage. Since quality is always difficult to achieve, the finest wines are those most affected by the unpredictability of the weather, such as the famous *vins de garde,* the *crus classés* of the Bordeaux region. Their greatness comes from their geography: Favorable conditions provide natural controls such as soils rich with minerals and water. These soils have improved over many centuries thanks to the winemakers' keen and nurturing attention. In these special regions, the winemaker is more "the midwife than the creator," helping nature express the supreme quality of the wine. The less the wine is manipulated, the finer the results. It seems *"the ultimate art of the enologist is to learn when to do nothing."* When this is mastered, the wine's color captures us as much as its liquid eases over our palate.

Count Gelasio Gaetani Lovatelli D'Aragona comes from a family that, for centuries, has been dedicated to the art of making wine. "Great wine can only come from a single vineyard that has slowly developed over the years, from vines whose roots have slowly expanded their reach (growing two meters a year) in order to draw more and more from the soil around them. What is most fascinating about wine is how similar it is to the human being. A son or daughter who has received a profound education based on strong grounds continues to grow without the need for high maintenance. Similarly, a vine will continue over the years to produce a good wine without too much experimentation. One knows which plants will bear the best grapes, just as in a family one knows which members can be counted on most. The best plants will be cloned (a piece of the old is grafted into the new) in order to preserve their qualities in the years to come.

"Today a plethora of well-made wines are born of manipulation, the offspring of continuous mixing of musts from many different vineyards. To gain commercial success, many winemakers like to experiment with different grapes to adapt their product to the changing market tastes. Their wine, alas, is born out of an insecurity and never develops any real personality. The truly great wine, however, exceeds the organoleptic taste of a given moment. For example, the great French winemakers have spent centuries developing a knowledge based on continual experimentation. Now they have ceased to experiment, knowing that from their vines they have already unlocked the best possible type of wine. Their creativity, however, has not run dry. Even if there is no more experimentation, they still must creatively orchestrate the many elements so influential in winemaking. Pure quality is born of the relationship between the gifts of Nature, the scientific know-how of the enologist, and the owner's own emotions and taste. It is the owner who selects from the entire crop which wine is destined to become great and which (the majority) is to become the second label."

In the complex business of creating outstanding products, sometimes a company has to learn when it's best to do nothing at all. For example, experimentation should not only acquiesce to the changing market tastes. This insecurity translates directly to the creation, since the product, or in this case the wine, can never fully develop any real personality.

PRODUCTS, no matter how fantastic they are, succeed only if they can stimulate our senses. The more senses that are stimulated, the more powerful the experience of the dream product or service. Understanding the product complexities associated with, say, jewels, perfumes, and wine means better appreciating the creative effort that goes into making these apparently simple products so emotionally special.

The technological revolution has also influenced the making of dreams. While in the past it was the hands of the skilled craftsmen who shaped dream products, today those hands have been replaced by advanced technologies and computers. What was once a gifted craftsman's chance intuition is now a company's continuous and organized search for innovation. Craftsmanship alone cannot tackle today's production volume. Technology must help improve handicraft production. Today's automation frees workers to better spend their time and skills on tasks at which machines can't compete. Companies now can optimize their creative resources while still controlling costs through the use of modern production technologies. The term "handmade" may no longer be entirely accurate, but the emotional input is there to stay. For example, deep in the labyrinth of corridors that snakes forty-four kilometers under Epernay, Burgundy, France, the gourmand monks of the past have been replaced by a maze of conveyor belts and robots responsible for opening cases of wine and microwave ovens where the heart of the corks are heated. Bottles are cleaned of impurities, filled, corked, and cased at a rapid-fire seventy thousand a day under vigilant electronic eyes. The stocking center, spreading over six levels and sheltering as many as 2 million bottles, is entirely computer-operated. Man's involvement is now limited to quality control and tasting. Champagne production has, however, not lost its charm. Automation here still pales compared to what mass-consumption companies can fire off. Alongside the most sophisticated robots, computers, and automatic production lines are still numerous craftsmen at work in this industry, balancing cutting-edge technology with their skilled handiwork. In some cases, handmade now means hand-finished, when the craftsman adds his special finishing touches to the object produced on an automated line.

As Piero Ferrari, the perceptive son of Enzo Ferrari, explains, "Automotive production technologies have made such improvements that today automatization has reached much higher quality standards with much more rigid and better-controlled tolerance levels than strictly handmade production systems." What has become critical is the thinking behind the entire project. In the past, the genius went into both conceiving a product and making it with skilled hands. Today, with machines replacing hands in the manufacturing of a Ferrari, the conception has become much more critical and now includes foreseeing, from the very inception of the project, all those production issues that were once addressed during the production process. Systems like CAD (computer-aided design) help engineers imagine, conceive, design, test, and verify a new Ferrari in virtual reality, long before they build the first prototype. Without the engineer's vision, the computer could never build an automobile as emotional as a Ferrari. If, in production, machines are more precise and efficient than man, man still plays a major role in the critical preproduction stage, and in determining the driving characteristics.

Ferrari invests almost 20 percent of its sales in Formula One racing and less than 0.5 percent in marketing. This distribution of financial resources would be considered suicidal in any other automobile company. However, racing plays a major role in the building of the Ferrari organization. F-1 racing is the most advanced type of racing, so advanced that the Ferrari F-1 department builds parts for NASA, the American space program.

* * *

As Mr. Ferrari explains: "More than 20 percent of Ferrari's workforce is employed in the F-1 department. My father built Ferrari exclusively as a racing-car company, creating racecars not only for F-1 but for all possible types of racing. Since racing is so expensive, with a huge R&D budget required, he was soon obliged to build street cars for very wealthy customers to finance his racing activity."

Racing, perhaps the sport that most ignites the dreams of the masses, has made Ferrari the most famous automobile company in the world. Racing has also infused our company with a very positive spirit, the spirit to constantly improve our performance, since racing never lets you stand still. It has disciplined us to measure our performances against an indisputable judge: time. Any new model must beat its predecessor around the testing track in less time.

Only then do we know we have objectively improved our performance. New models are not born out of revolutions but rather from constant evolution and improvements. Even though we sell technological dreams, customers have to be ready to accept them. Racing is a different matter. F-1 is so extreme that not all technologies developed can be transferred to the production of sports cars. For example, the carbon brakes are extremely light and can stop a car much better than anything else, yet they work only at very high temperatures, thus they are impossible to use in road-going cars.

"F-1 is fantastic for inspiring new ideas, creative stimuli, and scientific rigor in our young engineers. Those who are trained in F-1 and go on to design road-going Ferraris *'hanno una marcia in più'* [have that one extra gear]. Their minds are more intense, creative, and purposeful than their colleagues'. This is the most important contribution offered by being exposed to an extreme world!"

I had to know: "What is the Ferrari of your dreams, Piero?"

"My father always answered that question, 'It is the one I haven't built yet.' His mind was always looking toward the future. I believe mine would be the automobile that drives like a Ferrari, is beautiful like a Ferrari, and can be driven every day. I dream of a technology that allows us to dream every day."

While racing has become one of the most popular and effective ways of promoting and advertising products, for Ferrari, it still represents the best medium wherein to experiment with extreme conditions and forge toward perfection.

WHILE HARDLY BLESSED WITH the romantic image of the craftsman, computers and advanced technology do not interfere with the fundamental *raison d'être* of this industry: to reach the highest expression of creativity. On the contrary, these are indispensable tools that free the craftsman to dedicate all of his energies to his creations without the distraction of menial tasks. Computers, after all, have not encroached on man's most valuable freedom: creativity.*

* * *

*Computers may, in the future, help better redistribute the chance to create: Much as the Colt revolver in the Old West that gave even the weakest man an equal chance to fight against the strongest, computers could reduce the creative barriers by minimizing the experience component of creativity (for example, one might be able to paint without learning the technique). Is it possible to be an artist without technical knowledge? Where would the aesthetic value lie?

MOST OF THE COMPANIES in the business of selling dreams are small and flexible organizations, conducive to creative work. Even if they often reach significant sales volumes, they usually turn to outsourcing to lighten the load of production. The Italian fashion industry is the foremost example of outsourcing highly creative production. This industry owes its success partly to its essentially family-owned structure, in which today more than 70 percent of the workers are employed by companies with fewer than ten people. These small companies are supported by various consortiums, integrated networks that absorb production and provide working capital and the latest in research and development. The consortiums also purvey all marketing and commercial services that would otherwise not be available to those small companies due to their limited resources. Thus, creativity is often centrally developed, then shared through a computerized system with direct access to the various companies' machinery. Operating as a close network, these small companies can adjust to today's unstable environment, each one specializing in certain parts of the community's value chain. This electronic network helps each company concentrate on what it does best, allowing for efficient use of production equipment, reduction of fixed costs, and maximization of the creative and research effort (the last being equally distributed among the vast number of small companies that would otherwise not have access to these processes). This organized network, which, to a lesser degree, is also shared by other sectors (the high-end watch industry in Switzerland, the leather manufactures near Florence, the fashion industry in the Paris region, the movie industry in Hollywood, and so forth), effectively preserves the centuries-old system of craft production that still propels these small companies. It ensures future growth, with new technologies continuing to be centrally developed, while its great flexibility fosters individual experimentation and has secured the continuity of knowledge passed on from craftsman to craftsman over the centuries. This strategic wealth could have otherwise vanished due to the cyclical nature of the luxury business, which is always very sensitive to economic downswings. In other industries, during recessions, employees would have been fired or recycled into other areas of business, their knowledge lost forever. These craftsmen provide this industry with invaluable expertise that can hardly be replaced by cheaper labor from emerging economies.

Any company looking to succeed in the business of selling dreams looks to maximize its creativity. Building small and flexible organizations is instrumental in freeing collaborators from the adverse effects of excessive controls and bureaucracy.

DREAMS ARE A PERCEPTION. Because customers today are sophisticated, their perceptions have also grown more acute. They can no longer be influenced purely by a seductive message. The message must be substantiated by an outstanding product or service, rich with emotions and aesthetic value. For example, isn't it easier to be seduced by a bottle of Estée Lauder perfume than by a cheap whiff of apple-scented fragrance, or by a dinner inspirationally prepared by Daniel Boulud than a bowl of canned soup? Since seduction is more an art than a science, it draws its inspiration from an emotional environment rather than one of rationality. Understanding the exceptional quality that companies operating in this business infuse into their products and services leads us to search beyond the world of reason and into dissertations on emotions, senses, and passions. These highly unusual business book topics mark our obligatory path into the nature of this industry.

Many dream products are purchased for their symbolism rather than for their aesthetic value. But what is it about the way these products are created that captivates us so? Understanding the senses they stimulate and what motivates a team of creative and knowledgeable individuals is critical. Great products always require a labor of love. In these organizations, because the desire to create beauty precedes the need for financial rewards, artistic experimentation is not clipped by overly stringent cost controls. This discipline generates a "benevolent cycle" within the organization, in which more creative jobs attract creative people, which, in return, makes their collaborators more creative. Dreams are born because employees are encouraged to dream.

One common denominator that the successful companies operating in this business all share is a passion and dedication to the products they make. This cultural determination to create beautiful things breeds a type of organization dedicated to aesthetic experimentation, originality, and a fervent attention to details. What these outstanding products and services teach us is that long-term excellence resounds when the collaborators' passion for their work is met by an engaging creative environment that supports and encourages. Much like creators, who have spent lifetimes sharpening their senses and intellects to respond to their cultural environment, so must organizations learn how to feel and understand what excites the customer. Creators alone cannot create dreams, they can only inspire them. To transform their ideas into "commercial" dream products and services, creators must build a team of highly skilled individuals, just like Benuzzi at Ferrari, Cesaretti with Michael Mann, Garcia in the Cuban cigar factory, or Buccellati's engraver. Ensuring that their distinct and original taste will live on within the organization even after the creator has gone means developing a "memory" that is eternalized in the company's archives and thrives throughout the organization.

Creating dreams means producing beauty of an artistic caliber. Yet, unlike the beauty of art, this beauty is not about extremes or a revolution in originality. The goal here is not to glorify the creator, but to elate the customer. As Ferrari proves, even in the technologically advanced world of sports automobiles a dream product cannot represent a revolution but must represent a progressive evolution, since customers must be ready to accept and appreciate it. While creativity in art is often inspired by the artist's ego, in the business of selling dreams, creativity flows from the entire organization's desire to listen to its customers and encourage their imagination.

CREATORS AND THEIR COLLABORATORS can only create if they are supported by the owners of the company. Creating requires a long-term vision, not a common quality among shareholders, financial analysts, or financial directors. In the next chapter, we will determine which type of financial thinking a company requires to succeed in the business of selling dreams.

7

Financing Creativity

THROUGHOUT THIS BOOK we have shown how important emotions are in this industry. Succeeding in the business of selling dream products and services requires a creativity of an artistic nature that entwines the passions and the senses of the entire organization. However, unlike art, where the primary goal is to create beauty, here the focus is making a business. Therefore, all of these emotions must be rigorously channeled. Usually it is the financial department that must enforce this strict work discipline in any given organization. After all, it's hardly by chance that one of the greatest American clichés is "bottom line," meaning the only thing that really matters at "the end of the day" is the final line of the income statement. Financial people are often uninterested in how, when, or why, but yet they are completely fixated on the final result. Though the bottom line may be the gospel in many industries, in the business of selling dreams it does not tell the entire story. Here, profits must come from selling products and services that express the company's aesthetic values. In this business, the financial department must overcome the addiction to the traditional bottom line and short term that has plagued so many financial managers, shareholders, and analysts.

CREATING A PRODUCT or a service that ignites a dream tremendously affects the bottom line. As already discussed, dream products and services usually enjoy a very high added value, which translates directly into higher profits. Profits are maximized because the added value is maximized. To create those products, the company's financial directives must focus on the long term and allow the organization to take risks. It takes time for a company to pull together the expertise and credibility needed to create dream products and services. It also requires taking risks to experiment with the different aesthetic solutions that can stir our emotions and create the essence of a company's original taste. Without the time for long-term thinking or risk-taking, it is virtually impossible for a company to consistently create dreams. The financial department, in this case, must shatter the short-term, risk-avoidance mold in favor of risk-taking and the long term.

SELLING THE MOVIE IDEA *Titanic* to studios was the hardest part of Jim Cameron's job. Make a movie where everybody knows the ending and it isn't even a happy one? All the studios thought this guy was on the seaward side of reason. While Rupert Murdoch, owner of the film's production company, trusted Cameron's past successes, such as *Aliens, Terminator,* and *Terminator 2,* he was not ready to spend more than the already titanic budget of $120 million. Hollywood productions have become so outrageously expensive that a single flop can financially swamp a production company for several years. Look at Carolco, which rode high on its *Rambo* and *Lethal Weapon* hits only to bleed itself to death on the $92 million bomb *Cutthroat Island. Waterworld,* the 1995 $175 million floating flop, was another example of a near miss. Universal did squeak out with $225 million grosses worldwide, but that was a very disappointing squeak for what was then dubbed the most expensive movie ever.

Many critics believed that the movie *Titanic* was doomed to set sail on the same catastrophic course as the famous ship. Far from sinking the movie's financial supporters, Cameron's vision and fanatical determination propelled Viacom (the parent company of Paramount Pictures) and especially Rupert Murdoch's News Corporation (the parent company of Twentieth Century Fox) into the upper business stratosphere. Michael Mann, speaking more as a producer than a director, believes that "Rupert Murdoch's position globally has been improved by the *Titanic* success. His standing and ability to make deals now goes way beyond the already impressive financial benefits that the film has generated. His new title as 'head of the company that made the movie *Titanic*' may benefit him in terms of many other unrelated opportunities, even, say, as far as making a deal in China or a satellite operation in another part of the world."

Titanic, apart from being a perfectly executed film, can also be praised as the highest-grossing film ever. The risk News Corporation took brought such success that it completely changed the company's future. *Titanic* is an excellent example of a "product" that has ignited people's dreams.

In the scientific world of pharmaceuticals, Pfizer leads the way. Even if its 1997 sales were only $12.5 billion, half the sales of its main competitor, Merck (with 1997 sales of $23.6 billion), its capitalization is nearly identical to Merck's, with its stock trading at almost sixty times estimated 1998 earnings (the average for the U.S. drug industry is about thirty times earnings). The main reason for this fantastic financial performance? Viagra, the first FDA-approved pill to treat impotence, has excited the imagination of financial markets as much as it has its elated customers. Wall Street analysts predict that sales for the potency medicine could reach $5 billion a year by the year 2001, making it, by far, the most-sold pill ever. Pfizer's market value has increased by 160 percent over the last twelve months, almost triple Merck's 60 percent increase over the same period. In the very competitive pharmaceutical business, the hardest thing is usually recovering new-product investments, since companies must undergo extensive tests on their new drugs to avoid harm to their customers or being rejected by the very strict FDA (Pfizer consistently spends 15 percent of sales in R&D).

Success comes not only from the discovery of blockbuster new drugs but also from their proper commercialization. William Steere, Pfizer's CEO, argues that "the benefits of truly novel medicines, the stuff of blockbusters, often don't register with busy doctors until they get the story from well-versed sales reps." No risk this time, since media worldwide, from talk shows to President Clinton jokes, tripped a worldwide orgy for Viagra.

Is Pfizer's huge success based on scientific and medical facts or on cashing in on man's dream of unyielding potency and eternal youth? One thing is certain: Viagra has satisfied the dreams of investors, who are excited by the fact that after just a few months it has become the most famous pill on earth, and that its potential market is also unlimited, since, unlike any other drug, it will also be copped by the mass of horny customers who do not need it, but perhaps need the fix (we will call these customers rather than patients). Certainly Viagra is effective, since it makes sex more spontaneous and romantic than other treatments, such as vacuum pumps, penile implants, penis rings, gel suppositories, or injections.* Yet Pfizer has boosted its commercial success with creative dreamketing. First, forgoing the drug's scientific name, sildenafil, Pfizer substituted a brand name exploding with sublimity. Chemists at Pfizer define the word Viagra as "redolent of both 'vigor' and 'Niagara.'" Second, Pfizer has ensured that its customers can enjoy their dream by eliminating any possible hangups, such as guilt. It has even gone as far as requesting (and receiving) the Vatican's unofficial blessing. Third, by skillfully guiding the media *battage,* it has promoted its wonder pill without offending our prudish society.

Viagra is an interesting example of how, even in an industry as scientific as pharmaceuticals, products that spark our imagination best contribute to a company's bottom line and long-term growth. Morally, it's disturbing to think that a study showing that tamoxifen can prevent breast cancer (which is estimated to kill

*Injectable drugs can produce an erection regardless of context, as famously proved by Dr. Giles Brindley, a leading British impotence researcher, who once demonstrated the success of his experimental treatment by dropping his trousers in front of hundreds of astonished colleagues at a conference.

43,500 women in the United States this year) was announced only days after Viagra's approval by the FDA in March and has received only a fraction of the potency drug's exposure. Yet this industry, while it sells hope to many ailing patients, unfortunately always conjures in our minds the disturbing implication that sooner or later we will all get sick and need medication. The truth is that the dreams of the masses are not excited by drugs that cure diseases (since, right or wrong, we all expect to be healthy), but rather by wonder drugs that make our lives more exciting or more fulfilling. The dream of immortality and youth is energizing the pharmaceutical industry. Already the most profitable industry in the Fortune 500, with worldwide sales of $300 billion, of which one-third is in the United States, the pharmaceutical industry could see its sales double over the next five years thanks to such lifestyle drugs. As Steere says, "It struck me that a quality-of-life drug for aging would be a real winner. Look at the volume in cosmetics, which are nostrums that don't really do anything." Thus, Pfizer is increasing its market value by selling a better lifestyle through chemistry. It pays to sell dreams!

WHILE THIS BOOK is filled with companies that have fulfilled their customer's dreams, we are not implying that this is an easy feat. In the majority of organizations the financial decisions that set the business direction are often not based on the creative thinking that dreams require. The risk-avoidance strategies that harness typical financial managers, large boards of directors, most shareholders, and financial analysts are not very conducive to dreams. Since the investments needed to launch new products have increased to dangerous levels, business failures are usually met with mortal losses or merciless decapitation.

When successful, however, they can enhance a company's future. Once a company sells a product or a service that fulfills customers' dreams, it achieves not only extraordinary commercial success but also company visibility, credibility, brand acclaim, and a red carpet to the future. The Beetle, the dream car of the flower generation that made Volkswagen internationally famous, still defines the German company after more than twenty years—so much so that a modern version of it has just been relaunched. It is still too early to tell whether the new "Bug" will be the cause of another financial celebration, yet the car has received so much press, based on its glorious past alone, that customer awareness is already skyrocketing (a reason to be happy, since gaining customer recognition requires the highest financial investment when launching a new product). Or just think about what the Walkman has done for Sony's worldwide recognition. By mobilizing music, the Walkman catapulted Sony into the consumer market. Or take the 1983 introduction of the cellular phone by Motorola. Mobile communication has made Motorola one of the most famous U.S. brands.

EXPOSURE, especially at such levels as that of *Titanic* or Viagra, has become crucial in boosting a company's market value, since it ensures visibility, brand recognition, and long-term credibility (News Corporation and Pfizer will go down in history for their blockbuster successes). This type of exposure comes only from challenging common business thinking. And this comes only if the company's financial structure can withstand a possible flop. Selling dream products and services requires a different type of business mentality, yet when a company succeeds, its future is "Niagara."

* * *

SELLING DREAMS offers one promise that is any businessman's dream: high profitability. While any company strives for high profitability, very few can easily achieve it. The more markets become saturated by hypercompetition, the more companies tend to outprice one another in order to attract new consumers and gain market share. Price wars are hardly the way for companies selling dreams to increase sales. Companies in this business appeal to the customers' emotional and even irrational behavior (the *Homo ludens*): The price tag is not the deciding factor in the satisfaction of dreams. Mass-consumption companies, on the other hand, rely on consumer rationale (the *Homo economicus*), where the best possible deal is what motivates people to buy. Companies that sell dream products and services generate high profit margins by maximizing the added value. The higher the added value perceived by the customers, the more willing they are to pay the price. The products and services with the highest emotional content are those with the highest added value. Just think about art. It is the foremost example, in any business, of the maximization of added value. What is it about a wooden frame, a swath of canvas with some paint dabbed on it by an artist who was willing to cut off his own ear? Van Gogh's *Portrait of Doctor Gachet* is a good example, having been auctioned off for $82.5 million.* Since a company that sells a dream is actually selling an experience rather than

*In May 1990—and within three minutes this van Gogh was auctioned off at Christie's to Ryoei Saito, Japan's second-largest paper manufacturer. *The Times* of London reports that Saito recently resold the painting for one-eighth the price paid.

simply a product, it has ample opportunity to influence and magnify its customers' perception of the added value.

ONE OF THE MOST enlightening examples of how selling emotions can maximize gross margins is represented by the luxury industry. What's interesting about luxury companies is that while they command the highest prices, originally they were designed as organizations wherein artists could devote their time to creating beauty rather than solely generating cash. Price was not an issue as long as the company could satisfy its customers' most demanding requests. Never seeking primarily to operate at very low costs, these companies were certainly not the most economically efficient. Yet luxury companies have usually managed higher margins on sales than their mass-consumption counterparts, since they have historically based their entire business strategy on maximizing the added value to the customers by creating the ultimate products and services rather than the most affordable. In a wealthy society like ours, customers tend more and more to seek value in outstanding quality rather than in low prices. In a sense, the luxury company's main purpose is to sway customer attention away from the price issue. The high price could almost be considered a quality, bestowing exclusivity on the product and social distinction on the purchaser. This explains why the luxury segment should be, by nature, the most profitable of any business endeavor (if selling, say, computers were the most profitable business, then selling luxury computers would be even more so). Louis Vuitton, with its profits in excess of 40 percent of sales, is a perfect example of the high profitability found in the luxury business. This does not mean, however, that all luxury companies are that successful, since their market or policies might prevent them from reaching such results.

THE FOLLOWING TABLE offers comparative margins between indicative publicly traded luxury and mass-consumption companies.

Luxury		Mass-Consumption	
Jewels			
Tiffany	54.2%	Finlay	52.0%
Watches			
Movado	55.9%*	Citizen	33.6%
Fashion			
Christian Dior	42.1%	Liz Claiborne	39.5%
Shoes			
Gucci	63.7%*	Nine West	43.0%
Perfume			
Estée Lauder	77.1%	French Fragrances	33.0%
Luggage			
Louis Vuitton	46.0%	Samsonite	39.4%
Art of the Table			
Baccarat	41.3%	Williams-Sonoma	39.2%
Art of the House			
Poltrona Frau	42.4%	Ethan Allen	40.3%
Automobiles			
Ferrari	23.4%	Ford	19.4%
Hotels			
Ritz	12.1%	Marriott	6.2%
Food			
Petrossian Beluga	41.6%	Heinz	36.6%
Beverage			
Dom Perignon	51.2%	Coca-Cola	63.7%
Tobacco			
Consolidated Cigars	40.4%	Philip Morris	51.3%
Books			
Rizzoli	47.6%	Barnes & Noble	35.9%

*Estimated.

Luxury companies consistently post higher margins than the corresponding mass-consumption companies, explaining why mass-production companies are so eager to increase their margins by entering niche markets where they don't compete on price alone. While their accelerated growth has forced luxury companies to reach a wider customer base through products and services sold at more democratic prices, efficiencies in production and distribution have maintained their high margins.

Interestingly, Philip Morris and Coca-Cola have posted even higher margins than corresponding luxury companies: They may not sell luxury, yet they certainly do not sell commodities. Yes, Philip Morris sells cigarettes. Avid antismokers may suggest that consumer addiction to nicotine is the reason smokers are willing to pay a high price for their vice, yet even us fervid nonsmokers can agree that the success of Philip Morris might also come from the company's creation of such fantastic brands as Marlboro, which inspires much more than the simple need to smoke.

Likewise, Coca-Cola is not only selling a drink. Around the world, Coke has become an icon of the American Dream. Consumers may drink the soda because they are thirsty, yet they choose Coke over other brands because its powerful brand tantalizes their imagination.

Achieving high margins is the goal of any company. It is becoming more difficult due to the overwhelming saturation in many markets. To consistently achieve it means building a credible and exciting brand that can command premium pricing.

TARGETING THE HIGH-PRICED BRACKET is not easy work. The customer must be kept emotionally "hooked" at all times. In a sense, it is easier to increase margins by reducing costs, a most successful strategy in the past when the entire Industrial Revolution prospered on ceaseless cost cuts through increased volumes and improved production and distribution efficiencies. The latest wave in re-engineering has also increased company profits by optimizing the way companies are managed. The future might make it harder to increase profits based on these strategies, since companies themselves are already operating at optimal levels and consumers are now more attracted to low-volume, differentiated products. The relative shift in business cost structures is also making shaving expenses tougher. Because marketing costs, traditionally more complex to shrink, have become the most substantial costs for many businesses, achieving efficiencies is more and more challenging. It is certainly easier to recognize the improved efficiency of producing a given car in seven hours instead of twelve than it is to assess what happens as a result of an equivalent 42 percent drop in marketing costs: Is the message still as strong, does it reach the same number of consumers, and the right ones, is it as successful at building brand credibility?

OUTSIDE OF THE COMMODITY BUSINESS, a strategy based strictly on cutting cost is the sign of weak brand management and failing business vision. GM, the largest car company in the world, may now suffer from this ailment. Just like dry cleaners and hot dog stands, GM is also battling its eroding market share by waging rebate war. Yet its market share continues to slide, having gone from 58 percent in 1978 to almost 30 percent in 1998. While GM still has the best cost structure in the industry, its financial results are proportionally lower than those of its two main competitors, Ford and Chrysler, since the company seems to have lost the keys to car buyers' imaginations.

In comparison, Chrysler, a company legendary for its bout with bankruptcy, has increased its market share from 12 percent to a healthy 16 percent over the same twenty-year period. In spite of a less favorable cost structure, Chrysler's success comes from revving customers' interest and fulfilling their desires: First, Chrysler launched the mini-van, like prophets of the future family's desire for leisure time; then they went off-road with the Jeep, leading the sport utility pack. Both segments have been the fastest-growing in the automotive industry. Chrysler even managed to perform triage on the nearly dead Dodge brand by bringing us a dream car, the Viper, winning priceless exposure, and by launching other exciting models.

Discounting may be a short-term defensive tactic. It cannot be the business strategy that drives a company into the future. Through aggressive discounts, GM may momentarily fend off its competitors' market-share gains. To reverse this twenty-year slip, GM must throw off some sparks and learn how to launch something new and exciting in its automotive concepts. Discounts add up to one heavy toll on brand credibility. GM is not the only company to struggle with this. While price incentives totaled 8 percent of a car's sticker price a decade ago, they are up to 16 percent today. Cars no longer rank as high as they used to. Before they came in third (after a long foreign trip and owning a house) on a wish list compiled by CNW, while today they rank at only twelfth. If the industry cannot rev up its customers' imaginations, cars will be stalled in the commodities–low margins lane.

* * *

FROM THE FINANCIAL STANDPOINT, selling dreams requires managers to shift their business approach, incorporating a compromise between the traditional finance fixation with the short term, risk avoidance, and cost-cutting and the long-term, risk-fascination, and quality-driven mentality that dream creations require. David Pecker is the president of Hachette Filipacchi, the publishing company responsible for *Elle, George,* and *Mirabella,* among many other magazines. His financial background, and his successful career of restructuring and launching new magazines, makes him an authority on this subject.

"What is often difficult to understand is that, for a magazine that sells dreams, like *Elle,* success hinges on enhancing the readers' dream rather than achieving the ultimate cost efficiency. Aside from the editorial quality, it is also the quality of the paper, the ink, the photography, the styling, and combining all that creativity together that makes *Elle* so desirable. Even if the cost of a single page is more than ten times the cost of a page in other beauty magazines, we have to make that investment so that the reader feels she's in the front row at the runway catwalks when she picks up our magazine. It is difficult for financial people to understand all of these expenses, yet to cut any quality-related costs would result in a dangerous drop in the readership. The value of *Elle* is not in selling news, it is in selling dreams. That's why it requires distinct credibility.

"We are in a risky business: of the more than 660 new magazines launched over the past three years in the United States, only 5 percent are still being published today. Making a magazine is similar to making a movie: You have to finish it before you see the results. You need five years before you can assess the success. The cost of launching a new magazine is, on average, between $25 million and $50 million. To reduce the risks, we work with thresholds. First, we do a direct mailing to evaluate the response rate. If the targeted response rate is achieved, we invest the initial $10 million. If the project continues on target, we invest an additional $10 million, and so on. Success may come after substantial risks have been taken. For example, in 1989 I launched *Elle Decor* in the United States, a high-end prestige magazine targeted to the woman interested in international home design. Our biggest challenge was convincing the financial people to spend $15 million over the first nine months in order to promote the magazine. We had to invest heavily so we could build awareness through the organization of numerous events, ranging from private homes to museum designs. We were, after all, competing against two established institutions, Condé Nast's *House and Garden* and Condé Nast's *Architectural Digest.* We also had to build the credibility that would enable us to seize the exclusivity away from our competitors in order to present the dream houses people wanted to read about. After all, *Elle Decor* does not sell furniture, it sells a dream, the aspiration toward a certain lifestyle. When a reader see a beautiful estate in Palm Beach, a penthouse in Manhattan or Paris, a castle in England, or a villa in Italy, she admires the shapes, the colors, the mix of styles and tries to reproduce them in her own home, even if using much less expensive materials. Without an architect or a decorator she can re-create her own dream house and feel she has something in common with those multi-million-dollar homes. After a total investment of $22 million, in 1997 we achieved a circulation of 425,000 copies and eight hundred advertising pages a year and earned up to $2 million."

I was curious to learn what makes a magazine successful.

"There are two key points that determine the success of a magazine: the level of circulation and the advertising—not only its quantity, but most important, its quality, which is as important as the editorial. A magazine that sells dreams has to be consistent. It also has to advertise dreams, lest it lose its appeal."

I wondered whether the Internet and all the on-line services were bringing information to the readers in a more convenient way and whether Mr. Pecker was afraid that they might soon displace magazines.

"Magazines will always be here. Like I said, we do not sell information, we sell dreams. There are some forty-four hundred magazines that are published. The three big news weeklies, *Time, U.S. News & World Report,* and *Newsweek,* which have a combined circulation of some 10 million copies, are possibly the most vulnerable, since they are the ones that can be most easily displaced by on-line services."

I asked Mr. Pecker whether magazines command higher value. He agreed that magazines that start new trends, have global exposure, and represent the future will definitely command a higher p/e than newspapers selling only facts. Newspaper stocks trade between eight and nine times their earnings, while media companies selling magazines trade at fifteen to seventeen times. *Elle Decor* is possibly worth fifty times its earnings, or $100 million. Wall Street awards a premium multiple to those companies which sell something people dream about.

Mr. Pecker also agreed that the magazine industry has been very cyclical. "From 1969 to 1991, some very serious recessions have hit, like 1972 to 1974, 1989 to 1991. Every time there are two quarters of negative growth of the GNP, there is a decline in the luxury and fashion industries, our largest advertisers."

Michael Rena, chief financial officer at Chanel, agrees with this view.

"Luxury companies are more subject to economic downturns. Asia's latest recession has affected everybody, yet it has certainly affected more companies in our industry, which sells products that customers do not absolutely have to buy. To succeed in our business a company must have a financial structure that enables it to take these swings. It also needs to have a high profitability, to maximize its income during upturns. You clearly do not want to have enormous fixed costs, and ideally you want to be in a position where if the market suddenly changes you can cut on your variables, like advertising. If a company is private, like Chanel is, it is easier to cope with cyclicality, since public companies are more embarrassed by short-term results. For example, right now the LVMH management is exerting pressure on Louis Vuitton to maintain the overall profitability of the group, which has been compromised by the Asian crisis. In many public companies [probably not LVMH] stock options are very important, thus the management of the company is very concerned about the price of the stock and its short-term fluctuations. This may distract the long-term view that is required to succeed in our business."

Due to the cyclical nature of this business, companies must have strong financial structures able to withstand economic downturns. This dreaded cyclicality and its inherent risks often incite companies to diversify their activities early on, in terms of both markets and products, and to effectively control costs and inventory. Financial reserves and a top credit rating contribute to flexibility and security.

* * *

COMPANIES OPERATING IN this business all share very strong brands. They also share some other interesting financial characteristics. Since they often need ample resources in order to control the entire value chain, they all sell an experience, not just a product, because control limited to the production level will never secure their success. In the luxury and fashion industries, companies holding the highest profit margins (Louis Vuitton, Hermès, Ferragamo, and so forth), all strictly supervise their distribution. By directly selling their own products, they reap the profit margins of wholesalers and retailers while ensuring the best service for their customers. Sales volumes are inherently limited by the exclusive nature of this business, making margins critical to the company's economic success. This is why Louis Vuitton sells most of its products through directly owned and operated stores and why Vendôme is investing so heavily in controlling its distribution, both in retail and wholesale. Direct control over distribution also enforces strict pricing by avoiding the discounting strategies that affect most independent retailers.* This direct control can help reduce the short-term financial costs associated with high inventories, another calamitous effect that these discounting strategies can have on the credibility of many dream and luxury products and services. The ultimate **measure of success** in this business is the customers' **long-term willingness to consistently pay the (premium) price established by the company.**

*Interestingly, branded products are threatened by the competition from unbranded, commodity-type products in those industries in which distribution chains are strong—the food business, for example. The same fate could greet the automobile industry if manufacturers do not react promptly.

Only larger companies have the financial resources to control distribution. One of the reasons why smaller designers are closing their doors (Isaac Mizrahi, Kenar, Adrienne Vittadini) is perhaps the weak leverage they have with the distribution channels. Department stores place huge demands on fashion houses, especially for bridge collections, requesting that the houses foot advertising costs, take back unsold products at the end of the season, and pay for salespeople. Small companies can rarely compete. Liz Tilberis, the editor in chief of *Harper's Bazaar,* believes that "the saddest part is we are heading toward a kind of mediocrity. I mean commercialism. Of course, we have to have commercial clothes in the stores. But we must have a little madness."

Increased competition makes life for small, creative companies increasingly difficult. Sydney Pollack, also renowned as a movie producer (the Oscar hit *Tootsie,* for one), also expresses his concern: "Movies cost very commonly $100 million. That is a very scary economic venture. I do not like that type of pressure. What is happening more and more is that the risks are so high that studios are beginning to take partners—private investors, large corporations, or small consortiums of international investors. We have weeded out the middle ground of American movies, where the greatest ground of creativity was for years, what we called the B movies. It is very hard to get a studio interested in a $20 million film—they would much rather gamble on a $100 million film and spread their risks, or try a $5 million movie, distribute it and get somebody else to make it. We just did a film that was an enormous success in Europe but not in the U.S., *Sliding Doors,* with Gwyneth Paltrow, a picture that cost $8 million to make, and we have done $65 million as of yesterday. And I just finished a tiny little movie made for $6.5 million with Sean Penn and Kristin Scott Thomas from a Somerset Maugham novella called *Up at the Villa.* It was a movie I completely financed independently, just like *Sliding Doors.* So, at the same time that I am directing a $75 million movie with Harrison Ford, I am also producing a tiny little movie with independent money. In some ways, that is more fun."

DEALING WITH ESOTERIC PRODUCTS like dreams or luxury is not clear-cut from a financial point of view. The value of dreams and luxury products is intimately linked to their creative content, which is generated, to a large degree, in the R&D department. All costs relating to the development needed to transform ideas into salable entities, and the experimentation of new products and services, fall under the heading of R&D. These costs are not easy to control, because creators are usually reluctant to be inspirationally harnessed when it comes to their desire to experiment with new materials, designs, and styles. Given the impulsive nature of the creative process, there is a risk of stifling the inventive spirit with an overbearing set of controls. Thus, R&D costs are the most difficult to budget, yet they are critical to the company's profitability, due to the ever-growing demand for new models, whose inherently shorter commercial lives oblige companies to accelerate the amortization of R&D costs.

COST RATIONALIZATION is also tricky, since dealing with emotions forces controllers to be less draconian when it comes to slashing costs and understanding what really turns the customer on. Financial managers cannot be strict bottom-liners as is the case in most mass-consumption businesses. Yet this hardly means cost concerns are cast to the wind, since maximizing profits also includes withholding what is considered marginally important to the customer. For example, Rolex, one of the most profitable companies in the world, uses Zenith movements (certainly not the most prominent name in the industry) in many of its highly coveted watches. But Rolex has become one of the most popular watches more for its case design and image than for the sophistication of its movements. For Rolex, more sophisticated movements would mean increasing the price of its watches or having to accept lower profit margins. Rolex is so profitable because, while producing beautiful watches, it is highly disciplined in balancing its designers' and engineers' creative urges (they might prefer creating the most complete masterpiece watches in the world) with the owners' financial stipulations. Having an ego is a *luxury* that can only be enjoyed by artists, who always seek to produce the very best, not by creators, who must also abide by business rules. After all, it is what the customer perceives to be important rather than what gratifies the artist that decides the purchase.

ANOTHER IMPORTANT DETERMINANT is how much to spend on marginal items, those that have no return for the company, since they add no value to the customer, but are incurred just to glorify the ego of the company. In the commodity business, it is much easier for the controller to identify such an expenditure. For example, offering music at the gas pump may be nice but does not add value to the consumer, who just wants to refuel as quickly and as cheaply as possible. In the business of selling dreams, however, controlling marginal expenditures is much more difficult, since one does not sell low price but experience. Take the Ferrari dealer who has invested in the installation of a special air-conditioning system that can dispense the smell of a Ferrari interior, the Connolly leather, and the composite materials. It is a spiffy expenditure, which certainly helps create the special environment that sets the customer dreaming. Only financial managers with a keen knowledge of the products and services can properly determine the value of such seemingly marginal expenditures.

COMPANIES SELLING DREAMS are the toughest to evaluate, since so many emotional factors come into play. For example, the fact that most of these companies boast very strong brands helps ensure future earnings, while their glamour and appeal usually command premium prices. Take the following case.

In 1993, the French entrepreneur François Pinault (major shareholder of Pinault-Printemps-Redoute department stores, with 1994 sales of $13 billion) bought Château Latour, ousting Chanel, which was the first interested party. Chanel had been negotiating for six months with the seller, Allied-Lyons. Pinault offered $129 million (allegedly $20 million more than the famous luxury group had proposed) for the Bordeaux's first growth and gave the seller twenty-four hours to respond. Pinault justified the purchase price by saying: *"Latour is like a great piece of art; it is without price. There is only one Château Latour in the world. And I'd rather fight in the course of daily business to earn a few extra million so I can overpay for something like Château Latour. . . . The acquisition of Latour reflects first and foremost my passion for wine . . . an emotional, almost sensual rapport with this domain and the wine it produces."*

* * *

GOING PUBLIC is not easy in this type of business, where emotions often overshadow the strict business regimen. For example, Donna Karan, who runs her eponymous company, has proven very creative in promoting her brand and designing new products, yet much less so in keeping costs under control, a weakness not at all appreciated on Wall Street. A common fault of many private luxury companies is a high expense ratio: If strong in their higher gross margins, they are less preoccupied with paring costs. Shareholders are concerned with short-term results. The time frame has shrunk from the once three-to-five-year projection down to the next quarter.

THE FINANCIAL MANAGER of a company selling dreams faces the challenge of fully understanding the nature of the company's business. Traditionally, finance managers have had a reasonably easy time slipping from one company to another, even if they were operating in unrelated fields, because their technical expertise was not overly dependent on the type of business activity involved. Most financial managers are not usually expected to deeply understand the business—not like production or marketing managers, for example. The same is not true for financial managers employed in this business. They must thoroughly understand the entire value chain in order to succeed without threatening the creativity of the people or the quality of the products and therefore weakening the company's most "leverageable" assets: its artistic skills and brand.

More challenges arise today from financially powerful mass-production companies trying to compete in this high-margin, image-building business segment. These threats compel companies selling dreams to aim at higher financial rewards that can support important investments in new technology, distribution, and communication. Wall Street may not be as supportive unless companies can prove themselves through substantial growth. Thus, shifting their focus from selling luxury, which is limited in volume by its elitism and cyclical nature, to selling dreams, which are more democratic, may prove to be a winning strategy. Long-term success means these companies must leverage their resources in order to finance this business's single most important success factor: creativity. **Selling dreams is the business of maximizing the added value to finance creativity.**

TO ACHIEVE LONG-TERM GROWTH, companies must tame their traditional cost-cutting and hyperefficiency methods with a more artistic approach to business. Only by striking customers' dreams can companies really magnify their profits and maximize their brand equity. Stocks have had a compound real return of 16 percent a year for the last sixteen years, compared to 6.5 percent historically. Low inflation, low interest rates, the technology boom, and improved efficiency from sweeping restructurings have helped companies generate great margins. The future may not be as bright, since the rates of change are slowing considerably. Interest rates aren't likely to decline and gains from cost-cutting and increased productivity will hardly be as dramatic. Corporations will be hard-pressed by an epidemic lack of pricing power. Financial managers and shareholders will have to adopt a long-term view and a higher risk threshold if they want to outpace their competition. Constant changes in society are shrinking our attention spans and thus shortening the commercial life of products and services. Customers seek tailor-made products, forcing companies to produce more models in smaller volumes. At the same time, R&D costs are creeping up due to increased expectations, competition, and regulations. Worse yet, the communication costs for launching a new product are well beyond astronomical and headed for Mars. It is always expensive to gain customers' attention, yet, since our tastes are changing at an ever faster rate, companies must ensure that their product is immediately accepted in order to recoup their initial investment faster. Flops can be very expensive. Taking a conservative approach is not the solution: It may reduce short-term risks, but it may also endanger the company over the long term. Through prudent management, GM has suffered no flops over the past twenty years, yet it has seen its market share halved.

Selling dreams is not easy. Dreams are ethereal and often elude traditional business rationality. Yet when a product or service triggers the customers' dreams, the company's value skyrockets because the company gains pricing power and its brand recognition goes into orbit. Imagine the certain Viagra effect!

8

Conclusions

A JOURNALIST I SPOKE WITH ONCE smiled at me and said, "Allow me to ask you a stupid question. I drive a Lexus. How might I see the difference if I were to drive a Ferrari?" I answered the way Jesuits and politicians usually do, with another question: "How well can you drive?"

When a product or service can reach the customers' dreams, the answer to that question usually depends on the individual's skill, knowledge, and intuition rather than on the qualities of the product or the service. In other words, was this journalist experienced enough as a driver to really appreciate a Ferrari's performance or to understand Ferrari's sophisticated technologies and emotional engineering? A Ferrari becomes a dream car only when its refinement surpasses that of most drivers. To become dreams, products or services must surprise and challenge us. They must elevate customers to a maximum common denominator, to the highest expectations, rather than lower themselves to the minimum common denominator of the consuming masses.

CONNECTING WITH the customers' imagination is what it takes today to succeed in business. Technological miracles and the vicarious excitement of television have fed today's customers with a craving for excitement in their everyday lives, meaning even the most common products and services must excite them or be banished. Simply satisfying needs isn't enough. Today, customers want to indulge their dreams. Dreams are much more accessible to many more of us now, and fulfillment of them is no longer reserved for a secret society of spoiled rich people. The business of dreams has begun to substantially influence the rest of our economy.

Every company can create a dream product or service, because dreams are not fashioned of exclusivity or luxury. Yes, there are those companies, such as Ferrari, that focus solely on dream products and services. Yet there are also companies operating in the mass-consumption industry that are manufacturing products that also ignite their customers' dreams. With a single dream product, they establish their brand for years to come. Dreams need not be expensive. They just require a wealth of creativity, a resource every company can grow. Let's recap the seven steps to help you see how to fulfill your customers' dreams:

1. **Interpret the spirit of the time in order to understand which dreams will capture the customer.** Today, change quickly affects our culture, the force that shapes our dreams and helps

us express them. Fundamentally, dreams stay the same (as Disney has proven, Hercules excited crowds in 1998 just as he did several millennia ago), and we continue to dream of individuality (becoming our own heroes), power (social recognition), immortality (living longer and better), knowledge, freedom, and so forth. As technology nudges dreams closer to us, our expectations continue to build. Today, we want to be part of the creative process. We expect products and services to adapt to our individuality. Face it, we want more technology in our lives: in our homes, in our cars, in our pockets, even in the way we dress. To paraphrase Ralph Lauren, people want more technical stuff; a winter jacket is no longer enough, it needs to be made to climb Mount Everest. Running shoes are boring; today's customers want their sport shoes to be like cross-trainers developed for every single activity they do. Their dreams are much more specific: They don't want to become great athletes, they want to be the greatest golfer under par; they want to play eighteen holes in nineteen minutes, so they dream up a sport called extreme golf. We look for dreams to hit on many more levels today. A look isn't enough anymore; we want to see, hear, smell, touch, and taste. More senses must be involved in the experience, in order that we might be stimulated more intensely. Dreams mean fun, and today it's okay to have fun. Not as many people dream of becoming the president of the United States—more people want to be actors, singers, athletes, computer whizzes. Dreams need to carry us closer to an emotional brink, to an edge that keeps unfolding toward the extreme. Special effects will continue to challenge our imagination, and soon enough the spectator will peer at himself/herself featured in the movie. We want to dream on our own terms. The Internet has already begun to give us the world at a click. The easier our access to products and services becomes, the more we will search for those packing a stronger emotional charge. The time for selling dreams is now. Companies must strive to foresee and often provoke the changes that shape their businesses because interpreting the spirit of the times to get specific answers goes way beyond market study analyses or customer questionnaires. This lifelong exercise comes from intense curiosity, free of prejudice and bias, like that of an artist. There is no signpost guiding the way, only humility that lets the questions be asked, the risks be taken. This is the one discipline that a company must enforce, the institutionalization of curiosity and eclecticism. Companies must not fear the unconventional thinker: Spice up the board of directors with a multicultural mix of creative people, artists, and visionaries. Search beyond business for inspiration: Follow new trends; visit museums; participate in cultural activities; brainstorm with universities; attend shows and events hosted by leading or emerging industries; travel the world; learn what other generations are doing (hit the club scene, do the discos, visit retirement homes); follow sports; watch any kind of extreme sports competition; go to the movies, the opera, the theater, or any other artistic performance; search the Internet and download experiences. A company should teach each one of its senses to feel intensely. Educate emotions and train the imagination to perceive. Listen to the slightest whispers. Dream.

2. **Create products and services designed and engineered to convey intense emotions.** The Internet is speeding the polarization of products and services purchased to satisfy needs and those designed to fulfill desires. By arming us with knowledge, the Internet is helping us decipher what is advertising alchemy, letting us better distinguish commodities from dreams. Companies can no longer hype their products solely through cre-

ative marketing. Products and services must start out creative at the drawing board; only then can they express any sort of aesthetic value. By exciting us, these products and services will avoid becoming commodities forced to compete against the goods of huge corporations for very thin margins. With innovation, purpose, originality, beauty, fun, and passion, they must border on the extreme and represent risk-taking.

Even if customers demand instant gratification, products cannot give in to easy access. Commercialism and instant returns call for products that immediately captivate. Often, their passing is just as immediate. The goal is to create dreams, not gadgets.

Companies must listen carefully to their customers' dreams before they give even the slightest thought to design. For example, we dream of freely communicating, not owning a cell phone no matter how beautiful it might be. So instead of toiling over how to make that cell phone look better, companies should consider how to make that phone invisible (by, say, incorporating it into a jacket, weightless and undetectable).

Creating dreams does not come cheap. Companies must beef up their investments in R&D, not only to make their products creative, but also to develop new technologies that will bring profitability to even the smallest quantities of distinct, tailor-made products. Creating dreams is the best shield against becoming a commodity.

3. **Practice dreamketing.** New technologies will soon be available to every company that will make bringing products to the market much easier. The challenge is no longer to reach the market, but rather to ignite our dreams by sparking our emotions and imagination. A dream is not a product or a service. It is an extraordinary experience, one that the dreamketer

must build around the company's great products and services. A dream is not an objective entity, but rather a perception that exists only in the customer's mind. The dreamketer must influence that perception by becoming a great storyteller. Just like a successful Hollywood director who finds a script with an enthralling story, so must the dreamketer find the company with enthralling and emotionally engineered products. The director transports his audience to that fantastic place where they've never been before; the dreamketer must take his customers to a similar place. Creating these fantastic places requires originality and innovation. It means running the risk that the new creation will not be liked or understood. The dreamketer must launch each new product with a campaign that is as seductive to its customers as it is educative. Unlike artists, companies cannot count on posterity to secure customer approval. Companies usually have the resources to enhance the customers' perception so that they can better understand and enjoy the companies' creations (something artists surely cannot do). For example, when Gucci allowed Tom Ford to reinvent the company's style, it backed his innovative ideas with an advertising budget the likes of which no fashion house had ever seen before.

Exceptional brands can sway customer perception. Just as a powerful family name acts as a great calling card in society, exceptional brands lend credibility to a company's new products by tripping the customer's mind into dream mode. Just hearing the name Ferrari entices automobile enthusiasts to anticipate outrageous performance, sensuous lines, and the emotion of driving long before they even see the car.

Unfortunately, strong family names usually weaken after a few generations, as new members prove to be somewhat less driven than the founder. Keeping a brand exceptional means dreamketers must ensure that each new experience builds the brand's mystique rather than debilitates it. The dreamketer must work rigorously at keeping the momentum going and the brand exciting. Dreamketers are great seducers who sketch their creators' reality into poetry and their companies' history into a myth.

4. **Choose the customer.** Great customers force companies to become just as great. Companies must seek them out. This is not as easy as in the past, since today customers can pick from any number of alternatives, armed with ample information. Customers want value. They want to get more for what they are spending. And they do not want to spend their hard-earned money improperly. They will not accept spending more on commodities—just like some of the wealthiest women, who do their grocery shopping at Costco, the discount chain. Even they save when it comes to satisfying their needs so that they can spend on fulfilling their dreams.

Customers are knowledgeable and curious, always searching for new and intense experiences. They want to take part in the creative process so that products and services are tailored to their desires. They want to be in control of the purchasing relationship. Most important, they are not as faithful as they once were: Retaining them will mean a company must surprise, tease, amuse, and please them—constantly. They are much more vocal about their likes and dislikes: Through word of mouth, the Internet has armed them with the unprecedented power to make or break companies.

A customer revolution is afoot, marking a fundamental transformation in how people purchase and enjoy products and services. Millions of customers who are imposing their wills, tastes, and desires on companies are forcing a change in the way companies produce and sell. The relationship between the client and the company has swung around. In the past, consumers were a means by which companies achieved their financial goals; now companies are the means by which customers achieve their emotional goals. Like any other revolution, this one will crush those (companies) that cannot adapt and propel those (companies) with the vision and the creative might to seize the opportunity.

Selling dreams will help win the customer revolution!

5. **Choose a creator.** In this "instant information" society, intuition (the mind's immediate and unconscious assimilation of knowledge) is everything. Since knowledge is so readily available, outpacing competition requires that companies have the ability to see even before knowledge is formed. Intuitive people are rare. Meet the creator.

Creators have the vision to see farther and faster than anyone else. They are sensitive individuals who can interpret the spirit of their time and give form to their customers' unexpressed desires. Thorough understanding of the product and also the production process ensures that a creator's creations can be manufactured by the company's facilities. With a keen eye for details, the creator knows what works and what does not. Creators are passionate and extravagant, but not frivolous. Working quickly to respect the dreamketer's schedule, they are constantly busy with the innovation that keeps the creative engines stoked. Their knowledge lets them guide and motivate the gifted yet often egocentric craftsmen to respect their orders. They can build a team able to crystallize even their most extraordinary ideas. Creators possess the innate curiosity and the guts to constantly experiment and take risks: They respect the tradition of their companies, yet they aim for the future, searching for new ideas and ways to attract new customers. A strong conviction and passion for what they do lets these creators survive passing fashions and trends and any media-slung criticism. A creator guides a company through question and doubt, down uncertain paths to aesthetic excellence. Thanks to the creators, aesthetic worth is not sold out to commercialism, bottom-lineism, or the short-term vision that impairs so many larger organizations, shareholders, and financial analysts. The creator's voice and personal leverage with the company lets him or her impose aesthetic rigor with little compromise. Creators are quickly becoming invaluable spokespeople: Their personality, charisma, visibility, and glamour magnify brand appeal.

Creators do not peer into crystal balls, yet with their vision, sensitivity, and product knowledge they can convince the customer to see the same future that they are unfolding.

6. **Support creators with a creative organization.** Creators alone cannot create dreams. They can provide the vision and the inspiration, but dreams are not one person's doing. Dreams are emotional experiences that require teamwork from many gifted people participating at all levels of the experience. This takes an organization able to spread creativity. It's not a question of whether the company is creative, it's how to uncover that creativity that counts. Through rigorous training, sensitize collaborators to the company's aesthetic values and spread knowledge throughout the organization. Offer freedom and understanding, so that each individual can experiment without the fear of failure. Finally, build a passionate environment. Passion spikes the learning curve by intensifying the desire to learn. Passion motivates, inspires, and propels people to

go farther than their own expectations. Passion is contagious and pulls people to a common goal. Passion is essential if a company wants to maximize its creative resources and succeed.

Being part of an organization that creates dreams lets collaborators feel fulfilled and proud.

7. **Seize any possible chance to magnify the customer's perceived added value.** If you can touch customers' emotions, you will boost your influence on their perception of the added value and your company's pricing power. Companies are beginning to see that even doing all they can to shrink their costs isn't enough to generate the type of earnings growth investors expect from them. Such earnings are possible only if a company can count on a brand that commands a premium price.

The financial department must give the creator and the dreamketer the resources *and* the time to build an exciting and credible brand. A financial manager must not steer a company away from risk, but rather should build a financial structure that allows risk-taking. Without risks, there are no dreams. Dreams, by definition, are never born of the norm.

Building a powerful brand at times requires investing in image-building products even if they may generate a loss. Examples include haute couture, which operates at a loss but builds the image that sells perfumes and cosmetics at companies such as Chanel, Dior, or Givenchy, or the Viper, the expensive dream car project that re-established Chrysler as one of the most innovative automobile companies. By exciting customers and the media, these products carry brands for years to come. Once a strong brand is established, a company can leverage it to expand its product line (licensing) and to gain access to financial resources more easily.

In a market still giddy over the results delivered by Dell,

America Online, or Amazon stock, companies selling mere commodities have little hope of ever stirring any investor's imagination. Unless a company can increase its shareholders' value, it may be staring at a meager future with an underperforming stock. In the future, the pressure on stock prices will only grow stronger.

SELLING DREAMS MEANS striking a balance between rigor and passion!

This is an age of possibility we live in, a techno-jungle where all kinds of screens confuse our real life with Hollywoodesque cyber-desires. The rest of the world is adopting American culture. Lives are often sculpted like movie characters. Hollywood is washing over into reality; life is playing out like a movie script. People become actors, their environment a stage, products and services the props that help their performances or help make their lives more exciting. Superficial or not, Hollywood is showing us how to grab emotions by selling us dreams. Fashion designers are catching on quickly: Like movie directors, they first detect an interesting theme, then develop it through costumes and accessories, props that create exciting roles for their customers to play. Even designers and architects construct Hollywoodlike movie sets in stores, hotels, and restaurants wherein customers can perform activities like shopping, resting, or eating.

The business of selling dreams is headed for an impressive future. Our disposable income is bound to increase over the long run because income is slated to grow, despite transitory setbacks. At the same time, continuous re-engineering and technological advances will help reduce the costs of basic products and services. The risk of high inflation has been tamed, and the only fear seems to be that of deflation. Thus, we should have more money to spend on satisfying our dreams and on leisure and unnecessary items. The irrevocable "acculturation" of the free world will continue to stimulate our appreciation for products and services with heightened symbolic, hedonistic, and aesthetic value. While most businesses have reached saturation points and now grow only as fast as the population, selling dreams enjoys no limits. Customers just don't wait until they've "used up" one dream product before replacing it with a next one and a next. Dreams are not consumed—they are purchased because of a renewed excitement about a new statement, a new color, a new fashion, or even a change of mood. This business has grown less cyclical than before because, yes, dreams are not considered as superfluous as they were in the past. Dreaming is inherent in our very nature. Economic downturns may temporarily increase our concerns and darken our moods, yet the long-term trend calls for man to dream more and more.

UNFORTUNATELY, a vast majority in this world still cannot satisfy their barest needs. Yet this too is bound to change, simply because world economies are growing at a faster rate than the population. The ubiquity of television is bringing dreams into every household: Many cannot yet afford them, but they are already longing for them. Take China, for example. One of that country's hottest items today is a catalogue of luxury products. While most Chinese cannot afford luxury goods from the West, this certainly does not prevent them from dreaming, and their dreams are so strong that they will spend what little they have just to buy a simple catalogue. Even if many cannot afford them, there are still some 6 billion potential customers out there in the world craving dream products and services!

THE MOST INTERESTING THING about this business is that every company, no matter what its business activity or size, can learn something here. Any company can shatter the traditional business rationale and escape into the realm of intuition, feelings, imagination, emotion, seduction, and taste. Any company can learn that patience and long-term thinking are what build attention to even the slightest detail. Most important, any company can learn how to boost the creative energy within its organization in order to attract the best customers.

I've always believed the adage "Tell me how good your customers are and I will tell you how good your company is." The quality of the customers is the ultimate measure of business success. After all, a company's total worth is equal to the sum of its customers' purchasing power and their willingness to exercise it. Transforming otherwise common products into dreams is the best possible way to attract the best customers. A company need not be large and rich to achieve this, since, in this business, creativity and taste are often more important than capital. This is a business that really forces a company to listen to the customers and think horizontally in correspondence with their horizontal spending patterns. Companies thrive here not simply because of their production capacity but because of their ability to invite their customers to spend. Success in this business of dreams is not "owning" a product, it is "owning" a customer. By thinking horizontally, companies can better "own" their customers.

* * *

MAKING DREAMS fosters dream organizations in which creativity triumphs. Creativity is the most important quality for achieving business success (or any type of success, for that matter), and companies that sell dreams offer any type of industry key opportunities to learn how to enhance this most precious and scarce resource.

BREEDING THE MOST creative organizations, attracting the most generous customers, and building the most exciting brands is what makes the companies selling dreams so special.

The future is impossible to predict. However, one thing is certain: The company that can excite its customers' dreams is out ahead in the race to business success.

ACKNOWLEDGMENTS

WRITING THIS BOOK has helped open up my business experience by letting me contact all of those companies and people that, in many different ways, were after the same goal as I: to sell products and services that grip us emotionally. Simply put, to sell dreams. Since any kind of product or service can be shaped into a customer's dream, this study has brought me to a vast number of often unrelated fields, forcing me to develop an eclectic business view. At the risk of overextending myself, I tried to expand the scope of my research as much as possible. After all, my goal was not to narrow this down to one particular business subject, but rather to develop a vision that could be applied to all kinds of business activity.

Writing this book has been a great lesson in humility. When I realized that what I knew was far too limited to translate into a book that could ever grab an audience larger than my own mother, I turned to the knowledge that respected entrepreneurs, businesspeople, and cultural leaders kindly shared with me. I feel very lucky and grateful to have had the chance to speak with some of the most brilliant minds that influence the business world today. This book represents an exercise in brainstorming, intended to help the reader formulate engaging questions. It does not pretend to have all the answers.

This book started out as a Ph.D. thesis under the guidance of Professor Pierre Goetschin of l'École des Hautes Études Commerciales at the University of Lausanne. One of the most respected business professors in Europe, Professor Goetschin pushed me to develop a study that bent the rigid business rationale. His vast experience as consultant to many of the world's largest corporations, his eclectic appreciation of culture, and his sense of humor have helped me explore subjects usually swept deep into the corners of the business world, such as emotions, passions, and sensual impulses. To Professor Goetschin goes all my appreciation.

The Ph.D. thesis would have never become a book if my journalist wife, Kip, hadn't organized my sometimes nonlinear thoughts into some semblance of logic. Her curiosity, her flexible mind, and her desire to explore new fields of knowledge have proved invaluable to the structure of this book.

I would also like to thank Dominick Anfuso for the editorial guidance and vision that has brought this book to press, and my admired friend Christopher Buckley, a brilliant writer who, out of friendship and quite possibly pity, has tried to show me how to better articulate my concepts.

Writing this book has been a fantastic chance for me to talk with many insightful and accomplished individuals. I hope I've done justice to their views. I am deeply grateful to each one of them.

SELECTED BIBLIOGRAPHY

Abbagnano, N. *Dizionario di filosofia.* UTET, Turin, 1971.

Ackerman, D. *A Natural History of the Senses.* Vintage Books, New York, 1990.

Arieti, S. *Creativity: The Magic Synthesis.* Basic Books, New York, 1976.

Baudrillard, J. *Seduction.* St. Martin's Press, New York, 1979.

Belk, R.; Bahn, K.; Mayer, R. "Developmental Recognition of Consumption Symbolism." *Journal of Consumer Research,* vol. 9, June 1982.

Bennett, P. *Dictionary of Marketing Terms.* American Marketing Association, Chicago, 1988.

Bergmann, A. "Le management: un art ou une science?" *Revue Économique et Sociale,* Lausanne, March 1996.

Bourdieu, P. *Distinction: A Social Critique of the Judgement of Taste.* Harvard University Press, Cambridge, Mass., 1984.

Caillois, R. *Les jeux et les hommes.* Gallimard, Paris, 1967.

Deforge, Y. *L'oeuvre et le produit.* Collection Milieux, Paris, 1990.

Drucker, P. *Post-Capitalist Society.* HarperCollins, New York, 1993.

Dufrenne, M. *Esthétique et philosophie,* tome 1. Éditions Klincksieck, Paris, 1980.

Erasme. *Éloge de la folie.* Flammarion, Paris, 1964.

Finke, R. *Creative Cognition.* Bradford Books, Cambridge, Mass., 1992.

Guildford, J. P. "Creativity." *American Psychologist,* vol. 5, 1950.

Goetschin, P. "Art et management—Peut-on rêver?" *Revue Économique et Sociale,* Lausanne, March 1996.

Hanger, J. *The Little Book of Dreams.* Penguin Books, Harmondsworth, U.K., 1998.

Hirschman, E.; Holbrook, M. "Hedonic Consumption: Emerging Concepts, Methods and Propositions." *Journal of Marketing,* vol. 46, Summer 1992.

Hofstadter, A.; Kuhns, R. *Philosophies of Art and Beauty.* University of Chicago Press, Chicago, 1964.

Hume, D. *Les passions.* Flammarion, Paris, 1991.

L'industrie mondiale du luxe: l'impératif de la création face à la banalisation des marchés. Eurostaf, Paris, 1995.

Kapferer, J.; Thoenig, J. *La marque moteur de la competitivité des entreprises et de la croissance de l'économie.* McGraw-Hill, Paris, 1989.

Keegan, W.; Moriarty, S.; Duncan, T. *Marketing.* Prentice-Hall, Englewood Cliffs, N.J., 1995.

Kierkegaard, S. "The Diary of a Seducer," in *Either/Or.* Princeton University Press, Princeton, N.J., 1971.

Lipovetsky, G., *L'empire de l'éphémère.* Gallimard, Paris, 1987.

Longinotti-Buitoni, G. L., "L'industrie du luxe: qui est-elle et où va-t-elle?" *Bulletin H.E.C.,* Lausanne, no. 53, February 1997.

"Le marketing du luxe." *Revue Française de Marketing.* Paris, nos. 132–133, 1991.

McCracken, G. "Culture and Consumption: A Theoretical Account of the Structure and Movement of the Cultural Meaning of Consumer Goods." *Journal of Consumer Research,* vol. 13, June 1986.

Midgley, D. "Patterns of Interpersonal Information Seeking for the Purchase of a Symbolic Product." *Journal of Marketing Research,* vol. 20, February 1983.

Noori, H.; Radford, R. *Production and Operations Management.* McGraw-Hill, New York, 1995.

Perrot, P. *Le luxe, une richesse entre faste et confort XVIII–XIX siècles.* Seuil, Paris, 1995.

Rapp, S.; Collins, T. *Beyond MaxiMarketing: The New Power of Caring and Daring.* McGraw-Hill, New York, 1994.

Rivlin, R.; Gravelle, K. *Deciphering the Senses.* Simon and Schuster, New York, 1984.

Savage, C. *Fifth Generation Management.* Digital Press, Bedford, Mass., 1990.

Sekora, J. *Luxury: The Concept in Western Thought, Eden to Smollett.* The Johns Hopkins University Press, Baltimore, 1977.

Simonton, D. *Genius, Creativity, and Leadership.* Harvard Business Books, Cambridge, Mass., 1984.

Smith, A. *The Wealth of Nations.* W. R. Scott, London, 1921.

Solomon, M. "The Role of Products as Social Stimuli: A Symbolic Interactionism Perspective." *Journal of Consumer Research,* vol. 10, December 1983.

Souriau, E. *Vocabulaire d'esthétique.* Presse Universitaire de France, Paris, 1990.

Stanley, T. *Marketing to the Affluent.* Dow Jones–Irwin, Homewood, Ill., 1988.

Stern, R. "Artistes et managers: divergences, différences et connivences." *Revue Économique et Sociale,* Lausanne, March 1996.

Upton, D.; McAfee, A. "The Real Virtual Factory." *Harvard Business Review,* July–August 1996.

Van De Castle, R. *Our Dreaming Mind.* Ballantine Books, New York, 1994.

Van Horne, J. *Financial Management and Policy.* Prentice-Hall, Englewood Cliffs, N.J., 1977.

Vegetti Finzi, S. *Storia delle passioni.* Editori Laterza, Rome, 1995.

Weisberg, R. *Creativity: Beyond the Myth of Genius.* W. H. Freeman & Co., New York, 1993.

Womack, J.; Jones, D.; Roos, D. *The Machine That Changed the World.* Rawson Associates, New York, 1990.

Zandl, I.; Leonard, R. *Targeting the Trendsetting Consumer.* Business One Irwin, Homewood, Ill., 1992.

INDEX

ABC network, 86
Adam (first man), 23–24, 160
Adidas sportswear, 70
Adler, Alfred, 238*n*
Adonis/Venus dream, 46, 76
Adrienne Vittadini (designer), 292
Advance Publications, 102
Advertising, importance of, 134–36
A&E channel, 86, 88, 89
Aesthetica, 33*n*
Aesthetics, 33–35
  consumption, 109
  and play, 37*n*
Affluence, 161–64, 169–70
Africa, 78*n*, 193
Agnelli, Gianni, 154, 178, 218
Airplane industry, 72–75, 90–91
Alain Ducasse restaurant, 173
Alfa Romeo Spider, 59, 179
Allied-Lyons, 295
Amazon stock, 309
America, 12, 138, 169, 279, 292
  affluence of, 161, 162–65, 176
  consumerism in, 44
  culture of, 309
  entertainment in, 166
  individual in, 199–200
  as land of opportunity, 164
  magazines in, 287–88
  plastic surgery in, 79
  taxes in, 165
American Dream, 82, 188, 284
American Express, 105–6
America Online, 309
Americans, vs. Europeans, 218
Antarctic, 240

Antonioni, Michelangelo, 200
Aphrodisiacs, 258*n*–59*n*
Apparel business, 61
Arabs, 200
Architectural Digest, 101, 288
Arieti, Silvano, 196
Aristotle, 78, 227
Armani, Giorgio, 122, 201, 202, 220
Arnault, Bernard, 228
Arnell, Peter, 136–37
Arnell Group, 136
Art
  pleasure generated by, 38
  value of, 48, 281
Art Deco, 206
Artemis (goddess), 150*n*
Artists
  and entrepreneurs, 204–7
  function of, 42–43
  intuition of, 50–51
Art of the House, 283
Art of the Table, 283
Asia, 71, 116, 290
  See also Far East
Asprey, Edward, 171, 174
Asprey North America, 157–58
Astaire, Fred, 218
Athens, Golden Age in, 26
AT&T, 86
Auction houses, 47–50
Audemars Piguet Royal Oak watch, 177
Augustus, Emperor, 151, 178
Austrians, 200
Automobile industry, 11–14, 52–53, 59, 61, 62, 66–68, 75, 88, 126, 175, 184, 191–92, 202, 214, 236, 283, 291*n*, 304, 308
  and advertising, 134–36
  financing in, 285–86
  and ultimate dream, 142–43
  See also Racing; Sports automobiles

Babylonians, 214
Bacall, Lauren, 147
Baccarat (co.), 283
Bach, Johann Sebastian, 194*n*
Bacon, Francis, 141
Bahamas, 130
Balenciaga, Cristobal, 193
Banks, 57, 59
Bardot, Brigitte, 34, 104, 153, 178
Barnes & Noble, 283
Baron de Rothschild club, 117
Barter, 96
Basic Instinct (film), 126
Basinger, Kim, 152
Batistuta, Gabriel, 203
Baudelaire, Charles, 229
Bauhaus, 239*n*
Baumgarten, Alexander, 33*n*
Baywatch (TV show), 45–46
Beatrice Food, 61
Beauty
  aspiration of, 70–72
  expressions of, 216–18
  importance of, 77–80
  and jewelry, 249–50
  perceptions of, 115–16
  value of, 33–36
Beethoven, Ludwig van, 21*n*, 229*n*
Bensimon, Gilles, 89–90, 91

Benuzzi, Dario, 240–41, 244, 272
Beverage business, 61, 283
Blanc, George, 259
Blancpain (co.), 191*n*
Bond, James (fictional character), 44, 146–49
Books business, 283
Borgias, the, 197*n*
Bottom line, 274–75
Boulud, Daniel, 258–61, 271
Boussac (textile tycoon), 153
Brainstorming, 203*n*
Brand(s)
  dream, 138–40
  exceptional, 304–5
  home for, 136–38
  loyalty, 175
  management, 285–86
  personification of, 183–84
  positioning, 142–43
  power of, 44, 284, 291
  recognition, 92
Brando, Marlon, 178, 183–84, 187
Braque, Georges, 141, 206
Brazil, 250
Breakfast at Tiffany's (film), 146
Breaking the Waves (film), 84
Breast cancer, 278–79
Brecht, G., 239*n*
Breguet, Abraham-Louis, 216
Brindley, Dr. Giles, 278*n*
British, 187, 196*n*
  See also England; Great Britain
Brooks, Diana (Didi), 47–50, 181–82
Brooks, Mel, 46
Brooks Brothers suit, 180–81
Brunei, Sultan of, 24
Buccellati, Mario, 170–71, 250–53, 273
Buccellati jewel, 69
Buccellati North America, 250–53
Buckley, Christopher, 43–47
Buddhism, 226
Bulgari (co.), 253
Bulgaria, 254*n*
Business, polarization of, 63–67

Cable business, 88
Cameron, James (Jim), 202, 207, 208, 209–10, 275–76
Canada, 12, 165, 255*n*
Capital gains tax, 165
Capote, Truman, 57
Capri, 178
Caravaggio, Michelangelo da, 36
Card companies, 105–6
Cardin, Pierre, 193
Carolco (co.), 276
Cars. *See* Automobile industry
Cartier (co.), 237, 253
Cartier, Louis-François, 155
Casablanca, 211
Casablanca (film), 34
Casta, Laetitia, 104
Castro, Fidel, 56, 244
Catholic Church, 230, 262*n*
Catholicism, 35*n*
CBS network, 86
Celebrities, 80–82
Celine (co.), 194
CEOs, affluence of, 161
Cesar (artist), 141, 239*n*
Cesaretti, Gusmano, 211, 225–26, 241–43, 244, 272

Cézanne, Paul, 192
Chagall, Marc, 141
Champagne industry, 168–69, 266
Chanel, Coco, 57, 137, 193, 213, 217
Chanel (co.), 60, 62, 136, 190–91, 290, 295, 308
  dress, 60
  lipstick, 89, 114
  No. 5, 153, 255*n*
  tailleurs, 179
Change, 26–28
  and creativity, 221–22
Château Latour, 61, 62, 140, 159, 295
Château Margaux, 55
Château Pétrus, 159
Château Rothschild, 18
Château d'Yquem, 61
China, 26, 169, 201, 254*n*, 276, 310–11
Christ, 262*n*
Christian Dior fashion house, 70, 122, 152–53, 228, 283, 308
Christie's, 281*n*
Chrysler
  Dodge, 286
  Jeep, 286
  Viper, 286, 308
Churchill, Winston, 57, 178
Cigar Aficionado magazine, 100
Cigarette companies, 284
Cigar industry, 56, 99–100, 155, 243–44, 273
  See also Tobacco
Citizen (co.), 283
Cleopatra, 71
Clinton, Bill, 88, 178, 277
Clinton, Hillary, 34
Clothing industry, 104–5, 217–21
  See also Apparel business; Dresses; Fashion industry
Club Macanudo, 99
Clubs, ownership, 117–18
CNN channel, 61
Coca-Cola (co.), 12, 52, 53, 128, 137, 138, 283, 284
Cocteau, Jean, 141, 193
Cohiba cigars, 56, 155, 178
Colombia, 250
Colorstick, 115
Colt revolver, 269*n*
"Comic Relief," 180
Comoro Island, 254*n*
Companies
  and creativity, 195–96, 231–32
  and customers, 38–41, 50–51, 59–62, 184–85
  "dream," 128
  goal of, 183, 189
  and Internet, 129–34
  and long-term growth, 297–98
  luxury vs. mass-consumption, 282–84
  mass-consumption, 125, 172–73, 282–84
  quality of, 148
  See also Organization
Complications, 54*n*
Computers, 27, 76, 207, 282
  and creativity, 269
Condé Nast, 101, 102, 139, 288
Condé Nast Traveler magazine, 101
Connolly leather, 295
Consolidated Cigars, 283

Consumers, vs. customers, 158–60
Consumption
aesthetic, 109
hedonistic, 109
symbolic, 107–8
Cooper, Gary, 45
Cosmetic industry, 112–16
Costco (co.), 305
Cost rationalization, 293–94
Courrèges, 201
Cowboy image, 45
Crawford, Cindy, 34, 116
Creativity
boundaries of, 204–7
and change, 221–22
in companies, 195–96, 231–32
and computers, 269
description of, 190–93
eclectic erudition in, 222–24
evaluating, 194–95
and excellence, 272–73
factors promoting, 196–97
financing, 274–98
fluctuation of, 203*n*
and freedom, 237–38
and "geniuses," 198*n*
global, 200–201
and madness, 229–30
in movie/TV industry, 207–12
in organizations, 17, 234–45
and play, 37–38
role of, 202–4, 228
and sensory exploration, 214–15
successful, 213–14
and taste, 216–20
and work ethic, 224–26
Creator
choosing, 16–17, 306–7
organization support for, 307–8
Croesus, king of Lydia, 150
Cro-Magnon period, 27
Crowe, Russell, 57
Cruise, Tom, 184, 187
crus classés wine, 264
Crystal, Billy, 126
C-Span channel, 86, 88
Cuba, 56, 243, 273
Cullman, Edgar, Jr., 99–100
Culture, importance of, 50–51, 177–78
Customers
and affluence, 161–64
attention span of, 50
choosing, 16, 305–6
and companies, 38–41, 50–51, 59–62, 184–85
vs. consumers, 158–60
core, 184–85
and culture, 50–51, 177–78
dreams of, 38–41, 123–24, 300–302
emotional involvement of, 114–15
fame of, 150–53
and Internet, 129–34
listening to, 123–24
motivation of, 149–50, 156–57
nature of, 172–74
"owning," 311
quality of, 148, 311
reaching, 175–76
revolution of, 185–87
seduction of, 143–45
Cutthroat Island (film), 276

Dalí, Salvador, 141, 205*n*
Daniel restaurant, 159
D'Aragona, Count Gelasio
Gaetani Lovatelli, 264–65
Darwin, Charles, 79*n*, 247*n*
David (Michelangelo), 33
DB4 Aston Martin, 147
Dean, James, 45, 178, 184
Deflation, 166
de Havilland, Olivia, 153
Dell (co.), 308
Democratic National Committee, 88
Demoiselles d'Avignon, Les (Picasso), 192
Deneuve, Catherine, 33, 34
De Niro, Robert, 207
Denmark, 201
DKNY (co.), 136
Departures magazine, 105
Derain, André, 193
Descartes, René, 196*n*
Diana, Princess, 57, 157
Diamond, nature of, 68
"Diary of a Seducer, The" (Kierkegaard), 143–45
DiCaprio, Leonardo, 208
Dickens, Charles, 229*n*
Dietrich, Marlene, 34, 53, 153
Differentiate, vs. distinguish, 69*n*
Dionysus (god), 151
Dior, Christian, 137, 138, 174, 193, 201, 213, 217, 222
Discounting, 286
Discovery Channel, 86, 88–89
Disney (co.), 61, 62, 128, 237, 301
Distribution, 127–28, 291–92
 and Internet, 129–34
Dolce & Gabbana, 179, 215
Domino's pizza, 65
Dom Perignon, 146, 148, 149, 283
Donna Karan brand, 44
Dreamketer(ing)
 and marketing, 95–98, 106–7
 practicing, 15–16, 303–5
 and rituals, 116–18
 role of, 110–11, 123–24, 143–45
 strategy of, 111–12, 119
 and technology, 187–88
Dreams
 brands, 138–40
 business, 61
 carrying, 89–90
 of customers, 38–41, 123–24, 300–302
 definition of, 113–14
 and denominators, 90–92
 and dreamketers, 106–7
 as emotional experiences, 233–34
 ethereal nature of, 51, 298
 excitement in, 310
 and fashion, 30–32
 fleeting nature of, 119
 formation of, 50
 of freedom, 76–77
 fulfilling, 29
 as fun, 301
 function of, 21–22
 of heroism, 77
 interpretation of, 30, 50–51
 as market-positioning strategy, 68
 and materialism, 23–26, 35–38

as perception, 68–69, 271
price of, 124–27
products, 59
puzzling nature of, 97
and reality, 22
and seduction, 145
of social recognition, 76
status, 67–69
three fundamental, 76–77
use of, 70
Dresses, 69, 213
Drugs. *See* Pharmaceutical industry

Eastwood, Clint, 45, 83
eBay, 130
E! channel, 88
Edison, Thomas, 224*n*
Edward VII, King, 57, 155, 178
Egypt, 22, 77*n*, 200, 214, 256, 262*n*
Einstein, Albert, 21*n*, 221
Ekberg, Anita, 104, 147
Elegance, in clothing, 217–21
Elizabeth Arden brand, 135
Elle Decor magazine, 288, 289
Elle magazine, 89–90, 134, 287
Elway, John, 203
Emerald Coast, 178
England, 26, 201, 288
See also British; Great Britain
English Patient, The (film), 69, 82, 83, 91, 196
Enlightenment period, 197
Entertainment business, 61, 84–86, 89, 166
Entrepreneurs, and artists, 204–7
Epicurus cigars, 155
Erasmus of Rotterdam, 230
Escoffier (chef), 56
Esplendidos cigars, 155
Estée Lauder (co.), 70–72, 78*n*, 271, 283
E.T. (film), 81
Ethan Allen (co.), 283
Ethiopia, 255*n*
Europe, 64, 164, 165, 262*n*, 292
See also Western Europe
Europeans, 200, 258*n*
vs. Americans, 218
Eve (first woman), 23–24, 160
Excellence, and creativity, 272–73
Experience, vs. product, 94–95

Fabergé, Carl, 216
FAO Schwarz, 11
Far East, 258*n*
See also Asia
Far niente, 226
Fashion industry, 30–32, 38, 194–95, 201, 202, 215, 222, 270, 283
and senses, 248*n*
See also Dresses
FDA, 103, 277, 279
Feadship yacht, 34, 60, 62, 70
club, 117
Fellini, Federico, 104, 200
Fellow, Scott, 119–21, 123
Fellows, George, 112–16
Fendi (designer), 201
Ferragamo, Massimo, 53, 119–120
Ferragamo, Salvatore, 53, 119, 137, 138, 147, 214, 227–28
Ferragamo family, 119–23

Ferragamo brand, 53, 59–62, 124, 130, 138, 149, 160, 169, 215, 237, 291
Ferrari, 16, 33, 34, 64, 98, 128, 132, 138, 147, 155, 178, 272, 283, 295, 300
  and brand loyalty, 175
  club, 117
  customers of, 169, 220
  as dream product, 40, 59–61, 68–70, 72, 75, 77, 81, 87, 88, 90, 91, 97, 149, 273, 299
  as factory of dreams, 11–14
  F-1, 62, 162, 267–68
  as hot topic, 136
  luggage for, 236
  Mondial Convertible, 147
  name recognition of, 52–53, 66, 136, 304
  positioning of, 142–43
  "purity of purpose" of, 191–92
  racing, 267–69
  reasons for buying, 109
  reputation of, 126
  secrecy over new models, 182
  as status symbol, 184
  test driving, 240–41
  365 Gtb/4 Daytona, 152
  365 P, 154
Ferrari, Enzo, 126, 214, 267
Field of Dreams theory, 66
Films. *See* Movie industry
Financing creativity, 274–98
Finlay (co.), 283
Fitzgerald, F. Scott, 57
Florence (Italy), 270
Florio, Steve, 101–2
Flowers, 255–57
Fochon (co.), 61, 62
Food business, 61, 258–61, 283, 291*n*
Food & Wine magazine, 105
Forbes magazine, 161, 162, 181, 205
  400 list, 205
  FYI, 173
Ford, 283, 286
  Model T, 45, 97–98
  Mustang, 59
  Thunderbird, 89
Ford, Harrison, 80, 81, 293
Ford, Henry, 45
Ford, John, 200
Ford, Tom, 122, 201, 202, 215, 304
Fortune magazine, 131
  500, 279
Fox television, 87
Fractional ownership program, 74
France (French), 27, 30, 105, 151*n*, 165, 169, 198–201, 222, 254*n*, 255*n*, 258*n*, 262*n*, 263*n*, 265, 266
French Fragrances (co.), 283
Freud, Sigmund, 22*n*, 238*n*
Frey, Pierre, 216
Friedman, Milton, 239*n*
Fugu, 259*n*

Galliano, John, 122, 228
Galotti, Ron, 134–35
Garavani, Valentino, 213
Garbo, Greta, 53, 147
Garcia, Juan, 243–44, 273
Gardner, Ava, 34, 53, 147, 153

Gasoline business, 63–67
Gates, Bill, 87, 151*n*, 162, 163
Gatsby, Jay (fictional character), 164
Gauthier, Luc, 42–43, 47
General Cigar Holdings, 99
George magazine, 287
Gerard, Michel, 259
Germany, 42, 161, 165, 197, 200, 241, 280
Gift and inheritance tax, 165
Gifts, exchanging, 117
Girardet, Fredy, 55, 168
Girard-Perregaux watch, 34, 54, 59, 72, 90, 191*n*, 237
Givenchy fashion house, 228, 308
Glamour, attraction of, 92
Glamour magazine, 101
Glass products, 223–24
GM, 202, 285–86, 298
GNC (co.), 61
Goethe, Johann Wolfgang von, 21*n*
Gold digger, 42–43
Golf, 185, 301
Golf Club at Purchase, 185
Gourmet magazine, 101
Grand cru classé wine, 110, 140, 141
Grande complication watch, 35, 54
Grant, Cary, 218
Great Britain, 165, 255*n*
  See also British; England
Greeks (ancient), 22, 28*n*, 192*n*, 197, 200, 258*n*, 262*n*
Greenstein, Scott, 82–84, 91
Gres, Madame, 193
Griffith, Melanie, 152
Gris, Juan, 206
Gucci (co.), 32, 122, 139, 169, 215, 283, 304
Guerlain, Aimé, 216
Guerlain Shalimar perfume, 159
GUESS? Inc., 104, 138, 177
Guevara, Ernesto (Che), 56
Guggenheim Museum, 136
Gulfstream aircraft, 69, 72–75, 77, 90–91, 138

Hachette Filipacchi (co.), 287
Harley-Davidson, 128, 181, 183–84, 187
  club, 117, 118
Harley Owners Group (HOG), 118
Harper's Bazaar magazine, 134, 292
Haut-Brion wine, 140
Hayworth, Rita, 53
Health business, 61
Hearst, Mrs. Randolph, 153
Heat (film), 207, 242
Hebraic people, 214
Hegel, Georg Wilhelm Friedrich, 17, 34
Heinz (co.), 283
Heisenberg principle, 46
Hemingway, Ernest, 46
Hennessy cognac, 169
Hepburn, Audrey, 53, 146, 147, 149, 178, 218
Herculean dream, 77
Hercules (legendary hero), 301
Hermès (co.), 70, 89, 127, 138, 169, 174, 179, 180–81, 215, 291

Hershman, D. Jablow, 229*n*
Herzberg (intellectual), 239*n*
Hewlett-Packard 12C calculator, 180
Himalayas, the, 255*n*
Hindery, Leo, 86–89, 90, 91
History Channel, 86, 88
Hoffman, Dustin, 126
Hollywood, 29, 78, 82, 83, 91, 100, 101, 133, 162, 187, 198–201, 207, 209, 210, 270, 276, 309
Holyfield, Evander, 162
Hong Kong, 165
Horace (poet), 151
Horizontal business organization, 61–62, 66
Hotels, 56–57, 59, 283
House and Garden magazine, 288
Hughes (intellectual), 239*n*
Hume, David, 196*n*, 245
Huns, 200
Huston, John, 141
Hyundai car, 68

Iberia, 193
IBM, 12, 52, 53
Income tax, 165
Idleness, 226
Il Postino (film), 83
Imagination, 227*n*
Impressionists, 48
Income, discretionary, 167
India, 78*n*, 201, 223*n*, 250, 254*n*, 255*n*
Industrial Revolution, 23, 79, 98, 150, 185, 239, 285
Inflation, 166
Intelligence, 79–80
Interest rates, 165–66
Internet, 49, 96, 129–34, 176, 234, 289, 301, 302, 305
    and magazines, 101–2
Intuition, 205
Ironman watch, 102
Italy, 26, 165, 169, 197–201, 223*n*, 226, 254*n*, 258*n*, 262*n*, 270, 288
    See also Renaissance

Jacob, Max, 193
Jaeger–Le Coultre watch, 191*n*
Jaguar car, 89
Japan, 45, 52, 78*n*, 138, 161, 164, 165, 169, 187, 201, 259*n*, 281*n*
JC Penney, 60, 61
Jeans, 45, 104, 179
Jeffrey, Prince of Brunei, 152
Jericho Mile, The (film), 241
Jewelry, 109–10, 170–71, 174, 223, 283
    flourishing of, 250–53
    and power, 106–7
    and senses, 248*n*–49*n*, 249
    value of, 249–50
Jordan, Michael, 137, 162, 178, 203
Jung, Carl Gustav, 22*n*

Kandinsky, Wassily, 141
Kant, Immanuel, 33, 36
Karan, Donna, 296
Kasuga, Masahiko, 185
Kazan, Elia, 200
Kenar (designer), 292
Kennedy, Jacqueline, 49

Kennedy family, 49–50
Key to Genius, The: Manic-Depression and the Creative Life (Hershman/Lieb), 229*n*
Khan, Aga, 178
Kierkegaard, Søren, 143
Kirkeby (artist), 141
Knowledge, 227*n*
Koplovitz, Kay, 84–86, 91
Kors, Michael, 194, 195, 201
Kroeber, Alfred Louis, 197

Labels, 44
La Dolce Vita (film), 104
Lafite-Rothschild wine, 140
Lalique, René, 216, 223–24
Lanvin, Jeanne, 193
Last of the Mohicans, The (film), 159
Las Vegas, 211
Latin America, 116, 211
Lauder, Leonard, 70–72, 90, 181–82
Lauren, Ralph, 85, 201, 202, 217–21, 301
Leather products, 169, 270
Le Corbusier, 239*n*
Léger, Fernand, 239*n*
Le Girardet restaurant, 55
Leisure time, 28
Leonardo da Vinci, 197*n*, 223*n*
Lethal Weapon (film), 276
Levi's jeans, 14, 45, 59, 104, 128, 158, 178, 184
Lévi-Strauss, Claude, 106
Lexus car, 299
Lieb, Julian, 229*n*
Lievens, Jan, 194*n*
Light, properties of, 249*n*
Linen, Jonathan, 105–6
Lipstick, 114–15
Liz Claiborne (co.), 283
Locke, John, 196*n*
Loren, Sophia, 34, 53, 147
Louis XIV, King, 24*n*, 151*n*
Louis Vuitton (co.), 61, 62, 69, 138, 169, 282, 283, 290, 291
Lucas, George, 81
Luck, 227
Luggage, 283
Lusitanias cigar, 155
Luxury, 23*n*, 90
Luxury industry, 98–100, 137, 175, 215, 271, 290
  and gift-giving, 117
  vs. mass-consumption companies, 282–84
  and prices, 124–25
  and senses, 248*n*
  stores, 128
Luxury restaurants, 77
LVMH fashion houses, 228, 290

McDonald's, 43, 55, 173
McGregor (intellectual), 239*n*
McQueen, Alexander, 228
Madonna, 152
Maecenas, Gaius, 151
Magazines, 101–2, 105, 134–36, 176, 287–90
Magnani, Anna, 53, 147
Manet, Édouard, 193
Mann, Michael, 40–41, 57–58, 70, 72, 82, 91–92, 178, 202, 207–12, 219, 225–26, 241–43, 273, 276

Marciano, Paul, 104–5
Marcos, Imelda, 160
Margaux wine, 140
Marginal expenditures, 294–95
Marlboro cigarettes, 45, 137, 284
Marriott hotel, 283
Marx, Karl, 106, 221
Maslow, A. H., 239*n*
Mass-consumption companies, 125, 172–73, 282–84
Matisse, Henri, 192–93
Maugham, Somerset, 293
Maybelline mascara, 114
Medici family, 151*n*
Medium, and creativity, 193
"Memory," of company, 236, 273
Mercedes car, 102, 134, 139
Merck (co.), 61, 277
Mesopotamia, 262*n*
Miami Vice (TV show), 178, 207, 210–12
Michelangelo, 33, 197*n*, 201
Midas, legend of, 151
Middle Ages, 25, 60*n*, 256, 262*n*
Midler, Bette, 81
Midsummer Night's Dream, A (Shakespeare), 79
Mineral water, 68
Minghella, Anthony, 83
Mirabella magazine, 287
Miramax (co.), 83, 196
Mirò, Joan, 141
Mizrahi, Isaac, 292
Mobil Corporation, 63–67
Mobil I, 64
Modigliani, Amedeo, 36
Molyneux, Edward, 193, 217
Money supply, 165–66
Monroe, Marilyn, 53, 153
Mont Blanc pen, 180
Monte Cristo cigars, 178
Moore, Henri, 141
Morocco, 254*n*, 255*n*
Moss, Bryan, 72–75, 90
Motivation
  of customers, 149–50, 156–57
  for spending, 170
Motorola, 280
  StarTAC cell phones, 180
Mouton-Rothschild wine, 140–41, 142
Movado watches, 136, 283
Moveable Feast, A (Hemingway), 46
Movie industry, 40–41, 57–58, 82–84, 100, 169, 201, 202, 207–10, 241–43, 270, 275–77, 292–93
  and senses, 248*n*
  See also Hollywood
Mozart, Wolfgang Amadeus, 117, 224*n*
MTV, 219
Murdoch, Rupert, 87, 275–76
Museum of Modern Art, 191

Name recognition, 52–53
Napoleon, 224*n*, 258*n*
NASA, 267
NBC network, 86
Nero, Emperor, 24*n*
Newhouse, Si, 102
News Corporation, 276–77, 280
Newsweek magazine, 289
Newton, Isaac, 198, 229*n*
Niche channels, 86–87

Nicklaus, Jack, 185
Nightmares, as dreams, 85
Nike sneakers and sportswear, 14, 15, 41, 59, 70, 128, 137, 138, 158, 178, 180
Nine West shoes, 283
Nissan (co.), 202
Noah (biblical character), 262*n*
Normans, 200
Noto, Lucio, 63–67, 155

Object(s)
and creativity, 193
perception of, 68–69
Onassis, Aristotle, 49, 79–80
Oneiromancy, 30
Optical characteristics, 249
Organization
and creativity, 17, 234–45
horizontal business, 61–62, 66
support for creator, 307–8
vertical business, 61
Ownership rituals, 117–18

Pacino, Al, 147, 149, 207
Paltrow, Gwyneth, 292
Paramount Pictures, 276
Paris, and fashion industry, 270
Partagas Series 3d cigars, 155
Parton, Dolly, 45
Passion
function of, 307–8
past and present, 245–47
and rigor, 309
Passions (Hume), 245
Pasteur, Louis, 224*n*, 263*n*
Patek Philippe watch, 69, 83, 191
phases lunaires complication, 177
Paterculus, Velleius, 198*n*
Pecker, David, 287–90
Penn, Sean, 293
Pepsi-Cola, 61
Perception, 205
of object, 68–69
Perfume, and senses, 248*n*
Perfume business, 114, 254–57, 271, 283
Pericles, 200
Perigord (France), 258*n*
Perrier water, 108
Persia, 200
Peter Gunn (TV series), 211
Petrossian Beluga (co.), 61, 283
Pétrus wine, 110
Pfizer (co.), 237, 277–79, 280
Pharmaceutical industry, 103, 277–79
Philip Morris (co.), 283, 284
Physical fitness, 80–82
Picasso, Pablo, 141, 192, 193, 206, 224*n*
Pictet, Nicholas, 57, 59, 70
Pictet Bank, 57
Pinault, François, 295
Pinault-Printemps-Redoute department stores, 295
Pininfarina, Sergio, 216
Plato, 196*n*, 238*n*
Play, 37–38
Polarization, of business, 63–67
Pollack, Sydney, 199–200, 202, 292–93
Polo Sport, 220
Poltrona Frau (co.), 283
Portrait of Doctor Gachet (van Gogh), 281

Portugal, 255*n*, 262*n*
Possession, ritual of, 117–18
Possessions, material, 178–79
Power, importance of, 76
Practicality, selling of, 70–72
Prada (designer), 32, 201
Praise of Folly, The (Erasmus of Rotterdam), 230
Presley, Priscilla, 80, 81
Price, and value, 281–82
Products
  creating, 15, 302–3
  experience vs., 94–95
  and senses, 265–66
  symbolism of, 180–81
Protestants, 226
Puiforcat tableware, 237

Quaker Oats, 88

Racing, 240–41, 267–69
Radio, 102
Ralph Lauren brand, 135, 138
Rambo (film), 276
Ray-Bans, 184, 187
R&D, 293
Reagan, Ronald, 45
Rembrandt, 194*n*, 205*n*
Rena, Michael, 290
Renaissance, 25, 26, 151*n*, 197, 204*n*, 205*n*, 223, 252, 256
Restaurant, 258–61
  luxury, 77
  vs. supermarket, 94–95
Retail shopping, 133
Retail stores, 128
Reunion, 254*n*
Revlon, 78*n*, 112–16
Rimbaud, Arthur, 248
Rituals, 116–18
Ritz, César, 56
Ritz Hôtel, 56–57, 59, 60, 105, 178, 283
Rizzoli bookstores, 128, 283
Robb Report, 173
Robustos cigars, 155
Role playing, 180
Rolex watch, 69, 169, 294
  Oyster, 147
Rolls-Royce car, 60, 61, 62, 69, 102, 117, 138
Romans (ancient), 77*n*, 178, 262*n*
Rothschild, Philippe de, 141–42
Rubens, Peter Paul, 205*n*
Rules, 37
Russia, 45, 56, 57, 199, 255*n*
Ryoei Saito (co.), 281*n*

Saint Laurent, Yves, 201, 213
Saint Tropez, 178
Sales tax, 165
Samsonite (co.), 283
Saudi Arabia, 109–10, 240
Saving factor, 167
Savoir faire, 238–39, 244
Scent of a Woman (film), 147
Schiaparelli, Elsa, 193
Schiffer, Claudia, 104
Schubert, Franz, 224*n*
Schumacher, Michael, 162, 203
Secrets and Lies (film), 83–84
Seduction, of customers, 143–45
Self-image, 178–79
Seneca, 229*n*

Senna, Ayrton, 73
Senses, 247–48, 301
 and creativity, 214–15
 and products, 248*n*–49*n*
 See also Smell; Taste; Vision
Services
 creating, 15, 302–3
 symbolism of, 180–81
Setsuko (artist), 141
Sexual arousal, 108–9
 and food, 258*n*–59*n*
Shakespeare, William, 79, 80
Shanken, Marvin, 100
Shoe industry, 53, 59, 119–22, 137, 147, 214, 283, 301
Shoenberg, Cecil, 182
Siberia, 255*n*
Sicily, 200
Silenus (mythical figure), 151
Slate magazine, 102
Sliding Doors (film), 292, 293
Smell, as sense, 253–57, 262
Smith, Adam, 29
Smith, Anna Nicole, 104
Snapple, 88
Sneakers, 179
Social indifference, overcoming, 26
Social security tax, 165
Solgar (co.), 61, 62
Somalia, 257
Sony Walkman, 15, 41, 59, 69, 76, 280
Sotheby's, 47–50, 70, 129–30, 181–82
South America, 254*n*
Soutine, Chaim, 36
Spain, 262*n*
Spaniards, 200
Speed, Age of, 27–28
Speed Pass, 65
Spencer, Herbert, 30
Spending, motivation for, 170
Spengler, Oswald, 238*n*
Spielberg, Steven, 81
Spirit of the time, interpreting, 15, 41–42, 46–48, 300–302
Sports automobiles, 273
 and senses, 248*n*
Sports Illustrated magazine, 46
Sri Lanka, 250, 254*n*
Starbucks coffee, 65
Star Wars (film), 81
Steere, William, 277, 279
Steinberg, Saul, 141
Steinfeld, Jake, 80–82, 91
Steinway concert piano, 117
Stevens, Dorothy, 152
Stevens, George, 200
Stone, Sharon, 83, 126
Stravinsky, Igor, 193
Subject, and creativity, 193
Sumptuary laws, 24
Supermarket, vs. restaurant, 94–95
Swan sailboat, 69, 128, 177
Swatch, 69
Sweden, 165
Switzerland, Swiss, 55, 56, 101, 161, 169, 197*n*, 270
Symbolism
 of consumption, 107–8
 of influence, 178
 of products, 180–81
 of services, 180–81
Synthetics, 64, 257

Taste, 36
as sense, 257–62
Taxes, and wealth, 164–65
Taylor, Liz, 152
TCI (co.), 86
Technology, 49, 50, 83, 238
and dreamketer, 187–88
enrichment of, 85–86
and handiwork, 266–67
leaps in, 113–14
and limitations, 76
and speed, 27–28
Television industry, 86–89, 102, 210–12
broadcast, 86
cable, 84, 86
Ten Commandments, The (film), 147
Thailand, 250
Thomas, Kristin Scott, 293
Tiffany jewelers, 146, 149, 178, 283
Tilberis, Liz, 292
Time, 28, 32, 195
See also Spirit of the time
Time magazine, 289
Timex watch, 177
Tinguely, J., 239*n*
Titanic (film), 14, 175, 177, 207–8, 209–10, 275–77, 280
Tobacco, 283
See also Cigar smoking industry
Tolman (intellectual) 238*n*
Tommy Hilfiger (co.), 44, 136
Tootsie (film), 292
Town and Country magazine, 87–88
Toyota car, 60, 61
Travel & Leisure magazine, 105
Truffles, 258*n*–59*n*
Turkey, 254*n*
Twentieth Century Fox, 276
Tyrannosaurus rex, 48

U.K., 165, 255*n*
See also British; England
UNESCO, 226
Ungaro (designer), 201
United States (U.S.), *see* America
Universal (co.), 61, 276
Up at the Villa (Maugham), 293
USA network, 84, 88–89, 91
USA Today, 211
U.S. News & World Report magazine, 289
Utrillo, Maurice, 36

Valentino, Rudolph, 201
Value
defined, 125
of jewelry, 249–50
and price, 281–82
Vanderbilt, William K., 151–52
Van Gogh, Vincent, 36, 43, 229*n*, 281
Vanity Fair magazine, 134
VAT/GST/consumption tax, 165
Vatican, 278
Velázquez, Diego de, 204*n*
Vendôme (co.), 291
Verger, Roger, 259
Verne, Jules, 230
Versace, Gianni, 69, 201, 223*n*
Vertical business organization, 61
Viacom (co.), 276

Viagra, 14, 103, 109, 158, 179, 277– 79, 280, 298
Video conferencing, 74–75
Vieri, Lido, 203
Virgil (poet), 151
Visigoths, 200
Vision, as sense, 249
Vitamin business, 103, 158
Vogue magazine, 31, 101, 134, 139
Volkswagen, 135
  Beetle, 14, 70, 97–98, 280
Vostell, W., 239*n*

Walkman (Sony), 15, 41, 59, 69, 76, 280
Wall Street, 158, 179, 289
  and cost control, 296
  dress code, 180–81
  and growth, 297
  and people's dreams, 103–4
  and Viagra, 277
Warhol, Andy, 48, 49, 141
Warner, Philip, 157–58, 174
Warner Bros., 128, 177
Watchmaking industry, 54, 59, 83, 102, 169, 191, 270, 283, 294
Water, and satisfaction of drinking needs, 110, 149
Waterworld (film), 276
Wayne, John, 45
Wealth
  generation of, 97–98
  statistics on, 167
  and taxes, 164–65
  tools influencing, 165–66
  and world economy, 29
  See also Affluence
Wealth tax/net worth tax, 165
Wellcraft offshore racing boats, 211
Welles, Orson, 197*n*
Western Europe, 138
White Owl cigars, 155
Wilde, Oscar, 39
Williams-Sonoma (co.), 283
Windsor, duchess of, 174, 218
Wine, 18, 55
  aesthetic qualities of, 110–11
  and cooking, 261
  packaging of, 140–42
  quality of, 262–65
  and senses, 248*n*
Wine Spectator magazine, 140
Winslet, Kate, 208
Wintour, Anna, 31–32
Wolfe, Tom, 47
Woolf, Virginia, 229*n*
World War II, 42
Wyler, William, 200

Yachts, 102
Yugoslavia, 257

Zenith (co.), 294
Zinnemann, Fred, 200

ABOUT THE AUTHOR

GIAN LUIGI LONGINOTTI-BUITONI, PH.D., an entrepreneur with an international background, has studied in Italy, Switzerland, Germany, France, and the United States and has worked in various European, South American, and North American countries. He is currently the president and chief executive officer of Ferrari North America.